A Differ

CW00525101

Previous books by Trevor Negus

The Coal Killer

The Exodus Murders

FOR ROMAN

A Different Kind of Evil

Trevor Negus.

Trevor Negus

Published by Bathwood Manor Publishing

A CIP catalogue record for this book is available from the British Library.

ISBN 978-0-9955737-6-5

Book layout by Clare Brayshaw

Prepared and printed by:

York Publishing Services Ltd
64 Hallfield Road
Layerthorpe
York YO31 7ZQ

Tel: 01904 431213

Website: www.yps-publishing.co.uk

The book is dedicated to the memory of

PC 1570 Ged Walker

Nottinghamshire Police Dog Section

PROLOGUE

27th March 1986
Rampton Hospital, Nottinghamshire

The mournful wail of the second World War air raid warning siren rose and fell as the Police dog van was driven at speed through the entrance of Rampton Hospital.

It had been three quarters of an hour since the escape of Jimmy Wade and Clive Winstanley. Pc Carl Ryan was an experienced dog handler and his dog Blaze was considered to be one of the best working dogs on the section. The German Shephard was a big dog weighing over forty-three kilos, a brilliant tracker and very aggressive, everything a good land shark should be.

Carl Ryan was six feet tall, very fit and very strong, he needed to be a firm handler for the dog to respond. Together they made a formidable team.

The van stopped and as Ryan got out he glanced up at the sky. There were a few clouds, but it was dry, the sun was out and there was very little wind.

He grinned, conditions were virtually perfect for tracking, there was no sign of the heavy rain that had been falling the previous week.

'You took your time Carl, what kept you?'

The weary dog handler fixed the uniform Inspector who had addressed him with an icy glare and growled, 'The bloody accident on the A614 is what kept me boss! I couldn't get through, it was total gridlock. Drivers couldn't move out of the way even if they'd wanted to. Anyway, I'm here now boss. What's the story on the escape?'

Inspector Fraser looked harassed, he had the look of a man with the weight of the world's troubles pressing down heavily upon him. He gathered himself and quickly went into the details of the escape and the injuries inflicted on the men responsible for guarding the escapees.

As he got Blaze from the rear of the police van Ryan asked, 'Have we got descriptions of the two that have gone over the wall boss?'

'Jimmy Wade, the so-called Coal Killer is a white male, short blonde hair.'

Ryan interrupted the Inspector, 'Boss, we all know what Jimmy Wade looks like, his picture was never out of the papers when he was locked up. What about the other bloke who's escaped with him?'

'Clive Winstanley. He's a six foot five West Indian who weighs nineteen stone and has long dreadlocks, his four front teeth are all gold crowns. He is serving a life sentence for the abduction and rape of three schoolgirls in Northamptonshire. He's been in here for ten years now and is considered to be another extremely violent individual. The injuries they've caused to the guards are horrendous.'

'Right sir, we're ready, can you show me exactly where they went over the wire.'

The dog handler and his now very excited dog followed the Inspector to the concrete plant where Wade and Winstanley had overpowered their guards, scaled the wire fence and made good their escape. Other police officers were already milling about in the area, Ryan frowned and let out an audible sigh.

Seeing the frown and hearing the sigh Insp Fraser said quickly, 'Don't worry Carl, I've kept them away from the area the prisoners scaled the wire, so hopefully your dog will be able to pick up their track.'

'Nice one boss, that's the first bit of good news I've had since I got this call out.'

Carl Ryan then attached the harness to the dog and attached the twenty foot long tracking line. The change in Blaze was immediate. The dog immediately went in to track mode and his head lowered towards the ground.

Ryan then wrapped the leather lead and check chain around his body, bandolier style so he still had it to hand but not in the way. The experienced handler knew he would need the lead and check chain later.

He then bent down next to the dog and said quietly, 'Seek 'em. Good boy Blaze, seek 'em.'

Immediately the dogs large head went down and he began slowly traversing the area the other side of the fence.

Suddenly, Blaze turned and began to move purposefully across the area of open land moving away from the fence.

'We're on sir. I need three officers to follow me, not too close. I don't want them to distract the dog, but if he tracks them down and they're still together, I'm going to need some back up.'

Inspector Fraser turned and instructed three of the officers standing nearby to follow the dog handler. He then shouted, 'Try and keep in touch on the radio Carl, the signals aren't the best up here, lots of black spots.'

Carl Ryan waved a hand in acknowledgement. The other hand holding firmly onto the tracking line as Blaze increased his speed and began to track in earnest.

A quarter of an hour passed and the dog was still working hard to follow the scent, the track had taken Pc Ryan and his three colleagues over some rough terrain. All the men were scratched from tree branches and brambles, their boots and trousers were wet after traversing a couple of streams swollen from the recent heavy rains.

Each time they had encountered water, Carl had lifted his dog across the stream and again set the dog to track. Each time, Blaze had responded magnificently and within a few minutes had picked up the track.

The pace was relentless and all the officers were sweating profusely and pulling in lungsful of air.

Another ten minutes passed when suddenly Blaze stopped dead. The dog began to move first to the left and then to the right.

Carl Ryan held up his hand indicating for the three officers following, to remain where they were.

He shouted back to them, 'It looks like the two of them have split up, the dog knows there are two tracks. He will go for the strongest, just wait back there until we move off again.'

After a few minutes the dog stopped, then put his head down and turned to follow the track that led off to the right.

Ryan shouted back, 'Let's go lads! One of you radio it in, Wade and Winstanley have split up. One track is heading in the general direction of Retford, the one we're following is heading back towards Woodbeck.'

There was a shout of acknowledgement from one of the following officers, then all four were moving at pace again trying to keep up with Blaze.

The track was obviously strong as the dog increased the pace.

Suddenly, the police dog led the officers from the woodland they were moving through, out into a large open field that sloped down towards a small lake surrounded by tall bulrushes.

Once again Blaze stopped and lifted his huge head. His ears stood up and he began to sniff the air.

The experienced dog handler recognised the signs. His dog had now caught the scent of his quarry on the light wind that was blowing towards them, they were getting close.

Ryan bent down and removed the tracking line. Quickly he wound the long line between his wrist and his elbow before clipping it to his belt. He removed the leather lead and choke chain from around his body and held it in his right hand.

Carl shouted, 'Find him boy, go on!'

The dog immediately took off with Ryan sprinting after him.

Blaze raced to the edge of the bulrushes and began to bark fiercely.

Carl signalled for the other officers to remain back, away from the dog. He moved to the side of his dog and placed the check chain around the dog gripping the leather leash tightly, so he could control the dog easier.

He patted the dog, encouraging him saying, 'Where is he Blaze? Talk to me boy.'

The huge German Shephard was straining at the leash, snarling and barking. Continually lunging forward towards the bulrushes in front of him.

Still Carl could see no one.

He shouted over the dogs barking, 'Get yourself out here now, or I'll send the dog!'

Suddenly, the bulrushes parted and a huge West Indian with long dreadlocks emerged from shallow water at the side of the lake. The man had been lying down in the water next to the bank hidden by the tall rushes and surface weed.

'Get out of the water now Winstanley! Get on the bank and lie face down!'

Clive Winstanley snarled, 'Take it easy man, control that beast now!'

Very slowly he eased himself out of the water and onto the bank where he stood dripping wet.

He ignored the order from Ryan and made no attempt to lay down.

Blaze was going frantic, continually barking and leaping towards the huge West Indian. Carl Ryan needed every ounce of his strength to prevent the dog from savaging the man.

Winstanley stared at the officer and said, 'If that beast come near me man, I'll kill it stone dead, d'ya hear me Babylon!'

'Do as I tell you! Get on the ground and you won't get hurt.'

Winstanley took a step back, away from Ryan and Blaze and shouted, 'Fuck you man! I'm gone!'

Suddenly, he was sprinting away from Ryan, running full tilt back towards the village of Woodbeck. The first houses were less than two hundred yards away on the other side of the field.

Ryan shouted after the running man, 'Stop! Or I'll release the dog!'

Winstanley continued to sprint, his head was down and his arms were pumping, but his speed was severely hampered by the wet overalls clinging tightly to his legs.

Ryan bent down next to Blaze who was barking fiercely. He held his dog tight then released the check chain, at the same time he gave the dog the attack command, shouting, 'Passauf!'

Instantly, Blaze stopped barking and flew like a black and tan missile after the running man. The big German Shepard closed the gap in seconds and leapt from the ground, its jaws clamping onto the left arm of Winstanley. The force of the huge dog knocked the West Indian completely off his feet.

The dog released its grip on the man's arm and immediately clamped its jaws onto Winstanley's upper inner thigh, next to his groin.

Ryan and the other three officers sprinted after the dog and arrived less than a minute after Winstanley had been taken down.

Blaze was still latched onto the man's inner thigh and was shaking his big head vigorously. Winstanley was now howling in pain and shouted, 'Get ya beast off me man!'

Ryan shouted, 'Leave!'

Instantly, Blaze released his bite and let go of Winstanley. The dog moved two yards away from the stricken West Indian and continued to bark fiercely.

The dog handler shouted above the barking, 'Down!'

Blaze went down and lay on the floor, ears forward staring at the writhing man.

Ryan placed the check chain back on the dog. He then held the dog in the same position, so he was snarling just a couple of yards away from Winstanley.

Ryan turned to his colleagues and shouted above the snarling dog, 'Get him cuffed. One of you request an ambulance to join us at this location. This piece of shit is going to need a few stitches!'

The officers moved in and quickly restrained Winstanley.

Pc Ryan turned to his dog saying, 'Good boy Blaze, good lad!'

One of the other officers said, 'Carl, back-up's on the way with transport, and an ambulance is also travelling; what do you want us to do now?'

'Two of you stay with Winstanley, depending on how long the ambulance is going to be you might need to stem that bleeding on his leg.'

Ryan then turned to the other officer and said, 'You come with me, we'll go back to where the pair of them split up. I'll see if the dog will pick up the other track.'

Ryan began to jog back the way they had come.

Blaze had already forgotten about Winstanley and was now focussed on the next task.

The two officers and the dog reached the point in the woods where the escapees had gone their separate ways. Ryan took Blaze past the area where the track had split, he put the dog back on the tracking line and once again placed the check chain and leash around his body.

Ryan said quietly next to the dog's ears, 'Seek on'

The dog set to work immediately and within a few minutes had again picked up a track. Ryan and his colleague began following the dog through the woodland. Twenty minutes later Ryan could see they were approaching a hawthorn hedgerow.

Ryan checked the dog and said loudly, 'Wait!'

Immediately the dog checked and stood stock still. Beyond the hedgerow was a country lane; Ryan didn't want his dog to blindly run out into the road and run the risk of being struck by a vehicle. He returned the dog to the check chain and leash, once again winding up the tracking line.

The two officers and the dog then emerged onto the country lane. Once again Ryan said, 'Seek on.'

Blaze got his head down and again picked up the track. It now ran alongside the edge of the hedgerow at the side of the country lane.

They followed the track until it came to a layby near to the entrance to Haggnook Farm.

Suddenly Blaze stopped.

The dog lifted his head and turned to look back at Ryan.

The dog handler knew exactly what that look meant. The track had disappeared in the layby. The only explanation being that Wade had got into a vehicle at that point.

Ryan stooped down, he patted and fussed his dog, 'Good boy Blaze! Well done buddy.'

He then stood up and spoke into his personal radio, 'Pc Ryan to Inspector Fraser, over.'

'Go ahead, Pc Ryan.'

'Winstanley's been detained near to Woodbeck village, we've also followed what appears to be the track for Jimmy Wade but it's disappeared in a layby near a place called Haggnook Farm. My best guess is that Wade has either been picked up in a vehicle or he's abducted somebody with a vehicle. How soon after the escape were the road blocks established between Haggnook Farm and Retford?'

There was a brief delay as the Inspector studied the maps.

'Inspector Fraser to Pc Ryan, Haggnook Farm is three hundred yards past the established cordon. It looks like Wade has bypassed the road blocks that were set up by going on foot over the fields. There are no road blocks after Haggnook Farm.'

'In that case, Jimmy Wade is well and truly on his toes boss. At least we've collared Winstanley.'

'Received that Pc Ryan. Return to Rampton Hospital for a debrief and to sort out your statement for Winstanley's arrest. It seems his injuries are quite severe, he's currently on his way under escort to Retford General to have his thigh and his arm stitched up.'

'He shouldn't have run boss. It's a simple choice really, he chose badly.'

'Indeed, he did. A good job today Carl, make your way back into Rampton and I'll talk to you when you get here.'

Pc Carl Ryan, his colleague and police dog Blaze all began to walk slowly back towards Rampton Hospital.

Ryan was once again immensely proud of his dog. He felt a real sense of achievement that Winstanley had been detained. This feeling was tinged with a tangible mood of disappointment that he hadn't managed to track down and recapture Jimmy Wade as well.

CHAPTER I

3rd June 1986
Bleasby, Nottinghamshire

Voices.

The boy could definitely hear voices now.

They were gruff and guttural.

Men's voices.

There were several of them, all laughing and joking at something, or someone.

He still couldn't move, but slowly he began to regain other senses.

As well as hearing sounds, he could now smell stale cigarette smoke and beer. There was another stronger, pungent smell that he recognised immediately.

It was weed.

The men were smoking cannabis as well as tobacco.

It was a smell he remembered well from his mother's small, cramped flat in Hyson Green. It was an ever-present odour whenever she was in the flat entertaining his so-called uncles.

The boy knew he was lying face down on a mattress, it was damp and stank of mould. He had no idea where he was, or how he had got there.

As he slowly came to his senses he began to feel both the cold and the pain.

The cold was seeping through his body and the pain he felt below his waist came over him in waves. It started as a dull ache, but gradually got worse until it was almost too much to bear.

It made him want to scream out, but for some reason he held back.

He could feel a pressure bearing down on him. The weight he could feel on his back was forcing him down into the damp, dirty mattress. As the pressure bore down on his body, so the pain increased again.

Could he scream?

Should he scream?

He didn't know the answer to the questions swirling around inside his head.

He didn't move and he didn't scream, some instinct told him he needed to remain perfectly still and quiet.

Finally, the waves of pressure on top of him stopped. He felt the mattress below him rise slightly, as the weight that had been bearing down on him was removed.

Almost immediately he felt the mattress dip again, once more there was a pressure, more weight. Heavier this time, forcing him down into the mattress again. His face was enveloped by the stinking makeshift bed. He was struggling to breathe. Ever so slowly he turned his head so his face was looking to one side and he could at last breathe.

This time the waves of pain he felt were unbearable, still he stifled the agonised scream.

He still hadn't opened his eyes.

As the waves of pain continued to wash over his small, frail body, finally he plucked up the courage to open his eyes.

Everything was obscured by a blue haze.

Through the pall of cigarette smoke the first thing he saw were the three black legs of a tripod, on the floor, about a yard from his face. Moving only his eyes he looked up the legs of the tripod. Sitting on top of the metal legs was a black and grey metal box. On the box he could see a small red light that blinked on and off constantly.

The black box was pointing down at the mattress, pointing at him.

He daren't move his head, but flicked his eyes to take in what else he could see.

Just above his head he could see a man's forearm. It was covered in tattoos and moved slightly in time with the waves of pain he was feeling. He could see the muscles in the forearm bulging and contracting.

Standing next to the tripod he could see the naked legs and feet of a man. Once again, he allowed his eyes to move upwards, trying to see the rest of the man.

He was a fat, old man with a pot belly. He had no clothes on and held a can of beer in one hand and a cigarette in the other.

The boy continued to stare at the old man's face.

Suddenly he saw the man's eyes widen.

The boy could now see that the man was pointing at him with his cigarette.

He saw the man's lips moving and heard the gruff voice as he shouted, 'He's awake! The fucking kid's awake!'

Instantly the boy felt the weight on top of him lift off, the mattress rose slightly and the waves of pain stopped.

He began to try and turn over on the bed so he could see the whole room, but every movement he made racked his body with pain. His head throbbed and his eyes, now that they were finally wide open, were stinging.

Suddenly, he felt strong, rough hands grabbing him and heard angry panicked voices.

'Don't let him see our faces!' said one frantic voice from behind him.

The strong hands turned him quickly onto his front again. He felt a massive hand grab his hair and push his head further down into the mattress.

Finally, he found his voice and screamed.

The scream came out as a muffled shriek as his face was pushed deeper into the fetid mattress.

The boy stopped screaming, then he heard another voice saying, 'Get some more gear and get it into him. NOW!'

This voice wasn't panicked. It carried an air of command, leadership almost. With that sense of authority came real menace.

As his face was pushed deeper into the stinking mattress, the boy suddenly felt a stinging, sharp pain in his right thigh.

The needle of the syringe found a vein and the boy instantly began to feel light headed. The voices became distant once again, the pain slowly disappeared to nothing.

He could barely breathe now, his eyes began to feel heavy and slowly they closed, plunging him back into a sound proof darkness, where he felt nothing.

CHAPTER 2

4th June 1986
Tall Trees Children's Home, Bilsthorpe, Nottinghamshire

Pc Dave Bracewell drove the liveried Police car through the open rusting, wrought iron gates and along the treelined driveway towards the large Georgian house. The house was illuminated by white floodlights set in the ground.

The lights cast eerie shadows.

Looming out of the darkness, the old building looked like a haunted house from a 1960's black and white horror movie.

It had just turned two o'clock in the morning when he'd received the radio message to go to the children's home in Bilsthorpe and obtain the details for yet another missing person's report.

He cursed under his breath as he parked the police car outside the front of the building.

It was the fourth time this week that he'd been called to attend Tall Trees children's home.

He got out of the car and walked briskly towards the large wooden double doors. The hall light was already on and before he could knock, the right-hand door of the two opened.

Standing in the doorway, back lit from the hallway, was a middle-aged woman wearing a dark brown dressing gown and black fluffy slippers.

His mood lightened a little as he recognised the woman standing there. He was always pleased to see the home's matron, Caroline Short.

He said, 'Hello again Caroline. Which one of your little darlings is it this time?'

'Come in Dave. It's Evan Jenkins, again. I'll put the kettle on. It's coffee, white no sugar, isn't it?'

With just a hint of boredom in his voice Dave Bracewell replied, 'You know me too well Caroline, white no sugar it is.'

He walked into the spacious hallway and immediately heard scampering above. He glanced up and saw several young boys on the darkened landing, staring at him through the bannister rails, their faces lit by the hall light.

The matron also looked up and shouted, 'I won't tell you boys again, get back to bed!'

There was a chorus of farmyard pig noises as the boys disappeared back to their dormitories.

Caroline Short turned to the officer and said, 'Bloody kids, they've been waiting there for you to arrive, just so they could make them stupid pig noises for you.'

Dave shrugged his broad shoulders and with a resigned air said quietly, 'Now, why doesn't that surprise me?'

The matron grinned and said, 'Take a seat in my office Dave, I'll get your coffee. Do you want a slice of toast or anything?'

'Thanks, that would be great. I could murder a slice of toast.'

The policeman had come to know Caroline Short very well in the fourteen months she'd been the matron in charge of the home on his rural beat. The kids at the home were always absconding. Picking up the missing person reports and returning the boys to the home was part and parcel of the officer's routine work.

The fact that a lot of the times when the boys absconded, they were out committing petty thefts and burglaries in the area meant that the officer had come to quietly loathe the juvenile delinquents placed in care at the Tall Trees Children's Home.

Tonight, was no different.

No doubt this kid would be out there somewhere, committing crime or causing a bloody nuisance and as usual it would be down to him to try and placate the homeowner whose house had been burgled or the owner of the car nicked for a joyride and left damaged in a ditch. The actual crime they committed was serious, but going out to the children's home almost every shift was a real pain in the backside for Dave and the other uniform officers that worked the area.

As it happened, Dave Bracewell didn't mind getting called out to the home too much when he was on a night shift. Caroline Short was very easy on the eye and was always very welcoming with a hot coffee.

Dave was approaching middle age, was slightly overweight, wore glasses and had no confidence whatsoever around the opposite sex. Which probably accounted for the fact that he was still single and had never been married. Caroline always somehow managed to put him at his ease, he felt comfortable in her presence.

Some of the other staff at the home were right miserable buggers, but not Caroline. The matron always had a ready smile and made him feel welcome. More than that, she made him feel special.

Caroline's husband, Bill, was also employed at the children's home. He was the groundsman come handyman, who generally looked after the place.

The pair of them had moved to Tall Trees after transferring up from another local authority children's home they had run, just outside Looe in Cornwall.

That was another reason Dave liked chatting to Caroline; he was fascinated by her strong Cornish accent.

Caroline came back into the small cluttered office carrying a tray with two mugs of coffee and a plate filled with rounds of hot buttered toast.

'Look at the state of me Dave, why can't these bloody kids run off when I've had a chance to do my hair and put my slap on?' she laughed.

Dave took a sip of his hot coffee and looked at her closely over the rim of his mug.

She was slightly older than him, approaching forty years of age, had short jet-black hair and bright blue eyes with faint laughter lines at the corners. She was petite, just over five feet two but still curvaceous. Even under the old, dark brown dressing gown she wore, he could make out the sexy curve of her hips and her full breasts.

Dave was a single man and if it wasn't for the fact Caroline was married, he would have asked her out months ago.

He took another sip of his coffee, smiled and said, 'I don't know Caroline, you always look good to me.'

'Flattery will get you everywhere Constable', she giggled before continuing, 'Now eat your toast before it gets cold.'

Dave swallowed a mouthful of the warm buttery toast and said, 'When did you realise Evan Jenkins had absconded?'

'The boys were playing up around one o'clock. When I went up there to tell them off and get them all back into their beds, I noticed he was missing. Evan shares a room with two other boys. I like to keep all the younger ones together. It stops some of the problems you can get with the older boys. Bullying and the sex stuff, you know what I mean. I looked in his room and noticed he wasn't there. I've had a quick look around inside and Bill has checked the grounds. He's definitely gone.'

'When I got here you said, "Evan Jenkins, again!". I don't think I've heard that name before.'

'Haven't you? Well I'm surprised at that, the little darling's only been here for two months and he's constantly running off back home to Nottingham.'

'Nope, Evan Jenkins is a new one on me. What's he like?'

The matron then provided all the details and physical description the officer would need to complete the Missing Person Report.

Dave completed the form, sat back in the chair and said, 'Evan's only eleven years of age; that makes him very vulnerable. What's your opinion, Caroline, is he likely to come to serious harm?'

'That one; I doubt it very much! He's eleven going on twenty-five. Evan's as street wise as they come. His mum's a drug addict, a prostitute who lives in the Hyson Green flats complex in the city. Before he was sent here by the courts he was virtually fending for himself anyway. You'll find him hanging around Hyson Green somewhere, probably on a street corner in the red-light area on Forest Road. The courts were concerned that Evan was following in his mother's footsteps and prostituting himself.'

'He's a rent boy?'

'Exactly that Dave. Do you want another coffee before you get back on patrol?'

'It would be rude not to Caroline, thanks.'

She smiled and said, 'Coming right up'.

Dave shamelessly stared at her as she walked out of the office.

She was aware the policeman was watching and swayed her hips in an exaggerated, provocative manner. By the time she was out of sight Pc Bracewell had already forgotten about eleven year old Evan Jenkins.

Twenty minutes later he finished his second coffee and was leaving the home. He'd said goodnight to Caroline and was walking out of the building alone.

As he approached the front door he heard a movement above him. In the gloom he could see a face he recognised, looking down at him wedged between the bannisters.

It was another of the frequent absconders, Tommy Quinn.

Dave had lost count of the number of times he had returned the child back to Tall Trees after absconding.

The boy was staring down at him from the balcony.

'Hello Tommy, did you want something?'

'He won't be coming back.'

'What are you talking about?'

'Evan Jenkins, he won't be coming back.'

At that moment Caroline Short appeared in the hallway and shouted, 'Tommy Quinn, I won't tell you again! Get back to your room!'

Instantly the boy's face disappeared from between the bannisters and Dave heard him scuttle off back to his bedroom.

Caroline smiled at the policeman and moved in close, touching his arm.

She squeezed it gently and said huskily, 'Have you got everything you need Dave?'

Missing the obvious come on the flustered policeman replied, 'Yes, thanks Caroline, I'll see you soon.'

'I hope so, Dave.'

CHAPTER 3

22nd June 1986
Funchal Airport, Madeira

Danny and Sue Flint sat snuggled next to each other on two hard metal seats in the departure lounge at Funchal airport. It was a small airport with a very basic level of facilities. They had just over half an hour to wait before their flight back to East Midlands airport.

Sue had earlier managed to find a little coffee shop in the departure hall that sold hot beverages as well as a few books, magazines and souvenirs from the beautiful island of Madeira. She had resisted the temptation to buy a bottle of the famous Blandy Madeira wine or the heavy, honey flavoured Madeira cake and instead had returned from her impromptu shopping trip with just two cups of milky coffee.

The empty paper cups were now on the floor below the seats, the lukewarm coffee quickly consumed.

It had been three weeks of uninterrupted bliss for the newlyweds after the delayed start to their honeymoon.

Danny, with Sue's blessing, had postponed the honeymoon for three weeks after the wedding. Every hour of that time had been taken trying to locate and recapture the serial killer Jimmy Wade, after his audacious escape from Rampton Hospital at the end of March.

One of the guards attacked by Wade had been left seriously ill and in a coma as a result of his injuries and it

12

came as no surprise that Danny had been tasked by the Chief Constable to lead the Major Crime Investigation Unit in a bid to recapture the serial killer as soon as possible.

The wedding itself on the 7th of May had been a beautiful day and was everything the couple had wanted it to be, but there was a shadow hanging over the proceedings as Jimmy Wade continued to evade capture.

It was as if the infamous killer had vanished into thin air.

Danny had not felt at ease about taking time off and had postponed the honeymoon for three weeks in the hope there would be a breakthrough and Wade would be caught and returned to the high security hospital.

The escape of Wade had caused huge political rumblings and the Home Secretary had called for a huge revamping and upgrading of the current security arrangements at Rampton Hospital and other similar units dotted across the country.

The government had promised a huge budget to carry out this work as a matter of urgency.

All the political interest had kept the escape in the public eye for weeks and the longer it took the police to recapture Wade, the greater the pressure felt by Danny Flint and the small team of detectives on the MCIU.

The breakthrough hadn't come.

Eventually all lines of enquiry were exhausted and no other sightings were coming into the incident room.

Danny's boss, Detective Chief Superintendent Bill Wainwright had eventually insisted that Danny take his annual leave and fly off to Madeira to take his new wife on their belated honeymoon.

The couple had landed on the recently extended runway at Funchal airport on the 1st of June to begin their honeymoon.

Danny had booked the bridal suite at Reid's Palace, the famous hotel with the pink walls located on a cliff edge next to the ocean just outside the city of Funchal.

The hotel offered the height of luxury and was well known for the famous guests it had attracted over the years. The wartime Prime Minister, Winston Churchill, had regularly been a guest at the hotel and had stayed in one of the suites just along the corridor from where Danny and Sue had spent three blissful weeks.

Now as Danny waited for the flight information board to change, he began to feel a little trepidation about what would be waiting for him when he got back to England. There had been no messages from England outlining the news Danny craved, that Wade had been recaptured.

Before he left, Danny had left strict instructions with Detective Inspector Rob Buxton to contact him the moment Wade was caught.

He sat quietly, pondering how he was going to generate some impetus into a floundering manhunt. The detective fully understood the reason he felt so troubled. In his heart, Danny knew it would only be a matter of time before Wade killed again.

Their flight would arrive at East Midlands Airport at five o'clock that afternoon, Danny intended to be back at his desk by eight o'clock the following morning.

Disturbing him from his thoughts, Danny felt Sue squeeze his arm. He glanced at his wife and saw her staring into his face.

She asked with a measure of concern, 'Are you okay sweetheart? You've got that faraway look in your eyes.'

'I'm fine, don't worry. I was just thinking about what's going to be waiting for me when I get back to work tomorrow.'

Sue sighed deeply, 'The last three weeks have been absolutely beautiful. No interruptions, no telephone calls in the middle of the night, no long shifts. It's been heaven.'

'It has been wonderful, sweetheart, I wish it could be like this all the time. Do me one thing Sue; promise me that however manic our work lives get, we'll never stop loving each other.'

'That's an easy promise to make, detective, you know exactly how I feel about you.'

With a grin spreading over his sun-tanned features, he said, 'I still like to hear you say it though.'

'Oh, do you now?' said Sue teasing him.

'Of course I do', his grin got wider.

Sue giggled mischievously, 'Well I'm sorry detective, there's no time now, the information board has just changed. You'll just have to hold that thought and ask me again when we get home.'

'Don't you worry Mrs Flint, I will!'

Danny kissed her passionately on the lips, then said, 'Oh, I definitely will.'

The couple stood, picked up their hand luggage and made their way hand in hand to the boarding gate.

CHAPTER 4

23rd June 1986
South Lodge, Retford

The stone lodge was idyllic.

Its sandstone blocks provided a myriad of different amber and honey hues as they were illuminated by the rays of the early morning sun. The blocks contrasted beautifully against the dark green conifer trees and the lighter, emerald greens of the deciduous trees that formed the dense forest surrounding the building on all sides.

The lodge was situated in a natural clearing in the woods. It had originally been built to provide a residence for the gamekeeper employed by the Retford Hall Estate. Although still situated in the very heart of the vast country estate, South Lodge had long been sold off to the public.

The property had neat, tended gardens to the front and rear. Behind the small rear garden there was a field that contained two more stone outbuildings. This field was separated from the surrounding woods by the River Poulter, which in reality was little more than a wide stream.

The windows in the lodge were characteristically small and let in very little light. There was an entrance hall, lounge and kitchen downstairs; upstairs was made up of two bedrooms and a bathroom. A toilet had been added to this bathroom in recent years. The original outside privy was still situated in the rear garden.

The front door was the original solid oak and was set in an impressive stone archway. The rear door was a more modern stable door design, where the top half could be left open on hot summer days.

At the front of the property there was a parking area made up of black cinder. It was large enough to accommodate two vehicles and was situated directly outside the front gate.

Access to the Lodge was via a single-track dirt road that ran from one of the many country lanes that ran through the estate. Very few people knew of its existence; it was this very isolation that had first attracted Melissa Braithwaite to buy the secluded property.

Following the unexpected death of both her parents, she had been in a dark place and had sought isolation and solitude to try and come to terms with her grief.

That solitude had disappeared three months ago, Melissa now had a permanent house guest to share her isolation.

Jimmy Wade stared hard at his own reflection in the bathroom mirror.

He barely recognised himself.

His hair was now shoulder length and dyed dark brown, he had a full beard that had been dyed the same dark brown as his hair. The only thing he recognised about himself were the piercing blue eyes that sparkled back at him.

Three months had passed since his escape from Rampton Hospital.

As he stared at himself in the mirror he grinned as he recalled the way he had outfoxed the police. He knew that following their escape they would be tracked by police dogs, that was one of the main reasons he had involved Clive Winstanley in the escape.

Not only did he need the giant Winstanley to help him overpower their guards, he had also taken the calculated gamble that a police dog would track Winstanley before him. The West Indian was a huge man and Wade had calculated Winstanley's body odour would be stronger than his own. He had always believed that a dog would pick up on and follow the strongest track.

Still staring narcissistically at his own reflection, he ran his fingers through his long hair and tied it back in a tight ponytail. He didn't really care how it had happened, all the minutiae of the escape, he was just glad to be out of that hell hole.

Putting on a mustard coloured t-shirt he shouted, 'Mel, where are my Levi's?'

From the bedroom next door Melissa Braithwaite replied quietly, 'Sorry Jimmy, I've washed them. They'll be dry soon; can't you slip on some jogging bottoms for now?'

There was a tremor in her voice, she was now absolutely terrified of Wade.

It had only taken two weeks for Wade to get bored of her.

Braithwaite had been totally besotted by the serial killer and had willingly taken the massive step to assist him in his escape, firstly by providing him with a weapon and then secondly by providing transport away from the area surrounding the high security hospital.

At first, being alone in the lodge with Jimmy Wade had been everything she hoped it was going to be.

Jimmy had been considerate and passionate.

Melissa had never had a man make love to her the way that Jimmy Wade did. After hours of energetic lovemaking, she would lie on the bed totally spent.

He was insatiable. As she lay exhausted, he would begin to slowly caress her and would be instantly aroused again. Their lovemaking lasted hours, all night and on occasions all the following day.

Eventually she felt sore and was so exhausted she began to refuse his advances.

On one occasion after being refused, Wade forced himself upon her using violence to ensure he sated his all-consuming lust.

From that moment on whenever she hadn't complied, he used force and physical violence to get what he wanted.

Gradually, he began to be more domineering in every aspect of their lives together. The slightest comment or anything else he perceived to be wrong would result in physical violence. At first it was just a slap, then it became a punch.

Finally, all it took was one word out of turn or a single act out of place, for Melissa to be the subject of a sustained and savage beating.

The beatings got progressively worse until she had become a virtual shadow of her former self. She was not allowed out of the property alone. He would sexually assault her whenever he felt the urge and forced her into performing gradually more degrading and base acts with him.

Jimmy Wade now totally controlled her.

Melissa lived in constant fear that he would kill her.

Her existence was nothing like she had imagined it would be when she had assisted him to escape from Rampton.

The words of Stewart Ainsworth, constantly replayed inside her head.

On a previous visit to her home, the young social worker had warned Melissa that she should never forget that Jimmy Wade was a pure psychopath, a monster.

Now that it was too late, she had come to realise just how true those words were.

She now obeyed Wade's every word without question and she also knew that there could never be any escape from him.

Jimmy Wade had thoroughly enjoyed the transformation of Melissa Braithwaite. He had turned her from being an equally enthused lover to his own personal sex slave.

He had savagely manipulated her fragile mental state and bullied her at every opportunity. He was well aware that she had no family or friends who were likely to come calling or show an interest in her well-being.

As far as Wade was concerned, Melissa Braithwaite was naïve, stupid and ripe for exploitation.

It suited his purpose to have a totally subservient Melissa who would obey his every word instantly. He'd tired of having sex with her and merely used rough sex as a weapon to quickly take control of her.

It was far more pleasurable than beating her, was more effective and worked quicker.

He knew she no longer possessed the will or the nerve to try and escape his clutches, he had broken her resistance completely. She was now his slave and he could do to her what he liked, she would comply instantly and without question.

Enraged by her last comment, Jimmy now stormed from the bathroom into the bedroom and pulled Melissa from the bed by her hair. He screamed in her face, 'When did I tell you to wash my jeans?'

'I'm sorry Jimmy, they looked grubby so I put them in the washer last night, they'll be nearly dry by now.'

He slapped her hard across the face. The blow was delivered with such force that it left vivid red finger marks across her cheek.

'How many times have I got to tell you? You ask me first! You never think for yourself. Do you understand me?'

'Yes Jimmy, I'm sorry.'

'Go downstairs and find me something to put on!'

'Yes Jimmy, what would you like to wear?'

'You see, that wasn't too hard, was it? I would like to wear my grey jogging bottoms today, now get your fat arse downstairs and fetch them!'

Melissa ran naked from the bedroom and down the stairs, returning seconds later with a pair of grey jogging bottoms. She handed them to Jimmy who put them on. He then grabbed Melissa by the arm, gripping her tightly.

Instinctively she cringed away from him.

He drew her in closer to him and began to stroke her hair.

He whispered seductively, 'Don't flinch sweetheart, you know I love you more than anything else in the world. You have given me my freedom, I can never repay you for that my darling.'

With one huge hand he gripped both her cheeks and turned her face towards him. He kissed her passionately on the mouth. Her cheek was still stinging from the hard slap, but now she felt the same familiar urges coursing through her as she stared into his sparkling blue eyes. Even after all the beatings just looking at him filled her with a burning desire she had never previously known.

She doubted her own sanity every day.

'I'm sorry Jimmy, I didn't mean to upset you.'

'I'm sorry too Melissa. I don't know why you have to make me so angry. If you didn't make me angry I wouldn't have to slap you. Why do you do it sweetheart?'

'I don't know Jimmy, I'm sorry.'

'That's fine Mel, I know you're sorry. Go back downstairs and cook me some breakfast. Don't bother getting dressed today, I want to look at your gorgeous body while you're cooking, you know how much that always turns me on. Hurry along now, we've got a busy day ahead. I've waited long enough, it's time I started to settle a few old scores with those bastards from Rampton. Are you going to help me do that sweetheart?'

'Of course, Jimmy, you know I'll do anything for you, don't you?'

'Oh, I do sweetheart, I do know that.'

CHAPTER 5

23rd June 1986
Haywood Oaks Lane, Blidworth,
Nottinghamshire

Anne Parr was livid, literally fuming.

She could barely contain her anger as she opened the hatchback boot of her new Vauxhall Astra to let out Molly, her chocolate brown Labrador.

As she clipped the silver chain lead onto Molly's leather collar she reflected on the events of yesterday that had made her so angry.

It was still difficult for her to accept exactly how disgustingly she had been treated by the owners of the factory where she worked. After twenty years of loyal service as a machinist at Leigh & Oliver's Hosiery factory she had been handed her redundancy notice.

In just two weeks' time she would be unemployed.

Fourteen fucking days!

Didn't they realise that she had bills to pay?

Anne was approaching forty with two teenage daughters, she'd been a single parent for the last five years after her husband Ray had walked out on his family following a brief affair with his secretary. Just a week after he walked out, the young secretary dumped him.

Karma was a bitch.

Ray had come crawling back with his tail firmly between his legs. She never even considered taking the rat back.

It had been a struggle financially ever since and like most single parents, Anne always put her own needs last. She was only too aware that following the acrimonious split from her husband she'd let herself go a little. There was no spare cash for glamorous hair do's, manicures or new clothes.

She had no inclination to date other men, so what was the point in trying to glam herself up. It would have been a waste of the much-needed cash.

The one thing she had saved hard for was her new car.

It was her pride and joy.

To cheer herself up a little, she glanced over her shoulder at the brand-new Vauxhall Astra.

Almost instantly the black depression rushed back and she muttered aloud, 'I suppose that fucker will have to go back too.'

Her sombre mood remained as she walked with Molly along the single-track road deeper into the Forestry Commission woodland just off Haywood Oaks Lane. The woods were situated on the outskirts of the small village of Blidworth and were one of Anne's favourite places.

The track petered out to a dead end about twenty yards ahead and Molly would get to have her morning run in her own favourite area of the woods, undisturbed.

Most of the dog walkers used a different entrance into the woods. This area was quite boggy sometimes and was scarcely used. That was just how Anne liked it. A few months earlier Molly had been attacked by two Staffordshire bull terriers. As a result, the placid Labrador was now very anxious around other dogs.

Looking around at the woods surrounding her, Anne realised just what a beautiful morning it was. The sun was already out and even though it was still early it was starting to get warm. The hot dry spell looked set to continue. The birds were singing and the dappled sunlight streaming through the canopy of leaves was breathtakingly beautiful.

At the end of the track Anne bent down and unclipped Molly from her lead. Instantly the dark brown dog rushed off into the surrounding woodland. Anne slumped down on the trunk of a fallen tree and reflected a little more on her plight.

There was always the option of going to work at her father's jewellery shop. He'd asked her on many occasions to join the family run business as he wanted to work less hours and needed somebody he could trust to run the shop. The thought of being a shop assistant filled Anne with dread, but she needed a job so maybe this was the answer.

She resolved to call her father that day.

Her thoughts were interrupted by Molly barking furiously in the woods.

Molly never usually barked.

Anne stood up and walked into the woodland following the sound of Molly's now constant barking. Just twenty yards into the woodland she found the Labrador frantically scratching at some loose dirt and leaves.

She walked towards the dog scolding it as she got closer, 'Molly stop that! I haven't got either the time or the inclination to give you a bath today.'

Grabbing the collar of the dog she slipped the chain lead back on and turned to walk away.

Something made her stop.

Turning slowly, she looked back at the disturbed earth, where the dog had been digging.

An audible gasp escaped her mouth.

Sticking out of the soil was the badly decomposed hand of a child.

A morbid fascination at what she was seeing, now drew her back in closer.

Stooping down she could now clearly see the naked torso of a young child scarcely covered by the dry powdery soil and other debris.

'Oh God, no!' she cried and backed away from the grisly discovery.

Fighting back nausea and the urge to vomit she began to walk briskly back to her car, virtually dragging the still barking Molly behind her.

As she walked she spoke to herself to try and calm her unsettled nerves,

'Come on Molly, we need to get to a phone box. That poor, poor child.'

CHAPTER 6

23rd June 1986
Major Crime Investigation Unit, Mansfield

Danny Flint walked back into the large open plan offices of the Major Crime Investigation Unit, although he'd only been away for three weeks it still felt slightly alien walking into the already bustling office.

He exchanged a few pleasantries with the detectives beavering away at their desks before walking briskly into his office. He closed the door, took off his jacket and sat down behind his desk. He glanced up at the clock, it was still only seven thirty in the morning. Danny wasn't surprised when he noticed both Rob Buxton and Brian Hopkirk standing outside his office door already.

Both the Detective Inspectors were aware that their Chief Inspector would require a full briefing the moment he arrived back to work.

Danny beckoned through the glass for the two men to come in.

'Good morning gents, good of you to be here promptly. Let's get started shall we? Grab a seat.'

Both Inspectors returned the greeting and sat down.

Rob Buxton said, 'How was the honeymoon boss?'

'It was brilliant Rob, thanks. We both had a great time, it's a very relaxing place, but it's back to work now. So gentlemen, what exactly has been happening since I've been away?'

Rob spoke up first, 'I'll let Brian brief you on the new cases first boss, I've been working on the Wade case with my team.'

'Okay Brian, fire away.'

'Right sir, there have been two new cases referred to us in the time you've been away. The first happened on the day you left and was a pub fight that went tragically wrong. A "one punch scenario" I'm afraid. Two blokes squaring up outside the Black Bull at Mansfield Woodhouse. The first punch landed by Ricky Painter knocked out Michael Lincoln. He fell without any control and smashed his head on the kerb edge. Lincoln subsequently died that night from a brain haemorrhage while he was in hospital. The offender, Painter, had already been arrested outside the pub on the night by uniform officers. He's been interviewed and subsequently charged with manslaughter. The file's already been submitted. Painter is currently on remand at Lincoln Prison.'

'And the second?' asked Danny.

'The second case is a domestic murder, but with a difference. It only happened two days ago so most of my team are still tied up doing enquiries.'

'Why a domestic murder with a difference?'

'Because the deceased in this case is the husband. It would appear that the victim, Terrence Hartnell regularly assaulted his wife Charmayne. There are numerous calls logged to the address at Rainworth for domestic assaults and Hartnell has accumulated four convictions for actual bodily harm against his spouse. Seems that Charmayne got tired of the abuse and responded to the latest punch in the face by plunging a carving knife into the chest of her husband. The post mortem revealed that the knife pierced the left ventricle of his heart. He would have died almost instantly. Charmayne was arrested at the house by the two uniform officers who had responded to the call made by the next-door neighbours. They found the husband dead in the kitchen having bled out and Charmayne still holding the bloody carving knife. At the time of her arrest she made a significant statement to the officers along the lines of, "I'm sorry, I couldn't take it anymore, I had to do something to stop him".

'Has Charmayne been interviewed?'

'Yes boss, she has. She made full and frank admissions, but is obviously claiming she acted in self-defence.'

'You said this happened in response to the latest punch. Did Charmayne have any injuries?'

'Yes, she did. All her injuries were photographed when she was detained. She had suffered a broken nose and a severe black eye. A statement has been taken from the examining Police Surgeon and will obviously form part of the file.'

'It seems to me that Terrence Hartnell was very much the architect of his own demise Brian. Do you have enough staff to carry out the remaining enquiries?'

'More than enough sir, we're well on top of it.'

'That's excellent Brian, thanks.'

Danny turned his attention to Rob Buxton and said, 'Right Rob, where are we at with the ever-elusive Jimmy Wade?'

'It's as though he has completely vanished boss. There's been no new sightings since you left for your honeymoon. The general consensus of opinion is that once again he's somehow managed to slip out of the country.'

'I'm not sure I'd go along with that theory Rob. I know he managed to get out of the country before, but that was when he was in control. Nobody had ever heard of him let alone what he looked like and he also had plenty of spare cash to fund his enterprise. Everyone in this country knows what Wade looks like now. This is a man on the run, how exactly would he fund getting out of the country?'

'The only way would be if he had help on the outside, I guess.'

'My thoughts exactly, Rob. Remember how the dog handler, what was his name?' described the track disappearing at the layby near the farm.'

'The dog handler was Pc Ryan.'

'Yes, Pc Ryan described the track disappearing at the layby near the farm.'

'I've spoken to him at length boss, he's convinced that the reason for the loss of the track was that a vehicle had picked him up.'

'I take it there have been no reports of any new missing persons from the area around Woodbeck while I've been away?'

'No boss, there haven't.'

'So, I think it's fair to say we can now rule out abduction as a theory for Wade's vanishing trick.'

'I think so boss.'

'Right, I think we need to reopen the old Coal Killer case files and trawl through Wade's history. If he's had help, the answer may lie in there. Have all the enquiries been completed with staff at Rampton?'

'Yes boss, they have. All the staff have been interviewed. Nobody up there can shed any light on things. The escape was so unexpected and so violent, most of the staff seem to be in a state of shock.'

'What about visitors to Wade while he was held in Rampton? There was some talk before I left about a woman who had visited him on a number of occasions prior to his escape?'

'That woman was identified as Melissa Braithwaite. She was spoken to by detectives from this team two days after Wade's escape. Jeff Williams and Simon Paine visited her home address after checking the hospital visitor orders. Seems like she was visiting Wade to carry out a case study for her Masters in Psychology.'

'Anything from them? Any concerns about this Braithwaite woman?'

'Nothing. Other than the fact she was quite alarmed that Wade had escaped as they had argued on her last visit. This argument between her and Wade has also been confirmed by the staff nurse supervising that visit.'

'Rob, I think it's the easy option for us to all think that Wade has gone on his toes and is well away from here. Personally, I don't think that's the case.

Something's nagging at me that he's still around here. How are the injured guards?'

'Not good I'm afraid. Steve Thorne suffered the worst injury, he is still in a coma and doctors aren't sure if he will ever recover. The other three are all recovering physically but remain in a bad way mentally.'

'I know it's going to be a lot more work for your team Rob, but I want all the staff at Rampton re interviewed. I think there's something more to this escape than meets the eye. There must be an underlying reason how he got out so easily. Has a staff member helped him? How did he get hold of a weapon? There are still too many unanswered questions and loads of avenues to explore. I need you to get your team enthused again Rob. They need to understand that it's vital we locate and recapture Wade, because we both know it really is only a matter of time before that man kills again.'

'Right you are boss, I'll draw up a list of the new enquiries and get things organised.'

Rob was interrupted by a loud knock on the office door.

'Come in!' shouted Danny.

The door opened and Dc Martin Harper walked in, 'Sorry to disturb you sir, but we've just had a call out. The body of a young child has been found in woodland off Haywood Oaks Lane near Blidworth. Dc Baxter and Dc Jefferies are already travelling to the scene and Scenes of Crime have also been requested to attend. Fran Jefferies will make the decision re a Home Office pathologist when she's assessed the scene.'

'Okay Martin, thank you.'

Dc Harper left the room as Danny and his two Inspectors stood up.

'Right, Brian carry on with the enquiries into the Hartnell case. Rob, you can travel with me out to Haywood Oaks Lane. Let's see what we've got out there and then I'll make a decision about new enquiries into Wade's escape.'

Brian replied, 'Okay sir, I'll crack on with Hartnell.'

Rob said, 'Right you are boss. It's the holiday season so I'm a couple of Dc's down, but I'll brief the remainder to expect a briefing very shortly. Nobody's on rest days today so we should have plenty of manpower. Let's see exactly what we've got out at Haywood Oaks Lane first.'

'Okay Rob, grab some car keys, I'll be out in a minute.'

Danny was left alone in his office. He grabbed his jacket from the back of his chair and muttered, 'So much for being eased back in gently.'

CHAPTER 7

23rd June 1986
Haywood Oaks Lane, Blidworth,
Nottinghamshire

As Rob parked the CID vehicle, Danny could already see another CID car and a white Transit van parked in the small parking area at the end of the dirt track. The only other vehicle he could see was a new Vauxhall Astra with a very pale looking woman standing next to it talking to Dc Fran Jefferies. The detective was already wearing a white forensic suit, latex gloves and pale blue overshoes.

Danny got out of the vehicle and walked across to her, 'Good morning Fran. What have we got?'

Fran Jefferies moved away out of earshot of the pale woman and said, 'It's the body of a young boy, I'm guessing around ten to twelve years of age. There are no obvious marks of violence but decomposition is quite bad so any injuries that had been inflicted wouldn't necessarily be obvious anyway. I've already put a call into control to request the on-call Home Office pathologist. They've just informed me that Seamus Carter is en route and has an ETA of fifteen minutes.'

'Thanks Fran, who's the woman?'

'That's Anne Parr, she's the lady who made the call. I've just finished speaking with her. It seems this is a regular place for her to take her dog for its morning walk. She says it isn't used much by other dog walkers, that's why she likes it. The dog was let off its lead when they got to the other end of the track just before it peters out. It was the dog who found the body. Mrs Parr is understandably very shaken up boss. As you can imagine it was a gruesome sight for her to see.'

'Have you obtained all her details and made arrangements to get a full written statement?'

'Yes boss.'

'Right then, you can let her go on her way. Tell her not to go gossiping this news and what she's found all over town just yet Fran. I want her out of the way before the rest of the circus gets here.'

'No problem.'

'Where's Dc Baxter?'

'Phil's down with the body sir. We've put tape down to mark our route in. There's a good set of tyre marks that may be significant boss. Scenes of Crime are already looking at getting photographs and a cast of the mark. There's only one set of tracks down to the end of the lane and back out again. Most people use the parking area here.'

'Okay Fran, good work. Have you started a log?'

'The scene log had already been started by Pc Jackson over there boss.'

She indicated a uniform Pc standing next to a small Suzuki motorcycle.

'Pc Jackson is the rural beat man for this area, he was the first responder. He's very switched on for a young cop boss. He stopped us on the road to prevent damage to the tyre marks on the track and had already started the log.'

'That's great Fran, makes a nice refreshing change.'

Danny turned to Rob, who was approaching with two sets of forensic suits and overshoes.

As the two detectives donned the protective clothing, they were approached by Pc Jackson.

'Good morning detectives, can I have your names for the log please?'

Danny replied, 'I'm Det Ch Insp Flint and this is Det Insp Buxton from the MCIU. Well done on your work so far this morning Pc Jackson.'

'Thanks sir, it's not new to me I'm afraid. I transferred up to Notts from the Met two years ago for a quieter life. I spent four years on a Homicide Investigation Unit down there. Unfortunately, I've seen way too much of this.'

'Don't you fancy the CID up here then?' asked Rob.

'Not really sir, I enjoy the community side of the work I'm doing now. Far less stressful.'

Danny nodded, 'That's your choice Pc Jackson. Well done again this morning.'

'Thanks sir.'

Danny and Rob then followed the trail of tape that marked out the route into where the body was. As they moved down the track they saw two other people wearing forensic suits. Danny recognised Tim Donnelly from the Scenes of Crime department.

Danny said, 'Good morning Tim. What have we got?'

'The deceased is a young male, we've not gone near the body yet boss, we're hanging fire until the pathologist arrives. What we do have is a brilliant set of tyre tracks. It hasn't rained for over two weeks and the ground must have been soft when this vehicle was driven along here. So, we can say that these tyre marks must have been left over a fortnight ago.'

'Any idea of the vehicle?'

'Looking at the distance between the two tracks and the width of the tyres my best guess would be a wide wheel base van. Possibly a Ford Transit or something similar.'

Danny then heard a familiar voice booming down the track, the voice echoing back off the trees.

Rob said, 'Sounds like Seamus has arrived, boss.'

Danny replied, 'We might as well hang on for him and go into the scene together.'

A few minutes later, the larger than life character that was Seamus Carter came bustling down the track. He was dressed in a blue forensic suit that was straining to contain his huge nineteen stone bulk and carrying a black leather holdall.

Seeing Danny, he grinned and said loudly, 'Are you waiting for me, Danny?'

'I thought it best when I heard you arrive, Seamus.'

'Come on then, let the dog see the rabbit, detective.'

The three men made their way down the track until at the very end they found Dc Baxter.

Dc Baxter said, 'The body is just over there, sir'.

The young detective indicated an area approximately ten yards further into the woodland at the end of a length of blue and white police tape.

'Follow me gents', said Seamus.

At the end of the tape Danny saw the naked body of a young boy. Dc Baxter had moved aside some of the leaves that had covered the child on his first inspection.

Seamus Carter squatted beside the body. After a visual examination he announced, 'I can't see any obvious marks of violence, but it's very difficult to tell anything here because of the advanced state of decomposition and the animal interference. Looking at the general state of the body I would estimate the time of death was over two weeks ago, possibly nearer three.'

'Do you think he was killed here, Seamus?'

'On first inspection of the scene I would say no. This looks to me like the classic deposition site, there are no signs of a struggle, none of the surrounding vegetation has been damaged, there are no signs of his clothes nearby. No, in my opinion this is where he was dumped after the death.'

'Anything obvious on the body that might help with identification?' asked Rob.

'Nothing that I can see, identification will probably be down to dental records. You can ask your Scenes of Crime team to come up now Danny. I've seen all I need to see, thanks. Have you arranged for removal yet?'

'Not yet Seamus. I want Tim and his team to photograph everything in situ and to get samples of the leaf and soil debris used to cover the body. Once that's all done I'll arrange for removal to the mortuary at Mansfield for the post mortem. My best guess is that we'll be in position to remove the body in a couple of hours. Have you anything planned for this afternoon? Obviously, I want this post mortem to take priority.'

'Of course, Danny, without question. Everything else can wait. I'll remain here with Tim and his team until the child is removed. I'll see you later at the mortuary.'

'Thanks Seamus, much appreciated.'

Danny and Rob passed Tim Donnelly on the way back down the track.

Danny said, 'Tim, I want you to concentrate on the tyre tracks. Get a good cast and photographs. Make sure you also get soil samples from various points along the track from the base of the tyre marks. Seamus is of the opinion that this is the deposition site, so those tyre marks could turn out to be vitally important. Do you need anything else here before I resume?'

'No Danny, we've got everything covered here, thanks.'

As the two detectives got out of their forensic suits at the side of the car Danny said, 'Any first thoughts Rob?'

'I agree totally with Seamus; the kid's been dumped here after the act. Other than that, it's too early to say. First things first, let's get him identified and see where that takes us.'

'Radio ahead and start the ball rolling on any outstanding missing persons enquiries that fit the parameters of a white male, aged between nine and thirteen years. Also arrange for a section of the Special Operations Unit to be travelling. As soon as Tim and Seamus have finished here and the body's been removed, I want that whole area fingertip searched. Tell them to tape off ten yards either side of the track and search every inch.'

'Anything else for immediate action boss?'

'Yes, I want detailed weather reports for every day over the last three weeks and I want one of these new-fangled plant experts calling in. I want samples of all the plant life recovered from the body and the surrounding area. I was reading about it just before I went away. Seamus is an expert on infestation so he will be able to help us out with that side of things. He'll be able to narrow down the time of death quite tightly by what grubs and insects he finds in and on the body. Can you think of anything I've missed?'

'I'll arrange for a cctv trawl in this area, looking for a wide wheelbase van or similar over the past month.'

'Good call Rob, like you say, first things first, let's get the poor kid identified. Someone somewhere will be missing him. Do you know what flashed through my mind when I first saw the body?'

'Jimmy Wade?'

'Exactly that Rob. Jimmy bloody Wade!'

CHAPTER 8

23rd June 1986
South Lodge, Retford

The sun was high in the sky and very hot, so going into the stone outbuilding meant stepping into some welcome cool shade.

Jimmy Wade gripped Melissa Braithwaite's arm and dragged her inside growling, 'Come on Mel, get in here, I want to show you what I've done. I need you to cast your eyes over my handiwork.'

Braithwaite let her eyes become accustomed to the gloom inside the small outbuilding.

Built entirely out of the same sandstone used to build the Lodge, the building had originally been intended as a storehouse for tools and equipment used by the gamekeeper. It was a small space measuring only eight feet by eight feet square. Apart from the door the only other feature was a small six-inch square window that could not be opened and was set high above the floor.

Jimmy Wade had dug down into the floor and there was now a six-inch step down from the door. This meant that the solitary window was now at least seven feet from the floor and couldn't be reached.

As her eyes became used to the gloomy light, Melissa looked around. She stood with her back to the door and could see manacles fitted to the walls both to the left and to the right.

The steel manacles had been bolted into the stone wall and were on short lengths of sturdy chain that looked to be about eighteen inches in length.

She shuddered involuntarily and asked in a quaking voice that was barely a whisper, 'What are they for, Jimmy?'

Wade laughed out loud and said, 'They're for our guests Mel. When they come to stay, but before they come I need to test them out first.'

Unconsciously, Melissa backed away from Wade.

He shouted, 'Come here!'

Looking down at the floor she stepped forward towards her tormentor.

Wade grabbed her roughly and dragged her towards the nearest set of manacles. Braithwaite didn't resist, she knew if she tried to struggle he would simply beat her and then still do what he wanted.

She felt the coldness of the steel manacles clamp tightly around her petite wrists.

Because of the short length of chain, she was forced down onto her haunches, eventually she turned and sat on the cold dirt floor, her arms hanging limply suspended by the manacles.

'Well don't just sit there like an idiot! At least try and get out. Start yanking at the chain.'

Braithwaite did as she was ordered and began to pull with all her might against the fixings. Nothing moved. Soon her wrists were sore and starting to bruise and she stopped struggling.

'You're pathetic! Look at you, just sitting there with that stupid look on your face! I might just leave you in here for the rest of the day to teach you a lesson. Is that what you want me to do?'

'I'm sorry Jimmy, my wrists hurt, I can't do it anymore. Please don't leave me out here, it'll be freezing cold tonight. Let me come back to the house with you. I'll make you happy, I promise.'

'If I let you go, will you help me go and collect our first house guest?'

'Of course, Jimmy, you know I'll do anything you tell me to do.'

'Do you promise me?'

'I promise.'

'Very well sweetheart, let me unlock those restraints.'

He bent forward and kissed her as he used the small brass key to unlock the manacles, 'You know I love you with all my heart, don't you Mel?'

'And I love you too Jimmy.'

He helped her up off the floor, squeezed her tightly and whispered, 'It will be such fun tonight Mel, you're going to love it. Let's go inside the house and I can tell you what we're going to do.'

She smiled up at him but inside she was filled with dread.

CHAPTER 9

23rd June 1986
Public Mortuary, Mansfield, Nottinghamshire

A sombre, depressive mood hung over the examination room in the public mortuary at Mansfield.

Laid out on the stainless-steel examination table was the small body of a young boy. Standing to one side of the table was Seamus Carter in his green robes. The size of the Irish pathologist made the body of the child look even more insignificant. All the debris and dirt had been carefully removed from the body, samples being taken as they were removed.

Standing slightly back from the other side of the table were Danny Flint and Rob Buxton. They were also dressed in the surgical green robes. At the foot of the table stood Stephen Brewer; as the senior Scenes of Crime officer he would be responsible for making a video recording of the post mortem. The only other people present were Stephanie Bridges, Seamus Carter's assistant, who was ready and waiting with a camera to photograph anything her boss requested and Dc Nigel Singleton, who had been given the task of Exhibits Officer. He would be responsible for bagging and labelling each and every exhibit handed to him by the pathologist.

Seamus Carter took a deep breath and began to speak, his words recorded both on the video tape and also on his own Dictaphone.

'Gentlemen, if we're all ready. Presented is the body of a male child, estimated age between nine and twelve years old. The body was found face down and there are the usual signs of lividity present towards the top of the body. There is a high level of decomposition that compounds that discolouration. I would estimate the time of death to be well over two weeks ago, possibly nearer three.'

Leaning forward, he very carefully, with the help of his assistant, turned the body. Examining the back of the body he said, 'There is still a great deal of heavy bruising present along the entire length of the torso from the shoulder blades down to the buttocks. This bruising would not still have been visible had the child been left on his back.'

Looking closer at the marks he said, 'They appear to be numerous individual bruises as opposed to being one large bruise. They are definitely signs of physical assault and not a crushing injury.'

Leaving the body face down, the pathologist then examined the neck, wrists and feet.

He said, 'There are no obvious ligature marks anywhere on the body so the child was never physically restrained. This is interesting though.'

Carter leaned forward and looked closer at the back of the neck, 'These marks directly on the back of the child's neck look like hand marks. They are definite bruises as though the boy has been pushed down by a large hand on the nape of his neck.'

'Is that significant?' asked Danny.

'I'll know better later in the examination, but I've seen cases where downward pressure in that area of the neck onto a soft surface can cause asphyxiation.'

'Like suffocation?'

'Exactly, it's like the opposite scenario of placing a pillow over someone's face. If you were to force someone face down onto a pillow they would suffocate. Like I say, I'll know for sure later in the examination.

The pathologist then began to examine the area around the buttocks of the boy, 'As I suspected there's a lot of evidence of sexual assault. When I examine him closer I'll know more, but from first examination it would appear that this child has been raped anally on a number of occasions, that may also explain the heavy bruising to the back. Let's turn him back over, Stephanie.'

The young assistant again stepped forward and very carefully turned the dead child over.

This time the pathologist closely examined the mouth of the child, 'There's evidence that the milk teeth have in the main fallen out, but there are still molars at the back that show evidence of amalgam fillings. Some of the front teeth have already been replaced by second teeth. Again, this is an indication that this child is aged between nine and twelve years of age.'

Danny spoke up, 'Will we be able to identify the boy using dental records?'

'There should be a dental record somewhere, like I said there's evidence of fillings being carried out. As you know Danny, the arrangement of each person's teeth is virtually unique and like most of us, this child has already had fillings. There should be dental records available somewhere. I've an orthodontist friend, Linda Greenwich, who will assist me to make comparison with this child's teeth and dental records. I'm very hopeful that together we will be able to establish the child's identity from his teeth.'

'Right gentlemen, I'm going to start the post mortem examination proper now.'

The pathologist began the grisly but necessary task of carrying out a full post mortem, taking samples as he went.

Just over an hour later the examination was complete.

Seamus Carter turned to Danny and said, 'As I suspected Danny, the cause of death is asphyxiation by the method I described at the beginning of the examination. There's evidence to show that the child has been suffocated and because of the bruising on the back of the neck, I believe his face was forced down into something soft, a pillow or a mattress maybe. I'm still of the opinion that drugs are involved as well, so hopefully the toxicology on the samples we've taken throughout the examination will prove enlightening. Although there's evidence of serious damage to the anus caused by repeated sexual assault I can't find any viable semen for possible DNA testing. This is down mainly to the general level of putrefaction. Other than some internal damage where he's been repeatedly raped, this boy shows all the appearance of being a healthy child. All the major organs appeared to be, as you would expect, pristine. Like I said Danny, I suspect that drugs of some description are involved. I have found what could be puncture wounds on the right thigh and the upper right arm, but again it is difficult for me to state categorically that these have been caused by a needle. If you look closely, there are numerous puncture wounds all over the body caused by scavenging animals and birds. I've taken samples of insect larvae from inside the body cavities, I should be able to provide you with a more accurate time of death when I've completed my studies of these samples. Do you have any questions for me, Danny?'

'When will you be able to contact this orthodontist to help you obtain an identification?'

'I'll be on the phone to her as soon as we've finished here, hopefully either this evening or first thing this morning.'

'Could it be done tonight Seamus? It's vital that we identify this child as soon as possible.'

'I'll see what I can do Danny, it shouldn't be a problem, she owes me a few favours.'

'That's great Seamus, thank you. When will you know the results of the toxicology tests?'

'I will have those for you tomorrow morning. I'll let you have them at the same time as I submit my report. Stephanie will have developed all the photographs she's taken by then and they will accompany my report.'

'That's great, thank you. One final question. You've described how this boy was raped repeatedly. Is there any way of telling whether it was by a single offender numerous times, or by numerous offenders once?'

'That's a good question Danny, based purely on the different bruising and the inordinate amount of damage caused internally, I would lean more towards numerous offenders.'

Danny nodded thoughtfully, 'I was afraid you were going to say that Seamus. I'll talk to you tomorrow when I've received your report.'

'No problem Danny, I'll work on it overnight and hopefully we'll have an identification sooner rather than later. It doesn't matter how long I do this job, I don't think I'll ever get used to examining small children that have been defiled in this way. How could people do this to a defenceless, innocent child?'

'I've got no idea Seamus. It takes a different kind of evil, that's for sure.'

CHAPTER 10

23rd June 1986
Major Crime Investigation Unit, Mansfield

It was now early evening and Danny sat alone in his office, his mind was still reeling from the post mortem. There was something infinitely devastating about attending the post mortem of a murdered child.

He reached down to the left-hand drawer of his desk and took out an almost full bottle of Bushmills Irish whiskey and a glass tumbler. Danny was no drinker, but sometimes it was the only answer to dull an unforgiving sense of pain. He unscrewed the cap from the bottle and poured a single measure into the tumbler glass.

He replaced the bottle and closed the drawer. Leaning back in his chair he lifted the glass to his mouth and swallowed the fiery liquid in one gulp. He put the glass on his desk and made a quiet commitment to himself to catch the bastards that had defiled the young boy so horrifically.

Once again, he opened the desk drawer and replaced the unwashed glass.

He looked down at the blank page of his blue hardback casebook; picking up a pen he began to write strategies and possible lines of enquiry.

In big bold capital letters, the first word he scribbled down was "Identification".

There was a loud knock on his office door, 'Come in!' he yelled.

The door opened and Dc Rachel Moore walked in, 'Sorry to disturb you boss, but I thought you'd want to hear this.'

'What is it Rachel?'

'I've been running computer checks on outstanding local missing persons that fit our criteria. I've come up with three names that look the most promising.'

'Fire away', said Danny, reaching for his pen.

'First, there's a boy by the name of Stefan Batiskowski, he's twelve years old and was reported missing five months ago from his home in Worksop. His parents are Polish. This boy has never been missing before. Secondly, Evan Jenkins, eleven years of age, he's been reported missing since the 3rd June this year. He's a persistent absconder from the Tall Trees Children's Home out at Bilsthorpe. The worrying thing about this one is that he's normally found and returned to the home within a couple of days. The longest he's ever been missing is four days. Finally, there's a boy called Bryn Gower, another twelve-year-old who went missing while he was staying at his aunt's house in Mansfield after his mum and dad split up. There's a strong belief by the relatives, that this lad has run away back to his father's house in Wales, but he still hasn't turned up yet.'

'Thanks Rachel, do you have dates of birth for them all?'

'Yes.'

'Okay, pass their details on to Seamus Carter immediately, it might help him and his dentist friend to find the correct dental records for our dead child. Good work Rachel.'

'Thanks boss. I know that now probably isn't the best time to ask, but how was the honeymoon?'

'It was lovely, thanks Rachel. Madeira is a very special place, so relaxing. I've got to say though, that it already seems like a lifetime ago. That reminds me I'd better phone my wife and tell her not to expect me home any time soon.'

'Most of the troops will be coming back in for the eight o'clock briefing soon boss. Do you need me to do anything else?'

'No thanks, just get them names over to Seamus Carter, it's only just gone six o'clock, you never know he might be able to get back to us with a positive identification before the evening briefing.'

CHAPTER 11

23rd June 1986
South Lodge, Retford

The evening sun was sinking down towards the horizon and had already dipped behind the trees that surrounded South Lodge. It looked darker and felt colder than it actually was.

Jimmy Wade carried a cardboard box that contained the items he would need later. He walked over to the non-descript dark blue Ford Transit that was parked up directly outside the stone house. He'd chosen the Transit because of its sliding door on the passenger side of the vehicle.

Wade had been with Melissa when she purchased the vehicle two and a half months ago after part chopping her Ford Sierra. He couldn't risk her continuing to drive around in the Sierra in case somebody had seen him being picked up in it on the day of the escape.

Opening the slide door, he placed the cardboard box inside. The box contained a dark brown bottle of chloroform, loose cotton rags, cable ties, gaffer tape and a heavy pall pein hammer.

Looking at the contents of the box, Wade smiled.

He'd waited patiently for this night to come. He had spent three weeks going out with Melissa most evenings trying to spot his targets. Hours spent outside the place he loathed, risking recapture. Then last week there was finally a breakthrough, he had recognised one of the two male nurses who had regularly beaten him when he first arrived at Rampton.

Wade had observed Fred Barnes walk out of the hospital, across the car park on Fleming Drive and then get into a tatty Mini Metro.

Barnes was the older of the two men that he felt compelled to get even with. He had been the ringleader and the cause of the abuse he had suffered when he first arrived at Rampton.

Wade intended to flee to Ireland as soon as he had wreaked his revenge. He planned to use Melissa to help him achieve that, but afterwards there was no place for her in his long-term plans.

Throughout his time incarcerated in Rampton and since his escape, Wade had thought long and hard about the best way to achieve a revenge he wanted so badly he could almost taste it.

He had prepared something special for both Barnes and his younger sidekick Jack Williams.

He intended to make them pay dearly for their cruelty and abuse.

Having spotted Fred Barnes with his car, it then became much easier to keep observations on the Mini Metro. It turned out that Barnes was a creature of habit. At the end of every shift he would drive to the Crown and Anchor pub on Eastern Avenue, Retford, where he would have a couple of pints before walking to his house.

If everything went to plan tonight, Barnes would not be returning to his home address.

Wade closed the door of the van and walked back to the Lodge.

He knew exactly where his target would be at ten o'clock that night, he just needed to be sure that Melissa would play her part in the abduction and imprisonment of Fred Barnes.

CHAPTER 12

23rd June 1986
Major Crime Investigation Unit, Mansfield

Danny was just about to get up from his desk to address the gathered detectives next door when the telephone rang. He lunged across the desk to retrieve the handpiece, 'Chief Inspector Flint.'

A familiar voice was on the line, 'Danny, it's Seamus. Your detective Dc Moore has hit the jackpot. The dead boy is Evan Jenkins.'

'The young lad from the children's home?'

'The very same. Linda was able to match fillings on the dental records to the dead boy's teeth, it's definitely him.'

'That's great news Seamus, thank you for sorting that out so fast.'

'Glad to assist as always Danny. It was good work by Dc Moore, she narrowed the search down massively for us.'

'I'll mention your words of praise when I see her next. Thanks again my friend.'

'No problem, I'll crack on with my report now, I should have the toxicology reports in the morning so I'll be in touch then.'

The pathologist hung up.

Danny looked down at the scribbled name in his casebook, Evan Jenkins.

He said out loud, 'Now we're in business.'

Purposefully, he strode out into the briefing room and quickly called the meeting to order, 'Right listen up everybody. First and foremost, you need to know that we are investigating this as a murder enquiry. During the post mortem the pathologist has determined that our victim had been suffocated. The boy's face had been forced down into bedding or similar by a downward pressure on the back of his neck. The pathologist is of the opinion that this could not be done accidentally and would take a wilful act. I've just received a phone call from him and I'm now able to tell you all that he and an orthodontist have been able to positively identify our dead boy from dental records. The victim's name is Evan Jenkins. He is a reported repeat absconder from the Tall Trees Children's Home at Bilsthorpe. Obviously, this changes everything and we are now going to be extremely busy for the next few weeks, so don't make any plans. Well done Rachel for identifying Jenkins as a possibility for our victim; that has saved us all an inordinate amount of time. Rachel, I want you and Sergeant Prowse to travel out to Tall Trees immediately after this briefing and speak to the person in charge. I want to know everything they can tell us about Evan Jenkins. Make sure you take possession of all the missing persons reports filed under his name and any other clothes or other property at the home that belongs to him. I want to know exactly where he's been found each time and I want to know exactly which cops brought him back and what he told them about his activities while he was missing from the home. Take as much time as you need, talk in depth to the person in charge. Find out everything you can about Jenkins' general behaviour, how he got on with the staff and the other kids? What are his parents like? Who is his social worker? I want to know everything there is to know, okay?'

Tina Prowse replied, 'No problem sir, we'll leave straight after the rest of the debrief.'

'Thanks Tina, its vitally important to the success of this enquiry that this initial visit is carried out thoroughly.'

'I understand, sir.'

Danny continued, 'I would like the rest of you to finish off what you're doing and then get off home. It's going to be an extremely busy day for everyone tomorrow. I want everybody back here at six o'clock. In the morning I want to systematically question every member of staff and every child at Tall Trees. Rachel will obtain the list tonight and you will all be allocated people to question. Start with the other kids at the home first and then move onto the staff. We should have the pathologist's findings in full tomorrow morning and hopefully the toxicology reports will be quite revealing. I anticipate a lot of work off the back of that report. Tina and Rachel, I expect you to have a late finish tonight but I still want you back here for the morning briefing. It's vital that anything you learn can be passed on directly by you to the rest of the team. I want you to identify Jenkins' parents tonight and to concentrate your day tomorrow on interviewing them. Liaise with me before you go and see them, I will need to come along to deliver the death message myself before you speak to them fully. Does anyone have any questions?'

Nobody said a word.

'Okay everyone, you know what's required. Rob, Brian follow me, I need a quick word before you leave.'

Danny walked back into his office followed by his two Detective Inspectors and closed the door.

He said, 'Sit down gents. Right, we've just been given a huge lift. Making an identification that fast is a huge bonus, we need to make the most of it. Brian, I want you to prioritise the enquiries that need doing on the Hartnell enquiry, allocate the minimum staff you need to complete that. I want you then to allocate the remainder of your team onto this enquiry. Our priority has got to be finding the killer or killers of this young child.'

Brian replied, 'No problem sir.'

Danny continued, 'Rob, I want you to use all your team on this enquiry. After Rachel and Tina have finished with the parents of Jenkins tomorrow, I'm going to allocate to them the outstanding enquiries on the escape of Jimmy Wade. It will do Tina good to have to think about prioritising their time. I know that the two of them will approach it methodically and will at the very least make some progress while everyone else is working on this enquiry.'

Rob looked concerned.

Danny saw the look and said, 'Something troubling you Rob?'

'Is it wise putting Rachel on the enquiry to find Wade? There are twenty other detectives on this unit that could all do that job. I just think it's asking a bit too much of Rachel after her troubled history with Wade.'

'I know exactly where you're coming from Rob and trust me that did cross my mind. I have to trust Rachel and I believe she is made of strong stuff and will handle it okay. I know that Rachel and Tina work brilliantly together and if anybody can find a breakthrough in that stale case, it's them two. No, my mind's made up on that one. Rachel and Tina will work the Wade enquiry after tomorrow. Anything else gents?'

Rob shook his head and Brian said, 'No sir.'

'In that case I'll see you both here at six o'clock tomorrow morning.'

The inspectors left the room and Danny sat down. He hoped he was doing the right thing involving Rachel directly in the hunt for her nemesis Jimmy Wade.

He grabbed his jacket, turned off the office light and walked out.

CHAPTER 13

23rd June 1986
Tall Trees Children's Home, Bilsthorpe, Nottinghamshire

Caroline Short opened the front door of the Children's Home and saw the two smartly dressed young women standing outside.

'Can I help you ladies?'

'My name's Sergeant Tina Prowse and this is Detective Constable Rachel Moore, we're looking for the person in charge.'

'I'm the matron in charge here. Caroline Short, how can I help you?'

'We need to talk to you about one of your residents, Evan Jenkins.'

'Have you found him at last? What's he been up to this time? It must be serious if the police have sent a sergeant and a detective?'

'May we come in please?'

'Of course, sorry where are my manners? Come through to my office.'

The two detectives followed the matron into her small office.

Caroline Short sat down behind her desk and gestured for the two officers to take a seat.

'So, what has darling Evan been getting up to this time sergeant?'

'Mrs Short, I'm sorry to have to inform you, but Evan Jenkins has been found dead. We haven't contacted his parents yet so that information is strictly confidential. We're here tonight to find out everything you can tell us about Evan.'

Caroline Short gasped, took a deep breath and said, 'Bloody hell! I wasn't expecting that! Whatever's happened to him?'

'I can't go into specifics with you right now. Suffice to say, at this moment in time we are treating his death as suspicious. Have you got copies of the paperwork for each time Evan has absconded previously?'

'Yes, of course.'

Caroline Short stood up and walked over to a grey filing cabinet, retrieving a large manila folder.

She sat back down and opened the folder, 'Here you are, Evan Jenkins. He's absconded five times in the two months he's been here. Each time he went missing he was found later in the Hyson Green area and returned to us directly by officers from Radford Road Police Station. The boy was from a very troubled background. His father's way off the scene, nobody knows who or where he is. His mother's a drug addicted prostitute who plies her trade in the red-light district around Hyson Green. There's a strong indication that Evan is, sorry was, destined to follow in his mother's footsteps. The word I'm hearing from the other boys here is that Evan's already a drug user and rumour has it that he's been known to sell his body to pay for his drugs.'

'What drugs does he use?' asked Rachel.

'Rumours are that he's on heroin.'

An incredulous Tina Prowse said, 'Heroin, at eleven years of age?'

'Yes sergeant, heroin. It's sad, but that's the environment he's been raised in, I'm afraid.'

Rachel asked, 'Did Evan have a social worker?'

'Yes, her name's Bethany Jones, she works from the Social Services office at Strelley I believe. I've got her contact details in here somewhere.'

'That's great, have you got a current address for Evan's mum as well please?'

Again, Caroline quickly flicked through the paperwork in the file, 'Here it is. Mum is Tania Jenkins and she lives at 12, Valley Walk, Hyson Green flats. I've never been to Hyson Green flats, but I'm told it's a proper dump.'

'I used to work there Mrs Short, I know the area very well, it's not as bad as people say.'

'I'll take your word on that detective. Is there anything else you need?'

'Yes, there is. Before we go I'd like to see where Evan slept and we will need to take any property of his that's still here away with us. Finally, I'd like a full list of all your staff and all the other residents living here please.'

'Why do you need that?

'Obviously, we'll be sending other detectives to talk to everyone here about Evan tomorrow morning. That will include you again, Caroline.'

'Okay, I was just wondering, it's not a problem. I'll prepare you a list. Can you tell me where Evan was found? Was it in some shithole down the city as per normal?'

'We'll have more information for you tomorrow Mrs Short, that's all we need for now, thank you.'

'No problem officers, I'll try and make sure that all the staff are here at some stage tomorrow and that the fifteen other boys that live here don't go anywhere. If you need anything else from me tonight just give me a call, the number's at the police station.'

'Thank you Mrs Short.'

'I'll show you up to Evan's room. He shared a room with two other youngsters who are fast asleep at the moment. Any property he did have is in my office. We provide all the clothes they wear. So, all there is are a few personal things.'

'Such as?'

'He's got a couple of photographs and a bit of cash. That's about it.'

The two detectives had a quick look at the bedroom without disturbing the two other boys and then took possession of Evan's few, pitiful belongings.

Caroline said, 'If that's all you need tonight detectives, I'll show you out.'

Once in the car park and alone, Tina turned to Rachel and said, 'Wow! I'm glad I don't live here. That matron's a proper cold fish!'

'My thoughts exactly, the woman appears devoid of any emotion. I'm looking forward to showing you my old beat tomorrow though. Hyson Green flats, lovely. Bring your strong stomach!'

Both women laughed and walked back to their car, unaware that they were being closely watched from an upstairs window.

CHAPTER 14

23rd June 1986
Retford town centre, Nottinghamshire

Eastern Avenue was a side street and dimly lit.

Only two old street lamps were lit along its entire length. One was outside the entrance to the Crown and Anchor pub on the corner and the other fifty yards away.

Jimmy Wade had parked the Ford Transit in deep shadow between the front door of the Crown and Anchor pub and the Mini Metro owned by Fred Barnes. The distance between the pub door and the Metro was around thirty yards, there had been plenty of space for Wade to strategically park the van.

Wade and Braithwaite had followed Barnes from Rampton Hospital and had watched the burly, middle aged nurse park his car and as usual walk back to his local. Wade had then manoeuvred the van into the position it was now in, before swapping seats with Braithwaite.

'He's taking his time tonight', fretted Wade as he fidgeted in the passenger seat.

'Don't worry Jimmy, he'll be out soon.'

'No, something isn't right. You're going to have to go inside the pub and see what the holdup is.'

'Do you think that's wise?'

'Don't argue with me, just do it.'

Without saying another word Melissa started to get out of the driver's door, but before she got completely out of the van Wade grabbed her and pulled her back inside until her face was less than an inch away from his own.

He squeezed her windpipe and growled, 'Don't try anything smart in there, don't forget I'll be watching you. Just look inside the door and see what he's up to, then get straight back here, understood.'

A terrified Melissa nodded quickly.

Wade released his grip on her throat and she spluttered as she drew air back into her bruised windpipe.

'Go on then, get inside the pub', he growled.

Shaken and frightened, she got out of the driver's door and walked along the narrow pavement to the pub. Stepping inside the smoke-filled public bar she quickly glanced around, remaining in the doorway.

Fred Barnes was sitting alone at the bar, nursing the last remaining drops of his pint. She heard the barman say, 'You having another Fred?'

'No, that's it for me tonight Tom, I'm back at work in the morning.'

Melissa turned, hurried out of the pub and back to the van.

Opening the passenger door, she spluttered, 'He's on his way now Jimmy.'

'Good, wait by the front of the van. You know what you've got to do?'

The terrified woman nodded.

Wade got out of the passenger door, then got back into the van by the side door. Climbing into the back of the vehicle, he left the sliding door slightly open.

No sooner had he got back into the van than the pub door opened, a clearly tipsy Fred Barnes stepped outside. As the pub door was closing he waved his right arm and shouted, 'G'night Tom, see you tomorrow!'

Barnes walked slowly along the narrow pavement of the gloomy street towards the dark van. He fumbled in his jacket pocket for his cigarettes and lighter, stopping just at the side of the van he took a cigarette out of the packet and lit up.

A seductive voice floated softly out of the darkness, 'Can you give me a light sweetheart?'

Hearing the soft voice, Barnes looked up and for the first time he saw the gorgeous blonde standing by the front of the van. She held a cigarette between her full red lips and walked very slowly and very sexily towards him. He turned to face her fully. He couldn't quite believe what he was seeing.

She was stunning.

Having turned to face her, he'd now left his back facing the side of the van. Fumbling for his lighter he never heard the side door of the van slide open.

Wade emerged silently from the van clutching a chloroform soaked rag in his right hand. As Barnes stood statuesque, transfixed by Braithwaite's sexy charade, Wade slipped his left arm around the man's neck and with his right hand clamped the drug soaked rag across his face, instantly covering his mouth and nose.

Almost immediately the burly charge nurse went limp, his arms falling by his side. Wade supported the dead weight of the now senseless nurse.

He growled at Melissa, 'Get in and drive.'

Wade dragged Barnes backwards, off the dark street and into the rear of the van. He quickly checked that the street was still deserted before getting in the back and closing the side door. He shouted to Braithwaite, 'Get going Mel, I'll bang on the side panels when I want you to stop.'

The diesel engine of the Transit growled into life and she drove away slowly.

Neither Wade or Braithwaite had noticed Barnes lose his grip on the metal cigarette lighter as he was drugged. The stainless-steel lighter had been presented to Barnes when he left the Army and was engraved with his name and his regiment, the Scots Guards.

As the van was driven steadily away, Wade busily secured the still unconscious Barnes with cable ties, before gagging him with gaffer tape.

A grinning Wade, punched the stricken nurse hard in the face and growled, 'You're all mine now Nurse Barnes. I'm going to make you suffer so bad you'll wish you'd never been born.'

He banged on the side panel of the van and Braithwaite immediately stopped the vehicle. Wade got out through the sliding door and jumped into the front passenger seat.

He roughly grabbed Melissa by the hair and pulled her towards him kissing her hard on the mouth, 'You were awesome sweetheart, just as we'd planned. He's ours now darling, we're going to have so much fun with him and the others when we get them.'

Braithwaite smiled weakly.

Wade grinned and said, 'Come on sweetheart, let's get home, we need to celebrate this properly in our nice warm bed.'

Braithwaite started the van; she knew only too well what that comment meant.

She would have to endure another night of depraved, rough sex with her master.

CHAPTER 15

24th June 1986
Mansfield, Nottinghamshire

Danny turned over in bed and stared at the illuminated display of his alarm clock. It was still only four fifteen in the morning. Another hour and he would be getting up. He'd been wide awake since three o'clock.

Thoughts were racing through his head about his first day back at work. The discovery of the child's body, then the post-mortem and the full realisation and understanding that the young boy had been brutally raped before being murdered.

Already he could feel the pressure building to find the men who had committed the disgusting act. The words of Seamus Carter had been the most troubling, several offenders had raped the child. An organised paedophile ring that would be well used to covering their tracks would not be easy to identify and bring to justice.

Danny felt his wife stirring in bed next to him, 'Are you awake, Danny?'

'Yes. I'm fine sweetheart, go back to sleep.'

'What is it?'

'It's nothing, go back to sleep.'

'Listen Danny, when something's bothering you, you've got to talk to me. I'm wide awake now anyway. Let's go downstairs and have a coffee, we've both got to be up soon anyway. I'm on early turn at the hospital today.'

Danny sat up in bed, 'Okay, I'll go and put the kettle on.'

Ten minutes later Danny and Sue sat at the breakfast table sipping hot mugs of coffee.

'So, what is it that's keeping you awake after one day back at work detective?'

'The body of a young boy was found in the woods yesterday, he'd been raped and then suffocated.'

'Do you know who he is yet?'

'Yes, we found out late last night, he was only eleven years old for Christ's sake.'

Sue reached across the table and gripped her husband's hand.

Danny went on, 'Seamus reckons that the boy was assaulted by a number of men before he was killed.'

'That's awful Danny, where will you start to look?'

'We'll start where we always do, by looking at the victim and trying to find a link that somehow leads to the bastards that are responsible.'

'So, you know exactly what you're doing then Danny? How you're going to catch these men? How you're going to protect other innocent children?'

'I know what I want to do Sue, but will it be enough? Will I be able to catch them?'

'Stop doubting yourself Danny, I know you'll catch them. I also know that you won't stop until you do. Whenever you need to talk sweetheart, I'm here. I've seen plenty of death and heartache, too much. You've got to let me help you. We're a team you and me. When I took those vows Danny, I meant every word. I don't want you bottling things up inside you, that's when the pressure can become destructive. Always understand that you can confide in me. Don't worry, I'll definitely be unloading on you from time to time when things get too hectic at the hospital. Casualty is no place for shrinking violets Danny. Talk to me.'

'Thanks sweetheart. I suppose I'm just not used to having anyone to talk to about things, that's all. I do feel better now we've spoken. I will confide in you more and I will catch these bastards.'

'I know you will darling, now drink your coffee. We both need to shower before work.'

'It's a good job we've got a big shower then.'

They both stood up and holding hands made their way upstairs.

CHAPTER 16

24th June 1986
South Lodge, Retford

It was the freezing temperature that finally roused Fred Barnes.

He was shivering violently as he woke.

Horrified, he discovered that he was now totally naked and lying on a dirt floor. His eyes gradually became accustomed to the dim light and he started to scan the room he was in. He could see it was very small and the walls were made of a bare rock. The roof was way above his head and he could see bare wooden rafters beneath the tiles. The only door into the room, looked heavy and was made of some kind of hardwood. The only light coming in was through a very small window that looked to be about six inches square and was situated high above him. It allowed a single shaft of sunlight down into the gloomy room.

His arms were aching

He tried to stand and instantly realised why there was such a nagging pain in his shoulders. Both his wrists had been secured to steel manacles that were bolted into the stone walls. The movement he made as he tried to stand caused an agonising pain to fire through his wrists. He immediately gave up the attempt to stand and slumped back onto his side. He twisted his arms to the right to try and ease a little of the pressure caused by the manacles to the tender skin around his wrists.

As his eyes cleared and got used to the subdued lighting he made a closer inspection of the metal that secured him. He saw that the manacles were in fact secured to the wall on a short length of chain. He manoeuvred himself around until he was sitting in the best spot for comfort.

He looked down at his wrists and to his dismay saw that both were red and extremely sore. The skin around the bones on his right wrist had almost broken. Whoever had imprisoned him in this dungeon had taken no care about the condition he'd been left in.

Barnes sat in silence.

He tried desperately to control his shivering and come to terms with his predicament. Vainly he tried again and again to pull the chain securing the manacles from their fixings. All he achieved was to finally break the skin and cause his right wrist to bleed.

With a resigned groan, he gave up.

He breathed in deeply through his nose, the only smell he could detect was the damp earth he was sitting on.

Suddenly, a thought flashed into his mind. He had a vision of a beautiful blonde asking him for a light.

His head was aching.

Barnes could feel the blood coursing through his temples.

He strained his ears for any clues to his whereabouts.

The only sounds he heard, were birds singing and away in the distance he could hear the sound of running water. What sounded like a small stream falling over stones was definitely not far away from the building.

He took a deep breath and shouted at the top of his voice, 'Help me!'

There was no response.

Five times he shouted before he gave up, resigned to the fact that there wasn't a single person nearby to hear his cries.

Again, he tried to remember how he had come to be there.

As the fogginess in his brain cleared he started to recall the events of the previous night. He recalled leaving the Crown and Anchor pub after his usual second pint and walking along the dimly lit street towards his car.

He remembered lighting a cigarette.

Again, the vision of the gorgeous blonde burst into his mind.

'She asked me for a light', he said aloud.

Thoughts flooded in again.

Who the hell was she? How had giving her a light for a cigarette caused him to be here?

Who would want to capture him and hold him captive?

Nothing made any sense.

With a sense of real despair and hopelessness, once again Barnes shouted at the top of his voice, 'Somebody help me!'

Once again, his pitiful pleading was answered with a stony silence.

CHAPTER 17

24th June 1986
Major Crime Investigation Unit, Mansfield

Danny Flint walked into the briefing room at the Major Crime Investigation Unit. The clock on the briefing room wall showed it was now six fifteen. Every detective on the Unit was already present.

Sitting at the front of the room flanked on either side by Rob Buxton and Brian Hopkirk, Danny commenced the morning briefing.

'Good morning everyone. First things first. Tina and Rachel, how did you get on last night at Tall Trees?'

Tina answered, 'We spoke with the matron in charge, a woman by the name of Caroline Short. She's provided us with the list of staff who work there and the list of other residents that you wanted. She's assured us that none of the other residents will be going anywhere today and that she'll endeavour to ensure that all the staff will be available to be interviewed at some time today.'

'Thanks Tina, come and see me after the briefing with those lists so the enquiries can be allocated to their teams by the detective inspectors.'

Tina nodded.

Danny continued, 'Rachel, how was the Matron?'

'She was very helpful boss. She hasn't been in post that long, just over fourteen months I believe. She seems keen to help, but also comes across as being a little cold and aloof at times.'

'Did she have details of Evan Jenkins' parents?'

'There's only Mum. Dad isn't around anymore it would seem. Mum is Tania Jenkins, she lives at Valley Walk in Hyson Green flats. Caroline Short described the mother as being a drug addicted prostitute. I did some checks last night and Tania does have several convictions for soliciting and possession of Class A drugs. She's been cautioned numerous times and two years ago she received a twelve-month prison sentence for possession of drugs. No convictions over the last five months though.'

'Thanks Rachel, did you manage to ascertain who is Evan Jenkins' social worker?'

'Again, the information came from Caroline Short, she informed us that according to her records, Evans' social worker worked from the Strelley office. Her name's Bethany Jones.'

'What did Caroline Short have to say about the deceased?'

Tina replied, 'She was quite harsh in her assessment of Evan. She described how he was already using Class A drugs, namely heroin, and that whenever he absconded he was to be found around the red-light area of Hyson Green. Without actually saying as much she inferred that he was selling his body to pay for drugs.'

'That's interesting. When we've seen the mother this morning, I would like you and Rachel to track down this social worker and see if she confirms or refutes that rather damning assessment.'

'Will do sir.'

'Okay everyone, our priorities today are to find out as much as we can about our victim, Evan Jenkins. You will all be given either a member of staff or one of the residents to interview. Make sure you are as thorough as possible. The more we can find out about our victim today, the more likely it is we'll be able to find out who did this to him. Detective Inspector's Buxton and Hopkirk will see you all individually with your allocated subject. Until then, spend your time wisely and familiarise yourself with the location where Jenkins was found, the location of the Tall Trees Children's Home and the injuries sustained by the deceased. Are there any questions?'

The room remained silent.

Danny turned to Rob and Brian, 'Come into my office let's get these lists organised, so you can start allocating individuals to your teams for interview. I'm going to Hyson Green this morning with Tina and Rachel. I want to see Tania Jenkins to break the news about her son personally and tell her about our enquiries so far. I will call in at headquarters later to fully brief the Chief Superintendent and discuss how soon we release details of the victim to the press.'

Rob said, 'While you're at Hyson Green do you want me to chase up Seamus Carter for the results of the toxicology tests?'

'If he hasn't called by eleven o'clock, be my guest. He had quite a late night yesterday sorting out the identification. I'm sure he'll contact us as soon as he has the results, but chase him at eleven o'clock anyway. After that bombshell from Caroline Short about him already being a Class A drug user, those toxicology results could be very interesting.'

'Will do boss.'

CHAPTER 18

24th June 1986
Hyson Green, Nottingham

Rachel Moore drove the CID car into the large car park of the new Radford Road Police Station.

Danny was already waiting, he was leaning against the side of his car with his arms folded across his chest.

It was just after eight fifteen in the morning but the sun was out and it already felt warm. It was going to be another hot day.

'Come on ladies, what kept you? I've been here five minutes already.'

It was a joking rebuke and Danny grinned.

Rachel smiled back and said, 'When I've got a sergeant in the car with me I prefer to adhere to the speed limits boss.'

'This is your old stamping ground isn't it Rachel? I thought I'd better wait for the guided tour.'

'Oh yes, lots of unhappy memories working these streets. We can walk to the flats from here boss, it's not far.'

'Come on then, let's go and break the bad news to Tania.'

The three detectives walked out of the car park and along Radford Road towards Gregory Boulevard.

The grey concrete jungle that made up the infamous Hyson Green flats, soon came into view.

'Valley Walk's this end of the flats boss, we can get to it up that walkway.'

Rachel indicated a sloping ramp that led from the street up to the raised walkways that in turn led to the flats.

Danny noticed that many of the flats were now boarded up with secure metal grilles.

'Why are so many boarded up Rach?'

'Rumour has it that the flats are earmarked for demolition in the next couple of years. The council are gradually rehousing tenants and not filling the empty flats. Not before time if you ask me. It was the brainchild of some warped fifties architect, but for the people who have had to live here this place has always been a dump.'

Danny looked around him, the sense of deprivation in the inner city estate was everywhere. Litter blew along the stark, damp walkways. The stench of mould and rotting rubbish was everywhere. There wasn't a wall that hadn't been daubed with graffiti of some kind or another.

'Come on, let's get this done Rachel, this place is the pits.'

'This is Valley Walk boss, we want number twelve.'

Tina Prowse led the way onto the narrow walkway and began scanning the doors for number twelve.

Finding a red door with the number twelve painted on it in white emulsion she said, 'I think this is us, boss.'

Danny stepped forward and saw that the base of the red door had been on fire at some stage and was charred and blackened.

He muttered, 'Jesus Christ', and using his clenched fist, hammered on the already damaged door.

There was no reply.

The next door along the walkway opened and an elderly West Indian woman leaned around the door frame.

'Who dat banging the place down at this time of day?'

Tina replied, 'Sorry to disturb you, we're looking for Tania. Is this the right flat?'

'Who wanting to know?'

Tina took out her warrant card and said, 'We're police officers. We need to talk to Tania about her boy.'

'I thought you looked like Babylon. That's her flat alright, but you gonna have to bang harder to wake that girl. She been out all night working, if you know what I mean officer.'

'Thanks.'

Danny began to knock on the door even louder, then lifted the letterbox and shouted, 'Tania! It's the police. Open the door, we need to speak to you about Evan. It's important!'

A faint response came from within the decrepit flat, 'Just a minute, I'm coming.'

Very slowly several bolts were drawn back and the door was opened one inch.

'Show me your warrant, or I ain't letting you in.'

Danny wedged his foot in the small opening of the door to prevent it being slammed shut and said quietly, 'Tania open the door please. I'm afraid I've got some bad news about Evan.'

Slowly the door was opened.

The three detectives walked into the flat and followed Tania Jenkins down the hallway into the small lounge. She was dressed in old pyjamas; her hair was dark and lank and a half-smoked roll up cigarette dangled from her mouth.

The flat was barely furnished, a stained dark brown three-piece suite, a battered coffee table and a television in the corner made up the entire furniture in the front room. There was a large picture of Bob Marley on the wall over the two-bar gas fire. On the floor was a threadbare carpet, covered in discarded, unwashed clothes and half empty food cartons from the local takeaways. Stuffed in the corner next to the stained settee was an overflowing ashtray. Sitting to the side of the ashtray were a couple of used syringes. The room reeked of stale rotting food and a pall of blue cigarette smoke hung in the air.

The flat was disgusting.

Danny looked at the woman and asked, 'Tania Jenkins?'

'Yes, I'm Tania. You said it wasn't good news about my boy Evan. What's the little shit been up to now?'

'I'm really sorry to have to tell you this Tania, Evan is dead.'

'What you talking about copper? He's not dead, he's just run away from that poxy kids home again.'

'Tania, my name's Danny Flint. I'm the Chief Inspector in charge of the Major Crime Investigation Unit. I'm sorry, but Evan was found dead yesterday in woods near Mansfield. He'd been murdered, Tania.'

The enormity of what she was being told slowly began to register.

Suddenly, Tania let out a long low moan that turned into a high-pitched scream of a single word, 'Nooooo!'

Rachel stepped forward and put her arms around the distraught woman and eased her down until she was sitting on the settee.

After a couple of minutes, the sobbing stopped and Tania looked up at Danny, 'Who would do that to my lovely little boy?'

'We don't know yet, Tania, but we'll find whoever did it, I promise you that.'

'Can I see my beautiful boy?'

'These two detectives will arrange that with you today. I wanted you to hear this directly from me Tania. I want you to know you can call me or any of the detectives trying to find the people who did this at any time, night or day, okay.'

'Thank you, did you say your name's Flint?'

'Yes, I did Tania, it's Danny Flint. I'll leave you with Sergeant Prowse and Detective Moore now. It might take us a long time, but we'll find them I promise you.'

'If you do find them, it won't bring my boy back though will it?'

'No, it won't and I'm sorry I can't do that.'

'He was supposed to be in care Mr Flint. They said I couldn't look after him and they took him away from me and now he's dead! It's fucked up, that's what it is!'

'I know Tania, and I'm sorry.'

Danny walked out of the small flat followed by Tina, Rachel remained in the living room trying to comfort the distraught mother.

Once outside Danny said, 'Take it slowly with her Tina, take as long as you need. It's vitally important that we find out if she's aware of any drug abuse involving Evan. I want you and Rachel to ignore the evidence of drug abuse in the flat, the old syringes on the floor and anything else, we need to glean what we can from her without turning her against us. If you haven't got time to see Evan's social worker today, so be it. That enquiry will keep until tomorrow. You'd better get back in there with Rachel, I'll find my own way back to the car.'

'Ok sir, we'll contact you as soon as we leave here to let you know what Tania's got to say.'

'Thanks Tina.'

Danny put both of his hands in his pockets and walked off along the graffiti stained walkway.

The words from Tania Jenkins were still ringing in his ears, "He was supposed to be in care and now he's dead!"

CHAPTER 19

24th June 1986
Rampton Hospital, North Nottinghamshire

Jack Williams was puzzled.

It was nine thirty in the morning and he'd just started his shift at Rampton Hospital. He had worked at the high security hospital for three years now and throughout that time had always worked with Fred Barnes.

Fred was quite a bit older than he was, but he was ex-military and a good laugh. More importantly he took no shit from the nutters they had to look after. Fred was always quick to put them in their place and give them a slap. It was a part of the job Jack had come to enjoy and he now regularly joined in with Fred when a prisoner needed putting in their place.

The prisoners never complained anyway and it was good fun sometimes letting them know who was in charge. The odd smack around the back of the heads of the lunatics they had to deal with everyday wouldn't hurt.

It never did them any harm.

Jack was puzzled because the ex-Guardsman had not turned in for his day shift. In all the years they had worked together Fred Barnes had never missed a shift and he'd seemed fine when he left work yesterday.

The last thing he'd said to Jack was that he was nipping to his local for a couple of beers to help him sleep.

It was what Fred always said, he was a creature of habit.

Jack decided that if he didn't show up for work tomorrow morning, he would nip round after work to Fred's house in Retford and make sure he was okay.

He knew Fred had no family, so a quick visit to make sure he was okay was exactly what a good mate should do.

CHAPTER 20

24th June 1986
Mansfield Police Station, Nottinghamshire

Detective Sergeant Andy Wills walked into the canteen situated at the rear of the police station. The smell of recently fried bacon and sausage was drifting along the corridor and had enticed a very hungry Andy into the canteen.

Because of the early start, he'd missed getting breakfast at home, but now he had fifteen minutes where he could get something before he started his enquiries at the kids home in Bilsthorpe.

He smiled at the woman behind the counter and said, 'I'd like one of your delicious bacon cobs and a large coffee please Gina.'

'No problem Andy, would you like some tomatoes on your bacon cob?'

'Go on then, you've twisted my arm. I'd better grab a couple of napkins, I can't walk round all day with tomato juice down my tie, now can I?

'God forbid, the smartest detective on the CID with tomato juice on his tie, that would never do Andy', laughed Gina.

She continued, 'Grab a seat, I'll bring your cob over in a minute.'

Andy laughed and said, 'Thanks Gina.'

As soon as he sat down he saw a uniform officer walk in for his refreshment break. Andy recognised the officer as Pc Dave Bracewell who worked the rural mobile patrol that covered Bilsthorpe.

The constable ordered his breakfast and then sat down at the same table as Andy.

'Good morning sarge, are you working on the murder of that kid that had run away from Tall Trees?'

Andy nodded and said, 'You work that area, don't you Dave?'

'It was me that took the Missing Person's report for that kid when he ran off this time.'

'Has anyone from our office spoken to you yet?'

'No not yet, this is my first shift back. I've been away on holiday. I only found out the kid was dead when I came on duty this morning.'

Gina arrived at the side of the table carrying Andy's bacon and tomato cob and a mug of coffee.

She put the plate and the mug in front of Andy and said, 'There you go detective, enjoy. Your breakfast will be ready in a couple of minutes Dave.'

Andy said, 'Thanks Gina,'

Dave nodded in acknowledgement and then said, 'I won't disturb your breakfast sarge.'

'Dave, come and see me in our office when you've had your breakfast and we'll have a quick chat, okay.'

'Okay sarge, will do.'

Andy devoured his cob and stood up. He shouted to Gina, 'Okay if I take the mug with me Gina?'

'No problem, but bring it back when you get a minute please.'

Andy looked at Dave who was wading his way through a huge full English.

'Don't forget to come and see me when you've finished that Dave.'

With a mouth half full of sausage Dave nodded and said, 'I'll only be ten minutes sarge.'

About fifteen minutes later Dave Bracewell walked into the Major Crime Investigation Unit offices.

He looked around the office seeking out Andy Wills. He saw the sergeant sitting at a desk near the windows.

'Right sarge, what do you want to know?'

'Grab a seat, Dave.'

Dave sat down opposite.

'How long have you worked out at Bilsthorpe, Dave?'

'For the last three years, off and on.'

'So, you must get up to Tall Trees quite a bit then?'

'Way too much for my liking, the kids are always bloody running off.'

'Has it got better or worse recently?'

'We do seem to have to go up there more and more.'

'What reasons do the kids give for running off when you take them back?'

'It's a job to get anything out of the little bleeders, they don't want to know do they? Every time I go up there they make pig noises at me. They never say much when I take them back.'

'What about Evan Jenkins?'

'This was the first time I'd taken a misper report about him. Caroline said he was always running off, she was surprised I didn't know his name.'

'Caroline?'

'Caroline Short, the matron at the home. I took the report of Evan Jenkins absconding from her.'

'Is that usual?'

'I wouldn't say it was usual, especially on nights, its usually a member of staff, but sometimes it's Caroline who sees you and makes out the report.'

'That's twice you've called her Caroline and not matron. Do you get on well with her?'

'Yeah, Caroline's great. Not like some of the staff who can be a real pain in the arse. She's made a big difference since she started there.'

'How long's Caroline been in charge?'

'I'm not sure, a couple of years maybe.'

'Getting back to when you took the misper report for Evan Jenkins, was there anything out of the ordinary with the report?'

'Not with the report, that was standard stuff. I do remember something strange that happened as I was coming out of the home though. It came to me this morning when I found out that Evan Jenkins had been killed. It didn't seem to matter at the time.'

'What was that, Dave?'

'One of the kids was on the landing as I walked out. He whispered something that I just dismissed at the time, but like I say it now seems very relevant.'

'What did the kid say?'

'He just whispered that Jenkins wouldn't be back.'

'What do you think he meant?'

'I don't know, but bearing in mind what's happened to the kid, you've got to agree it's pretty weird.'

'Do you know which kid it was who made the comment?'

'Yeah, it's another one who's always legging it, a lad called Tommy Quinn.'

'Are you doing much this morning, Dave?'

'Only routine patrol, why?'

'Who's your sergeant?'

'Sergeant Davies.'

'I'll talk to her and see if I can take you off patrol. I want you to come with me and talk to Tommy Quinn.'

'No problem, if you can swing it with the sarge.'

'I'll speak to your sergeant, Dave, I think we need to know exactly what Tommy Quinn meant by that comment.'

Andy looked up from his desk and saw Brian Hopkirk across the other side of the office; he knew that the Detective Inspector was co-ordinating the interviews with residents and staff at Tall Trees Children's Home that morning.

He walked over and said, 'Boss, who's down to interview Tommy Quinn at Tall Trees this morning?'

The inspector glanced down at a sheet of paper on the desk, 'Lyn Harris and Simon Paine. They're down to interview him and another lad, Freddie Williams, why?'

'I'm going over to Tall Trees in a minute with Pc Bracewell, we need to talk to Tommy Quinn about something he said to Dave on the night Evan Jenkins went missing.'

'No problem Andy, Lyn and Simon are due to talk to Williams first, so I doubt they will have got to Quinn yet. With my compliments, tell them to interview Mrs Hilda Smith, one of the staff, after they've finished with Freddie Williams. You were down to interview Mrs Smith, I'll change the list so you can speak to Quinn.'

'Thanks boss.'

'What was said by Quinn, that's got you fired up Andy?'

'He told Pc Bracewell that Jenkins wouldn't be back.'

CHAPTER 21

24th June 1986
South Lodge, Retford

Jimmy Wade stood by the door of the stone outhouse and giggled quietly.

At his side, as always, was Melissa Braithwaite. She was shivering even though the temperature was rising steadily. She felt sore and bruised after her night of rough sex with Wade. He'd made her stop the van in which they were travelling on the way back from abducting the male nurse from Retford. He had then forced her out of the driver's seat and forced her to have sex pressed against the side of the van, where they could hear the moans of the bound nurse secured in the back of the vehicle.

When they finally arrived back at the Lodge, Wade had carried the burly male nurse from the back of the van and into the outhouse. He had then stripped the unconscious man and manacled him to the wall, leaving him naked and chained.

Braithwaite had watched in silence, fearing what was going to happen next. Her worst fears had then materialised; Wade, aroused by the capture of his tormentor, had then dragged her into the bedroom and raped her several times overnight. She had developed her own coping strategy and pretended to enjoy the rough sex, she knew if she tried to resist or complain it would only get worse.

She hadn't seen Wade this aroused for a long time and she dreaded what today was going to bring.

Wade smiled at her and said, 'We're going to have some real fun today Mel. I've been thinking about it all night. I don't want Barnes to know it's me that's got him yet. I want you to go inside and listen to what he's got to say. Don't speak to him, don't say a word just stare at him and let him ramble on. I'm going to watch through the little window.'

'Okay Jimmy.'

Melissa started to walk towards the door.

'Wait a minute Mel, come here.'

She stopped and walked the couple of steps back towards Wade.

He ripped her white cotton blouse, leaving her breasts exposed.

He laughed and said, 'That's better, let's see what Barnes makes of that.'

Almost trancelike, she turned once again and walked towards the heavy wooden door. Using the key Wade had given her she unlocked the big padlock that secured the door, leaving the key in the lock.

She opened the door and stepped inside, leaving it slightly ajar to allow a little more light into the small space.

Instantly she recoiled at the smell. Barnes had soiled himself overnight and the stench of human faeces was almost overpowering. Fearing what Wade would do if she stepped back out of the room, she steeled herself and stepped inside fully.

She could now see the naked man squatting on the dirt floor. His hands were out to his right, still encased in the metal manacles.

In a tremoring voice the man asked, 'What the fuck's going on? Who are you?'

As Wade had instructed, Melissa said nothing.

She stood facing the man with her back to the small window.

Barnes eyes constantly darted from the womans face to her breasts and back again, then almost with a whimper he said, 'Why are you doing this to me?'

Still she said nothing and just stared down at the stricken man.

Barnes began to beg, 'Please can't you just let me go? I've done nothing to hurt you. I'm sorry if I offended you when I gave you a light. I really didn't mean anything by it. You're a beautiful woman, I thought I was being polite.'

There was a faint tapping noise on the small glass window above her head.

Braithwaite took it as her cue to leave and walked out of the room.

Barnes wailed, 'Don't go, please. Just let me go. I'm begging you. I need water, can you get me a drink please?'

She ignored his pleadings and stepped back outside into the sunlight.

Wade was waiting for her when she got outside.

He was holding a claw hammer.

'Go back inside and tell him you're going to keep him here for sex and that if he does as he's told you'll let him live.'

Trembling, she asked, 'What's the hammer for, Jimmy?'

'You need to show him you mean business. Get back inside and give him a few whacks with the hammer. Don't hit his head though, go for his ribs.'

'I don't think I can do that that, Jimmy.'

'What did you say?'

In a voice little more than a whisper she said, 'I don't think I can do that to him.'

Wade's face flushed red and he growled, 'You've got a choice sweetheart. Get back inside and give him a couple of clouts or spend the rest of the day in there chained up with him. Your choice. Don't make me tell you again!'

Fighting back tears of fear and frustration she grabbed the hammer and turned to go inside again.

Wade stopped her, closed her blouse with the one remaining button and said, 'For fucks sake Mel cover yourself up, you look like a tart!'

She quickly straightened her ripped blouse until her breasts were covered and walked through the door.

Barnes instantly saw the hammer and recoiled.

Like a woman possessed Braithwaite launched a flurry of vicious blows at the defenceless man. The hammer landed squarely on the ribcage of Barnes and there was an audible crack as one of his ribs snapped under the force of the blow.

Hearing the noise as the bone snapped, she heaved and stopped her assault. Gagging, she turned and stepped out of the building.

Wade was laughing and snapped the padlock shut on the door.

He took the hammer from her, laughed and said, 'You see, that was fun, wasn't it? I knew you could do it. We'll come back again this afternoon, you can watch through the window when I introduce myself to Mr Barnes. I want some fun with him before we get his dopey sidekick this evening. Are you going to watch me have some fun Mel?'

'Of course, Jimmy, I wouldn't miss it.'

CHAPTER 22

24th June 1986
Tall Trees Children's Home, Bilsthorpe, Nottinghamshire

Detective Sergeant Wills and Pc Bracewell arrived at Tall Trees Children's Home and parked the CID car in the main car park in front of the home.

The home was already a hive of activity. Several CID cars were parked up alongside other vehicles that belonged to the staff at the home.

Andy and Dave walked towards the front door of the home and were met by Caroline Short standing in the doorway.

She was standing alone smoking a cigarette, leaning against the open front door.

Seeing Dave Bracewell approaching she took a long pull on her cigarette and said, 'Hello Dave, it's nice to see a friendly face this morning, your lot are everywhere inside talking to all the kids and the staff. What brings you out here?'

Dave glanced at Andy Wills and replied, 'I'm here with Detective Sergeant Wills, we need to speak to Tommy Quinn.'

With an almost smug grin Caroline replied, 'You'll have a job, Dave. Quinn legged it about an hour ago. I was just about to ring it through to your control room. I think he got pissed off at the thought of being spoken to by the CID.'

Dave exclaimed, 'Bloody hell!'

'Why do you need to see Tommy anyway? I thought the CID were dealing with this?'

Andy Wills interjected, 'I want to talk to Tommy about something he said to Pc Bracewell on the night Evan Jenkins went missing.'

'Tommy didn't say anything, he wasn't there that night.'

Dave said, 'Yes he was, Caroline. Don't you remember, you shouted at him to get to bed just as I was leaving? He said something to me as I was going out the door.'

'Well, I never heard anything, are you sure he was saying something to you?'

'Whether he did or he didn't is immaterial, I still want to talk to him', said Andy before continuing, 'Now, can we go inside to your office and have a look at Tommy Quinn's records so I can find out where he was found on the previous occasions he's absconded. I want to know where we can locate him.'

She allowed a strained smile to pass her lips and said, 'Of course, follow me. Do you want your usual cup of coffee Dave?'

'That would be lovely, thanks Caroline.'

'Detective Sergeant Wills?'

'I'm fine, thanks.'

Half an hour later and armed with the locations where Tommy Quinn had been found on previous occasions, the two police officers were in the CID car driving back towards Mansfield.

Andy was deep in thought, he'd noticed the smug reaction of the matron when she told them that Tommy Quinn had absconded and couldn't be spoken to.

Andy stopped the car at a set of traffic lights as they turned to red. He turned to Dave and said, 'Do you think Caroline Short heard what Tommy said to you that night?'

'I'm not really sure, sarge. She could well have done, I suppose. It was certainly loud enough for me to hear it.'

'What was her reaction on the night?'

'She never mentioned it, just bellowed at Tommy to get back to his room.'

'So, she never acknowledged that anything had been said?'

'No, not at all.'

'How did she seem to you today Dave?'

'Definitely not her normal self. She looked proper stressed out, but she's going to be with all this carry on, isn't she?'

'I suppose so Dave, I suppose so. Where's the best place to look for Tommy then?'

The lights turned to green and Andy drove on.

'Reading his file, he's been found on three previous occasions at the Spinning Palace, a slot machine arcade in Mansfield town centre.'

'Could he have got there yet?'

'It's doubtful, unless he managed to jump straight on a bus when he legged it into Bilsthorpe.'

'We'll go there first anyway. I'll have a word with the manager and get him to call our office as and when Tommy Quinn comes into the arcade. If he's that much of a regular the manager will know him. There's a photo in the file isn't there?'

'Yes sarge.'

'I haven't asked you Dave, what do you think Tommy meant by his comment?'

'I've been thinking about that all day. I just don't know. He was almost laughing when he said it to me. He definitely knew something I didn't.'

'Come on then, let's get down to the Spinning Palace arcade. With a bit of luck we'll be able to ask him that question ourselves sooner rather than later.'

CHAPTER 23

24th June 1986
Mansfield Police Station, Nottinghamshire

There was a loud knock on Danny's office door.

'Come in!'

Chief Superintendent Bill Wainwright opened the door and walked in.

Danny stood up and said, 'Good morning sir. I was just coming over to Headquarters to see you.'

'Well I've saved you the trip Danny. I fancied getting out of the office for an hour, so I thought I'd come over and see how thing are progressing with this dead child.'

Both men sat down and Danny said, 'Things are moving on Bill, we identified the boy late last night. His name's Evan Jenkins, he was in the care of the local authority and was a resident at the Tall Trees Children's Home over at Bilsthorpe.'

'Is it definitely a murder, Danny? I saw that he was found in woodland. It's not a case of an absconder getting hypothermia, is it?'

'Definitely not sir. I should have come over to headquarters and briefed you fully yesterday, but it was a bit full on and also my first day back. I know that's no excuse, you need to know what's going on.'

'I'm not going to argue with that Danny, the Chief stopped me this morning for an update when I arrived at work. Needless to say, I blagged it, but it was slightly embarrassing.'

'I can only apologise for that, Bill.'

'No harm done Danny. So, fill me in now, what do we know?'

'Okay, as I said we now know the dead boy is Evan Jenkins, eleven years of age. In the care of the local authority and a resident at Tall Trees Children's Home. His home address was Valley Walk in the Hyson Green flats. I've been there this morning to see his mother Tania. I wanted to break the news of her sons murder to her in person.'

'How was she?'

'Understandably, very upset. She made the point that the authorities had taken him into care to keep him from harm and now he was dead. I thought it was a very valid point.'

'Definitely. Some of those kid's homes are like a revolving door, aren't they? They're not secure accommodation, so the kids come and go virtually as they please, getting up to all sorts of mischief and crime as well as exposing themselves to all sorts of risks. How did the boy die? Have you had the result of the post mortem yet?'

'I've not received Seamus Carter's written report yet, but I attended the post mortem he carried out yesterday. He has verbally identified the cause of death as asphyxiation. The boy had been smothered. He'd also been badly sexually assaulted.'

'In what way sexually assaulted?'

'He'd been anally raped by several men.'

'Bloody hell!'

'Seamus Carter's of the opinion that the boy had been assaulted by several different men on a single occasion as opposed to a single man on several occasions.'

'I know the man is bloody good at what he does Danny, but how the hell can he tell that?'

'Something to do with the internal damage suffered by the boy and the different bruising on his back.'

'So, what are your thoughts? Do you think we're looking for an established paedophile ring?'

'Obviously I'm keeping an open mind, but yes that's the way I'm leaning.'

'Jesus Christ Danny, you're going to have your work cut out. These bastards really know how to cover their tracks.'

'I know sir, that's what's worrying me.'

'So what enquiries have you got running?'

'We're concentrating on background knowledge at the moment. My staff are all out at Tall Trees today, interviewing all the residents and staff at the home. Rachel Moore and Tina Prowse are still with Tania Jenkins getting all they can from her. I'm expecting the full post mortem report from Seamus Carter any time now. He thinks the toxicology reports will also be significant. The matron at Tall Trees, Caroline Short, has already inferred that Evan Jenkins, although only eleven years of age was abusing Class A drugs.'

'Bloody hell Danny, this just gets better. Have you considered a press release yet?'

'Now that Tania Jenkins has been properly informed I'm organising one for this evening. My intention was to keep it deliberately vague, you know the sort of thing, the police have launched a murder enquiry after the body of an eleven-year-old child was found in woodland near Mansfield yesterday. The relatives have been informed and police enquiries are ongoing.'

'Sounds spot on Danny, have you got any suspects yet?'

'Not really Bill.'

'That's a strange comment Danny, what do you mean "not really"? Either you have or you haven't.'

'Sorry. I mean no, there aren't any suspects. It's just that Jimmy Wade's still out there somewhere, Bill.'

'Surely this isn't his sort of thing though, is it Danny?'

'I don't know what his sort of thing is Bill. I know he's a bloody psycho and I wouldn't put anything past him.'

'Carter has said several offenders.'

'That's true. I suppose Wade will always be in my head until he's recaptured and locked away again.'

'I think we can probably discount that particular maniac from this enquiry.'

The Chief Superintendent stood up, 'I'd better be getting back to headquarters Danny. I'll go and see the Chief and brief him properly on how the enquiry is progressing. If you need anything, you know where I am. Good luck Danny.'

CHAPTER 24

24th June 1986
The Spinning Palace Arcade, Mansfield

The manager of the arcade had telephoned Andy Wills just over an hour after the detective had left his number instructing her to call him straight away, if and when Tommy Quinn came into the arcade.

She had recognised Tommy from the photograph immediately, he was one of her regulars, he loved playing on the new video games that were all the rage.

When they returned to the arcade Andy had sent Pc Dave Bracewell to the rear of the premises to cover the back door, before walking in through the front door.

The arcade was very noisy with loud sci fi sounds emanating from the machines. The arcade itself was gloomy. The only lights in the building were the flashing lights incorporated in the various games that were being used. It was surprisingly busy and the air was thick with cigarette smoke.

Andy stepped to one side of the front door and allowed his senses to acclimatise to the surreal surroundings.

The manager of the arcade, a young woman in her mid-twenties, had seen Andy walk in. She walked over to him and said above the din, 'Hello again, young Tommy came in about twenty minutes ago.'

'Where is he? I can't see him.'

'He's just nipped out the back to the toilet, he'll be back in a minute. He's asked me to make sure nobody goes on Alien Attack from Mars.'

'What?'

'It's the latest game, it's the big one over there.'

She pointed to a large machine in the far corner of the arcade.

Just as she did so, Andy saw a young blonde-haired boy emerge from the nearby toilet, he instantly recognised Tommy Quinn.

Unfortunately, Tommy Quinn knew a CID man when he saw one. As soon as he saw the manager talking to the cop, he turned and ran towards the back door.

Andy gave chase, racing across the arcade, dodging the other punters.

He followed Tommy out of the rear door and out into the sunlight.

Pc Dave Bracewell was standing near to the back door and was holding the wriggling Quinn securely by his right arm.

Dave grinned and said, 'Alright sarge, what kept you?'

'Well done Dave. So, this is the elusive Tommy Quinn.'

The blonde-haired youngster found his voice, 'What you after me for? I ain't done anything.'

'I know you haven't Tommy. I just need to ask you a few questions about something you said to my colleague here when he was at Tall Trees last week.'

Tommy grinned and replied sarcastically, 'I'm sorry Mr Policeman. I didn't mean anything by it. All the kids do the grunting pig noises when a copper comes in.'

'Yeah, very funny Tommy. Come on, let's get you to the police station where we can have a proper chat, before we take you back to the home.'

The three of them walked to the car in silence.

As soon as the car pulled away Tommy said quietly, 'I know what you're on about really.'

From the driver's seat Andy made eye contact with the boy in the rear-view mirror and said, 'Go on then Tommy, tell me what the comment was?'

'I just said that Evan wouldn't be coming back.'

'What exactly did you mean by that?'

'Look, Evan's a creepy little fucker. He doesn't talk to anyone. He's the matron's favourite. She's always taking him out for special treats. He never tells any of us what he gets treated to. He's a right mardy little fucker. He gets money from the matron as well as treats and he never shares fuck all. None of the other kids at the Trees like him. He's just odd, a bit weird.'

'I still don't understand why did you say he wouldn't be back?'

'I said it because matron had taken him out in the van earlier that night and when that happens he never comes back until the next day. Even then he's allowed to sleep in, while the rest of us either have lessons to do or gardening work with Bill.'

'How do you know the matron took him out? Did you see him go?'

'No, I didn't see him go, but he didn't come to his room after tea, so that meant he'd been taken out again.'

'Where does he go?'

'I don't know. Like I said, he's a creepy little fucker who never says anything.'

'Okay Tommy, thanks. Who's Bill, by the way?'

'He's the matron's old man. He makes us work around the grounds doing the gardens. He's a creepy fucker as well.'

'Why?'

'He just is, we all reckon he's one of them paedo's you hear about.'

'Why do you think that? Has he ever touched you Tommy?'

'Fuck off! I'd knock the old bastard out if he touched me. Nah! He's just a bit weird, always staring at you.'

The CID car was driven into the back yard of the police station.

'If I haven't done anything wrong, why have you nicked me?'

'Do you know what a witness is Tommy?'

'Course I do. It's another name for a grassing bastard!'

'I want you to be a witness and tell me about that night you made the comment to Pc Bracewell.'

'Sorry, but I ain't no grass.'

'This isn't being a grass Tommy, I just want you to let me write down what you've already said. I want to know about the special treats and the stuff that Evan got, that none of you other lads ever got. Will you do that?'

'Yeah, I'll do that. Evan's dead now isn't he? It's not going to affect him is it?'

'No, it's not going to affect him. You're dead right Tommy.'

CHAPTER 25

24th June 1986
Mansfield Police Station, Nottinghamshire

It was approaching four o'clock in the afternoon and the detectives from the MCIU were gathering in the briefing room. Danny had requested an afternoon debrief to assess how the enquiries were progressing and to bring the entire team up to speed with developments.

He had the press conference booked at five o'clock so he needed to get on with the debrief.

He walked into the room and brought the detectives to order.

He saw Rachel Moore and Tina Prowse sitting at the front of the room so he started with them, 'Tina, how did you get on with Tania Jenkins?'

'It went as well as could be expected sir. She's obviously very bitter about what's happened. She's adamant that there was never any real need for Evan to be taken into care.'

'Is that right though? The courts don't place kids into the care of the Local Authority without having a good reason.'

'That's very true, but Tania says Evan was never in any trouble with the police and that he was a good boy.'

'Well, that's a massive contradiction from what we're being told. What about the drug addicted rent boy we've all been told about?'

'Tania claims that's a load of crap. According to her, Evan was a sweet, likeable kid with no issues.'

'That sounds like a mother's love to me. Did you manage to speak to Evan's social worker?'

'No, we haven't. By the time we'd finished with Tania, it was time to get back here for the briefing. I did fire a call into the Strelley Social Services office and Bethany Jones is off work today, but back tomorrow.'

'Okay Tina, thanks. As a priority enquiry I want you both to see Bethany Jones tomorrow and find out exactly what the truth is about Evan Jenkins please.'

'Will do, sir'

'Have you got Tania's account in statement form?'

Rachel Moore answered, 'I've taken a preliminary statement from her just covering the timeline he was taken into care and her impressions of Evan, as Tina has described.'

'Okay. That's good work both of you. Get onto Bethany Jones tomorrow first thing, I need that enquiry sorting out asap.'

'No problem boss.'

'Rachel, I know Tania mentioned this morning that she would like to see her son; have you sorted anything out yet?'

'I've arranged to pick her up after this briefing, I'm going to bring her down to the mortuary myself. I've spoken with the coroner's officer and he's going to stay on duty and make sure Evan is ready for viewing.'

'Okay, thanks.'

'Right, listen in everyone. I've now received the full report of the post mortem findings. The cause of death is, as we thought, asphyxia. However, interestingly there were trace elements of cannabis found in the toxicology results. There was also evidence of a couple of prescribed drugs. The first of these is a drug called Thiopentone. This is an anaesthetic type drug that is normally found in cases where surgical patients have died under the surgeon's knife on the operating table. The second one is a drug called Suxamethonium, which can act as a paralysing agent.'

Rob Buxton shook his head slowly and said, 'So, are you saying that the boy was drugged before being sexually assaulted?'

'It would appear so; the levels of Thiopentone and Suxamethonium were quite high. Seamus believes that the boy would have probably been drifting in and out of consciousness and could also have been in a state of semi paralysis. The poor kid would have been aware of his surroundings and what was happening, but unable to move.'

'Bloody hell! How do you get hold of a drug like that?'

'That's a good question, Rob. It's a question that I've fired straight back to Seamus. He's looking into it for me. He's said already that the most likely place would be from a hospital. So, I want enquiries made with all the local hospitals to try and find out if any such drugs have been stolen or reported missing from their pharmacies. Rob, will you organise that enquiry please?'

'Yes boss, no problem.'

Danny then turned to Tim Donnelly, the senior Scenes of Crime officer and said, 'Are there any updates from you, Tim?'

'The main update is that we have now positively identified the type and make of tyre from the cast we took at the deposition site. It's a Goodyear Cargo Ultragrip and the size is 215/65. The good news is, this is quite an expensive tyre, so not that many are sold. It's still hundreds as opposed to thousands though'

'That's great work Tim. If we find such a tyre on a suspect vehicle will you be able to positively identify it as being identical to the one that left the track at the deposition site?'

'Yes, we should be able to. We're still working on finding unique markings at the moment, but we've already found five marks of wear and tear that will be unique to that particular tyre.'

'Excellent. Have all the soil samples taken from the deposition site been submitted?'

'Yes, they have sir.'

'Thanks Tim. Okay, Brian, how have the interviews gone at the home?'

'Everyone's now been spoken to and from the statements taken it appears that Evan Jenkins was widely disliked by the other kids but without any obvious reason. The staff all describe the boy as being sullen and withdrawn, somebody who refuses to engage and is quiet and moody.'

Andy Wills then addressed the detective inspector, 'Sorry to interrupt sir, I haven't had chance to talk to you yet about the statement I've just obtained from Tommy Quinn. It's quite enlightening.'

Danny said, 'Go on Andy.'

'I've been working with Pc Bracewell today after he approached me this morning and told me about a comment one of the boys at the home made to him on the night Evan Jenkins absconded. Pc Bracewell had gone to the home to take the missing person's report. He informed me that as he was leaving the home Tommy Quinn made a remark aimed at him saying that Evan Jenkins would not be back. Tommy

Quinn absconded from Tall Trees this morning but with the help of Pc Bracewell I tracked him down to a gaming arcade in Mansfield. He's now made a statement in which he describes how Evan Jenkins would be taken out of the home at night by the matron for special treats. Tommy has no idea what these treats were, but he's said that the reason for the other boys disliking Jenkins was because of this preferential treatment. He has also said that Jenkins would be allowed to sleep in the morning after being taken out on these treats and was also given money by the matron. He describes Evan as being mardy, not wanting to talk to anyone. He's also described Caroline Short's husband Bill as being a bit weird. All the kids at the home refer to him as the "Peedo". They all think he's a paedophile.'

'Now that's food for thought. Who interviewed the matron and her husband this morning?'

Dc Fran Jefferies said, 'I talked to both of them sir.'

'Was any mention made of these special treats?'

'No sir, but to be fair I only spoke to Caroline about the night Evan went missing and to both of them about what Evan was like.'

'Have you got statements from them?'

'Yes sir.'

'Okay Fran, I'll read the statements after the briefing.'

Danny then listened to the detectives as they gave their accounts of the interviews they had undertaken with the staff and children at the home.

After the last account had been given, Danny turned to Brian Hopkirk and said, 'When the kids were interviewed, did they have a member of staff present?'

'Yes boss.'

'Andy, when you spoke to Tommy Quinn, who was the appropriate adult?'

'Because we were at the police station I called out an appropriate adult from the appropriate adult scheme boss.'

Danny said, 'Brian, it seems a little strange that there's no corroboration for what Tommy Quinn told Andy. Tomorrow morning, I want all the residents at Tall Trees fetching in and re interviewing with an appropriate adult from the scheme and not a staff member. Let's see if we can find some corroboration for these special treats Quinn has told us about.'

He paused for a minute before continuing, 'Good work today everybody, finish what you've got to do before going home. Be back on duty at six o'clock tomorrow morning. It's going to be another long day of interviews and statements. Rob, Brian, come to my office after the briefing. Fran, I need a word with you before you go as well please.'

Danny walked into the office followed by his two inspectors and Dc Fran Jefferies.

'Fran, I want you to stay on for a couple of hours now and research Caroline and Bill Short. I want you to find out everything you can about them, any records either of them may have, their employment history, previous jobs in residential care. I want chapter and verse, you know the stuff. Are you okay to put a couple of hours overtime in tonight?'

'No problem sir, I'll get straight on it.'

As soon as the detective left the room, Danny turned to the two inspectors and said, 'Let's get stuck into those interviews tomorrow, gents. If we can find some corroboration for what Tommy Quinn has told us then we'll have a decision to make tomorrow evening.'

Rob said, 'Are you thinking about fetching the husband in?'

'I'm thinking about fetching them both in, let's see what tomorrow brings first shall we? Both of you sort out a list allocating a detective to each boy. Brian, let the cell block know that we'll need their assistance to arrange for plenty of appropriate adults in the morning. Rob, once you've sorted out the list for tomorrow with Brian I want you to concentrate on the hospital enquiry. Chase up Seamus Carter and see if he can be any more specific. It will help your task enormously if you know exactly what areas of surgery the drug would be recommended for. Don't be too late off tonight, I think tomorrow could be a very long day.'

The two inspectors left the office and Danny was left alone with his thoughts.

Once again, he heard the words of Tania Jenkins in his mind "He was in care, he should have been safe".

He pushed that thought to the back of his mind and picked up the sheet of A4 paper that contained the details he was about to release to the press ready for airing on the evening news.

He stood up, put his jacket on and grabbed the car keys. It would take him twenty minutes to get to headquarters, if he didn't leave now he would be late.

CHAPTER 26

24th June 1986
South Lodge, Retford

Jimmy Wade paused outside the door to the outhouse.

He could hear whimpering noises from inside.

He grinned as he thought of the surprise he was now going to give Fred Barnes. Payback was going to be so sweet. He planned on toying with him, making him suffer for the humiliating beatings he had subjected him to in Rampton.

There had been no reason for the physical abuse he'd been forced to endure at the hands of Barnes and the other male nurse, Jack Williams.

He turned to Melissa and said quietly, 'Can you see through the window okay?'

She shook her head, 'I can't see properly Jimmy, I'm not tall enough.'

'Just a minute. You've got to see this, it's going to be fun.'

Wade disappeared, before returning almost immediately with a sturdy wooden box for her to stand on.

She climbed onto the box and smiled, 'That's better Jimmy, thanks.'

Wade then unlocked the securing padlock and pocketed the key before opening the door in a very slow, almost theatrical manner.

For the full menacing effect, he remained standing in the doorway. The bright light from the sun was shining directly behind him and prevented Barnes from seeing exactly who it was that had opened the door.

Barnes instinctively recoiled away from the figure standing there and asked nervously, 'Who's there?'

Wade said nothing, but stepped inside the small room and slowly shut the door until it was almost fully closed.

He could see Barnes squinting, as the male nurse tried to focus on his face.

Wade said quietly in a mocking voice that held real menace, 'Come on Mr Barnes, surely you remember me?'

'Wade? Is that you?'

'You see. Even squatting there naked and manacled to the wall you can't help your rudeness, can you? It's not Jimmy or Mr Wade, it's just plain old Wade.'

'I'm sorry Jimmy, I was just surprised it's you. You look so different.'

'Do I Fred? Why do I look different?'

'It's your hair. Your hair has changed.'

'Is it my hair Fred? Or is it the fact that I'm not the one cowering away defenceless, waiting for another beating from you?'

'I never meant it personally Jimmy, I was just trying to keep order.'

Wade now exploded with rage, 'Keep order! Keep fucking order! What did I ever do that warranted you and that other halfwit to continually beat me?'

'Nothing Jimmy, you did nothing. I'm so sorry. What are you going to do to me?'

'I don't know Fred what do you think I should do?'

Barnes was frantically trying to think of a strategy to engage the psychopath that now held him captive, but he was already dehydrated, hungry and terrified.

He couldn't think of anything to say, so he started to beg, 'Please let me go, Jimmy. I won't tell anyone what's happened. I'm so sorry for what I did to you back then.'

Wade laughed, 'Do you honestly think I'm going to let you go? You're even more stupid than I thought.'

'Please Jimmy, it's not too late.'

'You see Fred, that's where you're wrong. It's definitely way too late for you, but don't worry, I'll be bringing you some company soon.'

'Company?'

'I can't let you be the only one to take responsibility for showing me a complete lack of respect, can I? That just wouldn't be fair, would it?'

'I don't understand?'

'You'll understand only too well very soon. Now get some rest and save your strength. You're going to need it, you piece of shit.'

Wade stepped forward and landed a heavy kick into the exposed ribs of Barnes. He then stepped outside and secured the padlock on the hasp. He put his ear to the heavy wooden door and could hear Barnes crying inside.

He helped Melissa down from the box and said, 'Did you see him squirm Mel?'

She smiled back and said, 'I did Jimmy. You were so calm and masterful. You were right, it was so much fun to watch him begging for you to let him go.'

'Are you ready for tonight Mel? Do you know what you've got to do?'

'I'm ready, I know exactly what I've got to do. I can't wait to see what you've got planned for them, when we've got them both.'

Wade smiled and put his arm around Melissa, 'Oh don't worry sweetheart, I've got something very special planned for the two of them.'

Melissa looked at the floor, averting her eyes, afraid they would give away her true feelings.

She was terrified of Wade and was simply saying whatever she thought he would want her to say.

As far as Melissa Braithwaite was concerned, she was in just as much a fight for survival, as Fred Barnes was.

CHAPTER 27

24th June 1986
Mansfield Mortuary, Mansfield

Rachel Moore pressed the doorbell on the mortuary door.

Standing directly behind her and shifting her weight from foot to foot was an extremely nervous Tania Jenkins.

Rachel felt the nervous tension emanating from the woman behind her so she turned, took Tania's arm gently and said quietly, 'Are you sure you want to do this Tania? I can just take you home if you want me to?'

'No, I'm fine detective. I need to see my boy. I need to tell him that I'm sorry before I say goodbye.'

The door was opened from within by the coroner's officer, Stewart Henson. Rachel had contacted Stewart earlier that day to arrange this evening's viewing for Tania.

Stewart opened the door wide and said, 'Hello Rachel, everything's ready for you and Mrs Jenkins. Evan is in the identification room. I've covered him with the purple sheet, remember to only expose the face nothing else. Do not under any circumstances, allow her to touch the body, okay?'

'Understood, thanks Stewart.'

She turned to Tania and said, 'Are you ready, Tania?'

Tania had her arms folded tightly across her chest. She nodded but continued to look down at her feet.

Rachel put a comforting arm around the nervous mother and guided her into the mortuary.

Stewart closed the front door and said, 'I'll leave you to it, Rachel. I'll be right outside the identification room, just call me when you're ready to leave.'

Rachel nodded before opening the door to the identification room.

The room was softly lit and in the centre, there was a single bench. On this bench was the body of Evan Jenkins. The body had been totally covered by a purple coloured, velvet sheet.

'Okay Tania, are you sure you want to do this?'

Tania nodded. She couldn't find any words and was barely able to take her eyes off of the small figure lying beneath the sheet.

'Remember what I told you Tania, please do not touch Evan, okay?'

'Okay.'

Very carefully, Rachel peeled back the velvet sheet so that just the face of Evan Jenkins was exposed.

The coroners officer had done his best to lessen the shock and had combed the hair of the boy's fringe forward to cover the wounds from the post mortem examination. However, even with Stewart's best efforts, the condition of the boy's face was horrific. The days of being exposed to the elements, scavenging animals and birds had all taken their toll on the youngster's features.

Rachel was standing right alongside Tania Jenkins and she grabbed her as soon as she noticed her knees buckle.

Just in time, she prevented the young mother from falling to the floor.

With Rachel supporting her Tania quickly regained some composure, but began to weep quietly.

She held a hand out towards the boy's almost unrecognisable face, but stopped short of actually touching him.

Between sobs, she said softly, 'My beautiful baby boy, I'm so sorry. I should never have let them take you away from me. I just wanted to see you and tell you that I'll always love you. I'm so sorry sweetheart.'

Rachel continued to hold and support her. She said in a voice that was little more than a whisper, 'Are you okay Tania? Are you ready to go now?'

Tania nodded and turned away from the remains of her once beautiful child.

Rachel did not let Tania go to replace the sheet, she just opened the door, continuing to support her as she left the room.

In silence, she passed Stewart and walked straight to the exit door.

At the door Rachel turned to Stewart and said, 'Thanks for arranging that Stew, I'll take her straight home now. I haven't covered Evan back up.

Stewart nodded and stepped into the identification room; he now had the task of returning the body of Evan Jenkins to the refrigerated drawers.

Rachel opened the main exit door of the mortuary for Tania and said, 'Come on Tania, let's get you home.'

Tania remained where she was, gripped Rachel's hand tightly and said in a trembling voice, 'Detective, do you think you'll ever catch the people who did that to my boy?'

'I never promise anything Tania, but what I will say is this; we'll never stop looking and we'll do our very very best to get them.'

Tania squeezed the detectives' hand and said, 'I know you will. Thanks for letting me come and say goodbye to Evan tonight, Rachel.'

With tears starting to well in her eyes, Rachel blinked hard and said, 'Come on Tania, the car's over here.'

CHAPTER 28

24th June 1986
Marsh Lane, Dunham, Nottinghamshire

Marsh Lane at Dunham was very quiet and very dark.

There were no street lights here and a mist was starting to roll up from the dyke that ran alongside the lane and fed into the nearby River Trent.

Jimmy Wade had parked the Ford Transit van about fifty yards from the small cottage that Jack Williams called home. He'd followed the male nurse, the week before, as he drove home from Rampton Hospital.

The cottage was one of only three dwellings on Marsh Lane, the nearest house neighbouring the cottage was almost a hundred yards further down the lane.

It was now just after ten o'clock at night. Wade had been parked in the same location for an hour. During that time, not a single vehicle had driven along the lane.

Wade knew that Williams was a single man and lived alone.

He'd often heard the young nurse bragging to his older colleague Fred Barnes of his sexual exploits at the cottage. Desperate to ingratiate himself with his older colleague, Williams had severely beaten Jimmy Wade whenever he had the opportunity.

Wade had made a promise to himself on more than one occasion, that eventually he would kill Jack Williams.

Tonight, he'd been patient.

He had deliberately waited to make sure that on this particular night Williams didn't have any female company.

He turned and looked at Melissa Braithwaite sitting next to him, 'It's time Mel. Do you remember what you've got to do?'

Braithwaite nodded, but there was an anxious look on her face.

'Come on Mel, for Christ's sake we've gone through it a hundred times. Do you know what you've got to do or not?'

Recognising the rising temper behind his voice, she quickly nodded towards Wade and said, 'I know what I've got to do Jimmy, sorry.'

'That's more like it sweetheart. Trust me, this is going to be a piece of piss. Just do it exactly how I told you. I'm telling you Mel, this prick can't resist a pretty face.'

'Okay Jimmy, I'm ready.'

Wade started the van and drove it slowly along the lane with the lights off. He stopped directly outside the cottage owned by Williams and turned off the engine. He got out of the driver's seat, walked round to the side door and retrieved a bundle of rags and a brown bottle from the rear of the van.

Braithwaite also got out of the vehicle and stood quietly by the side of the van. Wade reached over and undid the buttons of her blouse exposing her ample cleavage.

He grinned and said, 'That's better Mel. There's no way he'll be able to resist those.'

Slowly and stealthily they made their way up the garden path towards the front door of the cottage. Braithwaite walked directly up to the door while Wade hid behind a nearby conifer in the garden. As soon as he was out of sight from the front door he glared at Braithwaite and nodded.

Almost trancelike, she began hammering on the front door with her balled up fists.

After a few seconds of the persistent banging, a light came on in the hallway of the cottage. She continued her furious knocking and heard a voice inside shout, 'Just a minute, I'm coming!'

Suddenly, the door was flung wide open.

Jack Williams stood in the doorway bare-chested, wearing a pair of grey jogging bottoms and a pair of untied training shoes.

He stared at the blonde woman with her breasts exposed beneath the unbuttoned blouse and said, 'Are you alright? What the hell's going on?'

Without saying a word Braithwaite pushed by him, walked down the hallway, collapsed to the floor and began sobbing.

Williams turned his back to the door and rushed to help. In his haste to help the poor woman, he failed to close the front door behind him.

In a flash Jimmy Wade was through the door and behind Williams.

He clamped the chloroform soaked rag over the face of the young male nurse. In seconds, the chloroform took effect and Williams slumped to the floor of the hallway, unconscious.

Wade shoved the drug soaked rag into his jacket pocket, stepped forward and landed a single, massive kick to the side of Williams' head.

He shouted, 'That's the first of many, you bastard!'

He pulled Braithwaite to her feet and said, 'Come on Mel, get moving, don't just sit there. I'll bring this tow rag. Make sure you pick up the bottle of chloroform from outside the front door.'

She nodded hastily and scuttled out the front door.

Wade picked up the male nurse and threw him over his shoulder in the classic fireman's lift. He paused at the front door and looked both ways along the dark, quiet lane.

It was still as silent and dark as the grave.

Nothing stirred.

Quickly, Wade carried Williams down the path to the Transit van. He slid open the side door and threw Williams into the back. He passed the van keys to Braithwaite and said, 'Get in and drive home. I'm staying in the back with this piece of shit. I owe him big style.'

Without saying a word Braithwaite got in the driver's seat and started up the van, driving slowly along the now foggy lane.

Behind her, the front door of the cottage remained wide open and the hall light was still on. From the back of the van she could hear the sound of Jimmy Wade administering a brutal beating to the already unconscious Jack Williams.

By the time they arrived back at South Lodge, there was only a deathly quiet from the back of the van. She parked the van outside the lodge and with a real sense of trepidation walked to the side of the van.

She paused momentarily and then opened the sliding door.

The moon illuminated Jimmy Wade as he sat in the back of the van next to the unconscious male nurse. Both of Wade's hands and his face were covered in blood spatter, that looked black in the moonlight. He had a demonic look on his face and grinned at his unwilling accomplice.

Braithwaite could see that Wade's teeth were also covered in blood.

Wade jumped out of the van and said, 'Let's get the bastard into the lock up.'

He took hold of Williams under the armpits and gestured for Braithwaite to grab his legs. She took the weight of his legs, gripping him behind the knees and helped Wade to lift him out of the van.

As soon as they emerged from the van out into the bright moonlight she could see that both of the man's ears were now missing. Wade had bitten them off in his frenzied rage.

She felt her legs go weak and almost gagged.

Controlling herself, she glanced away and helped Wade carry Williams behind the lodge and down to the stone outbuilding where Barnes was already captive.

Unceremoniously Wade allowed Williams to drop to the floor, before he unlocked the padlock that secured the door.

He flung the wooden door wide open, waking the sleeping Barnes.

Moonlight flooded into the room through the open door and Wade could see Barnes staring at him, his eyes wide with fear.

Wade growled, 'I told you I'd bring you some company.'

He then dragged the unconscious and badly beaten Williams into the room. Dragging his arms up to the manacles on the wall, Wade secured his wrists before letting him hang limply from the metal restraints.

Once Williams was secured to the wall Wade stripped him of his training shoes, jogging bottoms and boxer shorts leaving him bloody, battered and naked.

Barnes whispered, 'Is he dead? Have you killed him?'

'Not quite, he'll get over it and when he does I've got a special treat lined up for you pair of bastards.'

Wade then picked up the clothing he'd taken from Williams, stepped outside, slammed the heavy wooden door shut and replaced the padlock.

Melissa Braithwaite followed him meekly back to the Lodge.

CHAPTER 29

24th June 1986
Mansfield, Nottinghamshire

The chimes of the iconic Big Ben signalled the start of the ten o'clock news on the television.

Danny turned to Sue and said, 'I'll put the kettle on, do you want a coffee?'

Sue stood up from the sofa they were sharing, 'I'll go, you catch up on the news.'

No sooner had she left the living room than the telephone started to ring in the hallway. Now it was Danny's turn to drag himself off the sofa. He walked into the hallway and picked up the phone, 'Hello, Danny Flint.'

'Hello sir, it's Inspector Howson in the control room, sorry to call you at home so late.'

'What's the problem, Inspector?'

'I've got a woman on the phone demanding to speak to you urgently. I wouldn't normally have called you at this hour, but she says it's about the dead boy, Evan Jenkins.'

Danny knew Inspector Howson and knew he wouldn't have called unless he felt he had no choice, 'Don't worry about the time Mick, what's the woman's name?'

'Bethany Jones.'

'The social worker?'

'Yes sir. She saw your press release earlier this evening and is now worried that the murdered boy is Evan Jenkins.

I didn't deny or confirm her fears over the telephone, but she insisted that if it was Evan she needed to speak with you urgently.'

'Okay Mick, is she still on the phone?'

'No sir, I've got her home number. She's asked me to contact you and ask you to return her call tonight.'

'Pass me the number.'

Danny scribbled down the phone number and said, 'Thanks Mick.'

He put the receiver down, picked it straight back up and dialled the number he'd just been given. The call was answered immediately, 'Bethany Jones.'

'Hello Mrs Jones, it's Chief Inspector Danny Flint, I've been asked by our control room to give you a call.'

'Thanks for calling me back, Chief Inspector. I saw the press release you did earlier, I'm extremely worried that the murdered child you spoke about is one of my cases.'

'Ms Jones, surely you must know that I'm not going to discuss the identity of the child over the telephone. For all I know, I could be talking to a reporter or a journalist.'

'I understand that, but if it's Evan Jenkins, I need to speak with you urgently.'

'I'm not confirming or denying anything tonight, if you want to speak with me I'll be in my office at six o'clock in the morning. I'd be glad to see you there and discuss anything with you then.'

'Thanks for nothing, Chief Inspector. I'll be in your office at five past six.'

'I look forward to seeing you.'

Danny put the telephone down just as Sue walked past with the two mugs of coffee, 'Who was on the phone sweetheart?'

'It's work. That was Bethany Jones, a social worker, she wants to see me urgently about Evan Jenkins. I think she's the woman responsible for putting the kid into care.'

'I'm sure she didn't make that decision lightly, Danny. I think you need to maintain an open mind about that, don't forget what the conditions were like in that flat at Hyson Green. I could tell you were shocked by it, when you described the state of the flat to me.'

'As always, you're right Sue. I'm just so pissed off about that kid's death I feel like I need to apportion the blame to someone.'

'The only people responsible are the men who actually did it. Thousands of children end up in care for any number of reasons, none of them deserve what those men did to Evan. Concentrate on the real criminals involved, the men who abused Evan. Now come and get your coffee before it gets cold.'

'I will Sue and thanks. It's got me wondering though, what could be so urgent that an experienced social worker felt the need to call me tonight. She must have known I wouldn't be able to talk to her. Something's rattled her cage, I wonder what it is?'

'Now that's more like the Danny I know and love.'

'Very funny, drink your coffee, Mrs Flint.'

CHAPTER 30

25th June 1986
South Lodge, Retford

The morning light was just starting to filter through the small window way above his head. As the light became stronger and illuminated the cramped space inside the outbuilding, the hopelessness of his situation became more apparent to Fred Barnes.

He was wide awake, he'd been kept awake all night listening to the ragged breathing and groans coming from the man who was chained to the wall opposite him.

Now as the daylight flooded in he focussed on the injured man's swollen and bruised face. He could now see that both ears had been ripped from his head and dried, caked on blood stained his entire features.

There was something familiar though, about those now distorted features.

The injured man began to stir and very slowly eased himself into a more comfortable position.

Fred Barnes spoke quietly, 'Are you okay?'

There was no response. Realising the damage to the man's ears may have impaired his hearing, he tried again. This time he spoke a bit louder, 'Are you okay?'

The man opposite shook his head slowly and tried to speak, but the sounds that escaped from his battered mouth were unintelligible.

Even though the words came out in a series of groans, Fred recognised something about the tone of the voice.

He asked, 'Is that you, Jack?'

Again, the man opposite responded with a nod.

'For fucks sake Jack, what's he done to you?'

Jack Williams shook his head and made a sound, he made it again and this time Barnes realised it was a question. Williams repeated the sound again, 'Who?'

Barnes responded immediately, 'It's that fucking psycho Jimmy Wade, he got me a couple of days ago. We're properly in the shit here mate.'

Williams let out a single whimper and then fell silent again.

CHAPTER 31

25th June 1986
Mansfield Police Station, Nottinghamshire

Danny had just walked into his office, taken his jacket off and sat down when the telephone on his desk started to ring.

He picked it up, 'DCI Flint.'

'Good morning sir, it's Sergeant Leigh on the front desk, you've got a visitor.'

'Don't tell me, Bethany Jones.'

Leigh chuckled and said, 'Correct, your psychic powers are definitely improving sir.'

'I'll come down, take her into one of the interview rooms please.'

'Will do sir.'

Danny put the phone down and put his suit jacket back on, he grabbed his blue case book and left the office.

Rob Buxton was just walking into the briefing room, he saw Danny and said, 'Going somewhere boss?'

'Evan Jenkins' social worker, Bethany Jones, is here to see me. Keep your jacket on, you can come downstairs with me and hear what she's got to say as well.'

'A social worker out and about at six o' clock in the morning, that's never been heard of.'

Danny grinned at the feeble attempt at humour, 'It gets better Rob, she was phoning me at ten o'clock last night telling me she had information about Evan Jenkins and could

I confirm whether or not he was the dead child referred to in the news bulletin.'

'Like that kind of information is ever going to be confirmed over the phone.'

'Exactly. I just told her if it was that urgent she could come in and see me at six o'clock today.'

'And here she is, right on time.'

The two detectives found Sgt Leigh and he showed them into the interview room where the social worker was waiting.

Bethany Jones was an Afro Caribbean woman in her mid to late thirties. She was quite plump and had an open, friendly face. Her hair was fixed in neat corn rows and she wore a very smart, navy-blue two-piece business suit.

As the two men walked into the interview room she stood up.

Danny extended a hand, smiled and said, 'Good morning Mrs Jones, I'm Detective Chief Inspector Flint, I hope you understand why I couldn't tell you anything last night and that I wasn't being deliberately obstructive.'

She smiled and said, 'It's Bethany. My mother is Mrs Jones. I understand, detective and I shouldn't have phoned you, but I was shocked when I realised that the dead child you spoke about could be Evan.'

Danny gestured for her to sit back down and said, 'Bethany, it's bad news I'm afraid. Your instincts were correct, the dead child I was referring to is Evan Jenkins. As I said on the news last night we're treating his death as suspicious and have launched a murder enquiry.'

She looked down at the floor and then back up at Danny. He could see tears welling in her large brown eyes.

Danny said nothing more and waited until she had composed herself.

Bethany Jones brushed a tear from her cheek and said, 'I'm sorry, detective, give me a minute please.'

Danny said quietly, 'Take as long as you need, Bethany.'

Finally, she took a deep breath and said, 'I'd arranged to meet Evan on the 6th of June to talk over a few things but he never showed up. When I contacted Tall Trees, and spoke to that woman she told me that Evan had absconded. She promised to let me know when he came back. I take it she knows he's dead?'

'Sorry Bethany, when you say that woman, who exactly are you referring to?'

'Caroline Short, the matron at Tall Trees.'

'Caroline Short was informed two days ago.'

'You see what I mean, that bloody woman! Why didn't she tell me straight away?'

Rob Buxton said, 'I'm sorry Bethany, I'm not sure of all your protocols. Is she obliged to tell you or should she leave that to us?'

'I guess you're right Inspector, I suppose it's down to the police to inform me. You've got to realise that this has been a major shock for me and I'm bloody angry.'

Danny said, 'Can we get you a drink of tea or coffee? You've obviously got something you need to tell us, it might help us all if we have a minute and then discuss whatever that may be.'

'Thank you, Chief Inspector, I'd really love a coffee please.'

'Please, call me Danny. Rob, would you do the honours and make us all a coffee please? How do you take it, Bethany?'

'White, two sugars. Thanks.'

Rob stood and left the room, returning five minutes later with a tray containing three mugs of coffee. He set them down on the table and sat down.

Danny said, 'Okay Bethany, what's this information that you want to share with us?'

She took a sip of the hot coffee and said, 'The meeting I was due to have with Evan was about getting him placed in a different care home.'

'Why did you think that was necessary?'

'Ever since he was placed there, Evan has constantly absconded and returned to Nottingham. At first, I thought he was just homesick and that he would settle down. That never happened. Every other week he would run off again and be found hanging around the streets of Hyson Green.'

'Most of the kids in residential care homes abscond at some time.'

'Very true Danny, but this was constant. I formed the opinion that he wasn't running to get back to something, but rather running away from something.'

'Did you talk to him about it?'

'Of course, I did, but he was a very shy, timid kid who was always reticent to talk.'

Rob said, 'That's a very different picture of Evan Jenkins than we're currently being provided with.'

'What do you mean, detective?'

'The information we're getting about Evan is that he was on the cusp of being a full time rent boy and that he would readily sell his body to men so that he could pay for his Class A drug addiction.'

With an incredulous look on her face Bethany Jones exclaimed, 'What!'

Rob continued, 'I can see by your face that doesn't sit right with you, Bethany. Is our information wrong?'

'I'm sorry, but your information couldn't be any more wrong!'

Danny interjected, 'Why don't you tell me about Evan?'

'I will Danny, but first I want to know where you heard that crock of shit. Cos I've already got a good idea!'

Danny said, 'At the moment we've only spoken to Evan's mum, the staff and residents at Tall Trees.'

'I knew it, that bullshit's come from Caroline, hasn't it?'

Danny ignored the question, 'Tell me about Evan, why was he taken into care in the first place?'

'Rather ironically, in view of what's happened, it was for his own protection.'

'I've been to his home address and I've met Tania', said Danny quickly.

'Well in that case you'll understand some of the reasons. His mother Tania is a good woman, but she has serious self-esteem problems. Unfortunately, these problems manifest themselves in addiction. Tania is a heroin abuser and constantly has Class A drugs at her home, which she injects. As a result, the house is generally littered with used needles. She has no income other than benefits, so to fund her habit she works the streets around Forest Road as a prostitute. Quite regularly she will take punters back to the family home. So, you see, from a very young age Evan has been exposed to all sorts of risks, both from drugs and strangers in the family home.'

'Who made the decision for a care order?'

'I submitted the care order and placed it before the court. It was upheld and Evan was subsequently taken into care. I've worked bloody hard ever since to try and help Tania through her issues, but I don't see her changing her lifestyle anytime soon.'

'When you spoke to Evan the last time, what did he tell you that made you consider switching his care home?'

'Evan never said anything to me directly. Like most kids he constantly dropped hints. There was never anything concrete to take further.'

Rob said, 'Well, what did he hint at?'

'He made insinuations that everything was not as it should be at Tall Trees.'

'Come on Bethany, stop beating around the bush, what insinuations?'

'He made suggestions that Bill Short sometimes acted inappropriately towards him and the other boys.'

'What exactly do you mean Bethany? Give us specifics.'

'This is the problem detective, there never were any specifics. Evan told me he always felt uncomfortable around Bill Short and hated being left alone with him. He told me all the other kids felt that way too.'

Danny said, 'What did you do about it, Bethany?'

'Without a specific allegation there was nothing I could do. I spoke to my bosses and they fobbed me off, saying Evan was a fantasist. I shouldn't have let them deter me though, I knew Evan and he was a good kid. When I said earlier that you couldn't have been further off the mark with your description of him, I genuinely meant it. He was a lovely, quiet boy. In any other home environment, he would have shone. He was an intelligent, articulate boy who never got into any trouble.'

'Why would he be described to us as the polar opposite?'

'You're the detective. I would suggest it was done in some ill-conceived feeble attempt to deflect you from where you perhaps should be looking.'

'Tall Trees Children's Home?'

'Exactly. One other thing you should know Danny. When I started having genuine concerns about the regime at Tall

Trees, I started doing a bit of digging into Caroline and Bill Short. They came to Nottinghamshire from Cornwall almost two years ago. I contacted the local authority down there and it appears that they both left under a bit of a cloud from their last employment.'

'What were they doing in Cornwall?'

'The same as here, running a local authority care home.'

'Did you find out exactly why they had left that employment?'

'They wouldn't disclose anything to me, they're not obliged to. The woman I spoke to would only say that they would never be employed in a similar position in their region again.'

Rob said, 'That's ludicrous, why can't they disclose that information?'

'I didn't say couldn't, I said wouldn't. They're not obliged to, so they don't.'

'Before you go today Bethany, I'd like you to sit down with Rob and provide him with all the details of the people you've spoken to in Cornwall. We'll look deeper into that and all of their previous employment history. Is there anything else Evan disclosed to you that we should know about?'

'There was never anything he said. Behaviourally, though there was a massive change in him. He went from being the likeable intelligent kid I spoke about earlier to being a sullen, withdrawn, sulky brat who couldn't be bothered to utter a word to you in conversation. Something or someone changed that little boy, Danny.'

'Thanks for coming in so early Bethany, are you okay for time to sit and talk this all through with Rob?'

'I've got all the time in the world Danny, thanks for listening.'

CHAPTER 32

25th June 1986
Marsh Lane, Dunham, Nottinghamshire

Wally Hastings walked slowly up the path to the cottage.

He was feeling every day of his sixty-three years today. He was tired and his back ached under the weight of all the mail in his sack.

One more bloody year and he could retire.

Wally couldn't wait for retirement. It couldn't come fast enough as far as he was concerned. He was sick of the early mornings. The only thing about working for the post office he would miss would be the conversations he had with the people on his round. Ever since his wife died he had lived alone so there was never any possibility of a conversation at home. The brief chats he had with his customers were like getting small glimpses into other people's lives, he relished talking to people.

As he approached the cottage, the elderly postman noticed that the front door was wide open and the hall light was still on. Very strange; it was now daylight and had been for some time.

He looked down at the name on the envelope, Jack Williams.

As soon as he saw the name on any envelope, he could instantly put a face to the name.

Jack Williams, young, dark haired, good looking chap. Always friendly, mad keen on football.

He knocked on the front door, ready for a chat.

There was no reply so he shouted, 'Post, Mr Williams!'

Still no reply.

Feeling slightly disappointed that he'd missed out on the chance to talk to someone, he threw the bundle of letters onto the floor of the hallway. He got the next bundle out from the mail sack that was biting into his right shoulder. He saw that the next delivery was for the detached house further along Marsh Lane, about a two-hundred-yard walk.

Marsh Lane was a dead end and he groaned inwardly when he realised he would have to walk two hundred yards there and then another two hundred back carrying the hefty sack, just to post two letters.

'Fuck that!' he said aloud.

Wally put the heavy bag down on the floor just inside the gate of the cottage and began to walk off down Marsh Lane carrying just the two letters. If he got caught leaving the mail unattended he would be for the high jump.

He didn't care, it would be fine. He was only going to be five minutes. It was far better than carrying that lot all the way down the bloody lane and back.

He delivered the letters and made his way back to the cottage where Jack Williams lived.

He was surprised to see the front door was still wide open.

He walked up the path and shouted inside, 'Is everything okay Mr Williams?'

The letters he'd delivered were still untouched on the floor.

A growing sense of unease came over the elderly postman.

He took the decision to step inside the house and see for himself. He needed to make sure everything was okay.

He found the living room light still on as well and the television blaring away to itself. He could see the remains of a cigarette that had been allowed to burn completely out, it had left a four-inch line of ash in the ash tray.

Something was definitely wrong, he could feel it.

Tentatively he made his way through the house checking every room.

It was like the Marie Celeste.

There wasn't a trace of anyone. The house had been abandoned.

Nobody in their right mind would go out and leave the door wide open and all the lights and television on.

He went downstairs to the hallway and picked up the telephone.

He dialled three nines and said, 'Police please.'

The operator put him through and when a police officer came on the line he said, 'My name is Wally Hastings, I'm a postman. I'm on Marsh Lane at Dunham, not far from the bridge. I'm at a house that's been left wide open, it looks like it's been abandoned, somethings' not right. Could you send someone out please?'

There was a pause and then Wally said, 'Yeah that's fine, I'll wait here until they arrive. Thanks.'

Wally walked back down the path and retrieved his mail bag.

He returned to the cottage and with a sigh sat down on the bottom stair in the hallway of the cottage and waited for the police to arrive.

CHAPTER 33

25th June 1986
Mansfield Police Station, Nottinghamshire

From his office Danny saw Tina Prowse and Rachel Moore arrive for work. Not wasting any time, he opened the door and said, 'Rachel, Tina, I need a quick word.'

The two women walked into the office.

Danny said, 'Close the door and take a seat.'

When they had sat down Danny continued, 'I'm taking you two off the Evan Jenkins enquiry. I want you to start looking into the escape of Jimmy Wade again. I'm conscious that enquiries into the escape have been put on hold since the murder of Evan Jenkins. I need two of my best people to kick start the enquiries up at Rampton.'

Tina said, 'What about the social worker Bethany Jones? We're due to see her today as a priority enquiry.'

'Bethany Jones came into see me this morning, Rob Buxton is with her now.'

'Okay sir, when do you want us to start on the Wade enquiries?'

'There's no time like the present. I've just taken a very interesting phone call from the duty Inspector who covers the area around Dunham Bridge. He's informed me that one of his officers has just been to a house in Dunham that's owned by a man called Jack Williams. The front door of his house was left wide open and there's no sign of him.'

Tina asked, 'What's the significance of that in relation to the Rampton enquiry? Am I missing something?'

Danny continued, 'The Inspector also informed me that Mr Williams is a nurse at Rampton Hospital. It could be a coincidence with a perfectly innocent explanation. Me, I don't really go for coincidences. So, there you are ladies, your starter for ten. Go and see Inspector Eastwood at Newark Police Station, then travel to Dunham and find out what's happened to Jack Williams.'

They both stood up and Rachel said, 'Is there any reason why you're putting myself and Tina on these enquiries boss?'

'Like I said Rachel, you're two of my best people. I know I can rely on you to work unsupervised and to get the enquiries done. Get yourselves up to Newark and keep me in the loop please.'

'Will do boss.'

CHAPTER 34

25th June 1986
Mansfield Police Station, Nottinghamshire

It was approaching midday.

The results of the interviews with the other boys from Tall Trees were starting to filter back into the MCIU offices.

Danny had called a meeting with Rob Buxton and Brian Hopkirk to discuss their next move.

'What's it looking like so far, Brian?'

'It's different again from yesterday. Without exception, the boys have been far more willing to talk to us without having a member of staff breathing down their necks.'

'Any corroboration for the information provided by Tommy Quinn yesterday?'

'Yes. Two other boys have made statements about Matron's special treats. They don't know much, but what they're saying is that on a number of occasions, Evan Jenkins has been taken out of the home late at night and then gets to lay in bed the next day as well as getting other special privileges.'

'Do any of the boys have any idea where Evan has been taken?'

'None.'

'How are they saying he is taken out of the home?'

'Apparently, Tall Trees has a mini bus. He is always taken out in that.'

'What make is the mini bus?'

'Would you believe, it's a long wheel base Ford Transit.'

'Has any of the team seen this vehicle?'

'No, they haven't. Fran Jefferies has told me that there are two garages situated behind the main building of the home at the back of the property with big shiny padlocks on.'

'Are the garages big enough to put a Ford Transit in?'

'Yes, they're big enough. Fran spotted them when she was looking for Bill Short to get his statement.

'Right, talking of Fran, how's she getting on with the background checks into Caroline and Bill Short?'

'She's come up with some very interesting stuff boss. I've spoken with Rob after he'd finished talking to Bethany Jones and it seems that Fran is ahead of the game. She's already discovered the reason why they were both asked to leave their last job in Cornwall. It would appear that Bill Short was getting too many complaints about his inappropriate behaviour and comments around the boys. There wasn't enough to involve the police but the local authority was satisfied that something untoward was going on. The old no smoke without fire thing. Quite tellingly though, the Shorts didn't make any fuss or attempt to dispute the decision. They just moved on, left the county and obtained the job at Tall Trees.'

'Didn't anybody in Cornwall think it might be a good idea to let the authorities in Nottinghamshire know about their reasons for leaving?'

'They're not obliged to, so they don't. It's crazy.'

'Well, maybe one day in the not too distant future, that sort of information will travel ahead and stop these people flitting from one offence to the next.'

'That certainly needs to be the case sir, but I think it will take something horrendous to make it happen.'

'As horrendous as the murder of an eleven-year-old boy perhaps?'

Danny was fuming.

He needed to calm down.

He sat down and took a minute.

Neither of the inspectors spoke, they recognised the signs and knew when to stay quiet.

Eventually Danny said, 'Unless either of you can give me a good reason not to, I propose that tomorrow morning we arrest Caroline and Bill Short on suspicion of being involved in the murder of Evan Jenkins.'

Rob had anticipated this statement and replied, 'Do you think we've got enough for a charge of murder?'

'For a charge? In all honesty, no, I don't. I can't afford to risk missing the opportunity to seize that Ford Transit. If the vehicle used by the home is the same vehicle that left the tyre tracks in the mud at the deposition site then we're really making progress. I'm prepared to gamble, fetch them both in and then search the property. We can then seize the Transit and subject it to a full forensic examination.'

Brian said, 'I agree Danny. Every day we delay, it gives them the opportunity to thoroughly clean down the vehicle and get rid of any evidence.'

Rob said, 'Personally, I think there's more merit in playing it softly softly. I think we should initially invite them both in for questioning rather than arrest them and get their backs up. We can then get financial enquiry forms signed while they're cooperating. I think we should invite them in and at the same time have the Special Operations Unit execute a Section 8 PACE warrant to search for evidence of a serious arrestable offence. I don't believe any Magistrate would refuse to grant one under these circumstances.'

Danny looked thoughtful and then said, 'I like that idea, Rob.'

Brian spoke up, 'I think it's a good idea, but I think it might fall down around the warrant. I think the magistrates will argue if you've got enough for the warrant why not just arrest them? They will see it as a tactic by us to delay the detention period.'

'It's a good point Brian, but I think we should try anyway. Let's start getting things organised. Rob, I want you to get to court this afternoon and swear out a Section 8 PACE warrant as discussed. If we get that issued by the magistrates then first thing tomorrow morning we invite them both into the station to be questioned, initially not under arrest. Brian, I want you to arrange for Special Ops to search the property, have a word with Tim Donnelly and the Vehicle Examiners, tell them to be ready should we need a full lift to transport the Transit back to headquarters forensic bay for a full examination. Let's get cracking, there's a lot to organise for tomorrow. Brian, once you've organised Special Ops, Scenes of Crime and the Vehicle Examiners, I want you to make a start on the operational order.'

'No problem sir, who do you want for the interviews?

'For Caroline, I'd like Glen Lorimar and Phil Baxter and for Bill let's have Lyn Harris and Simon Paine. I'll see you both back here at three o'clock to see how we're progressing.'

CHAPTER 35

25th June 1986
Bilsthorpe, Nottinghamshire

The two detectives from Newark Division drove onto the car park of the Limes Café on the Old Rufford Road.

The informant had been insistent when he phoned in, he would only speak to either Detective Sergeant Malky MacLaine or Detective Constable Jimmy Finn.

Malky MacLaine had always been considered a loner and a maverick by other detectives on the CID.

The straight-talking scot had moved to Nottinghamshire from Glasgow when he was seventeen and had joined the police force when he was twenty. He'd moved on to the CID just four years into his service and had spent the last six years there, achieving a promotion to sergeant and remaining on the department.

MacLaine shunned the suits and ties normally worn by members of the CID and came to work in old ripped jeans and an equally battered leather jacket. He had long blonde hair down to his shoulders and a full beard. His methods were as unusual as his attire, but he got results. His bosses would continue to turn a blind eye to some of his more irregular ways just as long as he continued locking up criminals on a regular basis.

The key to his success was the vast network of informants he ran. It had been said that Malky ran as many informants as the rest of the Division put together.

Jimmy Finn was more than happy to go along for the ride with his sergeant and had also taken to dressing in the same casual manner and developing his own string of informants.

Between the two of them there wasn't much criminality they didn't know about in Newark and the surrounding areas.

It was one of these informants, a drug addict named Lenny Jansen, who had contacted him earlier that day and given a nugget of information that could turn out to be pure gold. When he was finally put through, Jansen had described how a drug dealer by the name of Billy Monk would be arriving at the café in a gold coloured Ford Capri to take delivery of five kilos of heroin.

Malky MacLaine's eyes had lit up at the prospect of seizing such a large haul.

Heroin was only just starting to flood into the area, being driven over from Manchester by dealers anxious to tap into a previously little used market.

The only problem for MacLaine was the informant had only called it in half an hour ago. There'd been no time for him to formulate a proper plan with the right amount of resources. Both men had decided to wing it and had raced to the café car park in the hope of making an arrest.

Malky MacLaine saw the gold Capri first, 'Looks like we're too late Jimmy, the fucker's already here.'

Just as he spoke three men walked out of the café and down the steps to the car park. All three shook hands, before two of the men walked off, heading away from the Capri. One of these two men carried a black briefcase.

The third man of the group walked back towards the gold Capri.

He was a squat, powerful looking individual with crew cut hair and a badly broken nose. He was wearing a black cargo coat and blue jeans. More importantly, he was carrying a large brown leather holdall.

Finn asked, 'What do you think sarge, do you reckon that's Billy Monk?'

'I don't know, but if he looks like he's getting in that Capri, let's nick the bastard and take a look inside that bag.'

'Right you are sarge.'

The man with the holdall continued to walk directly towards the gold coloured Capri

He got to within five yards of the car and took out a set of keys from his coat pocket.

MacLaine said, 'That's it. I've seen enough, get the bastard!'

Both detectives jumped out of their car and raced across the car park.

The man with the holdall looked at them, but had no time to react.

MacLaine reached him first and unceremoniously dumped him on the ground. The holdall flew from the man's grasp. Thinking he was being robbed the man began to fight back aiming punches at MacLaine.

The tough scot with a little assistance from Jimmy Finn quickly overpowered the man, handcuffing him as he lay on the ground.

Jimmy Finn continued to restrain the struggling man who shouted, 'Are you fuckers cops?'

MacLaine grabbed the holdall.

He unzipped it and examined the contents. Inside the leather bag he could see several brown coloured blocks wrapped in clingfilm. The experienced detective knew exactly what he was looking at.

MacLaine's face broke into a wide grin and he said, 'Billy Monk, I'm arresting you on suspicion of possession with intent to supply Class A drugs, namely heroin.'

He cautioned the still struggling Monk who said angrily, 'Who's the bastard who grassed me up?'

'It doesn't really matter does it Billy, the bottom line is you're fucked!'

Monk growled as he was hauled to his feet, 'Listen Jock, why don't you go fuck yourself!'

MacLaine chuckled and said, 'Really Billy, that's not very polite is it? I reckon you need to think about your situation here. This little lot's got to be worth about eleven years in the nick. I think some co-operation might be in order, don't you? Why don't you start by telling me the names of the people who dropped this gear off for you?'

'Not a chance. If I told you that, I'd be a dead man within a month!'

Finally, the drug dealer stopped resisting the handcuffs and began to calm down.

MacLaine said, 'Get him in the car, Jimmy.'

Jimmy Finn opened the back door of their scruffy CID car and put the prisoner in the back of the car. MacLaine put the holdall in the boot and climbed into the back of the car next to Monk.

Monk scowled at the tough Scot and said, 'Look, I've never met you before. I can't be doing eleven years in the nick. Is there anything you can do for me? I can make it worth your while, if you know what I mean?'

'Really Billy, I hope you're not trying to bribe one of the Queens men, are you?'

Monk growled, 'Very funny.'

MacLaine growled back, 'Listen to me, you piece of shit, the only thing I deal in is information. Tell me who you've just met?'

'I can't tell you about the people you saw me with, I would be a dead man. I do have something you might find interesting.'

'Go on Billy. I'm all ears.'

'I've got a client who buys a lot of gear off me, heroin, cocaine and amphetamine. She can't get enough of the stuff. You lot need to have a serious look at her for all sorts of disgusting stuff.'

'Look Monk, if you're gonna mess me about with some Jackanory story, I'm not interested!'

'Seriously, this ain't no bullshit. The word I'm hearing is, after she buys it from me she sells it on to a load of blokes that get their kicks abusing kids. Real dirty bastards.'

'You mean paedophiles?'

'Yeah that's 'em. Dirty scummy pieces of shit. It wouldn't bother me one bit grassing them fuckers up.'

'Okay Billy, that might be something I could be interested in. What's your punter's name?'

'Not so fast Jock, what's in it for me? I'll talk alright, providing you can make some of this shit go away for me.'

'Listen, Billy, if you don't tell me the name of your punter in five seconds flat, it won't be going anywhere and I won't be able to help you, do you understand?'

'Alright, alright! I don't know her actual name but I do know that she's the matron of that big kids home just up the road. The word I'm hearing is that dead kid was from that home too, if you get my drift?'

MacLaine went quiet, thinking things through.

He looked into Monk's eyes and said, 'Oh, I get your drift Billy. Come on, let's get you over to Mansfield nick. I need you to talk to someone over there.'

'I won't talk to anyone until I'm guaranteed some help with this lot. I mean it, I want a deal before I say a fucking dicky bird. That's fair, detective.'

'Let's just see when we get there, Billy. If anybody can help you it will be Mr Flint.'

CHAPTER 36

25th June 1986
South Lodge, Retford

Jimmy Wade placed the jogging bottoms, boxer shorts and training shoes into the small brazier that was already blazing fiercely, the fire boosted by a squirt of petrol.

He grinned as he watched the flames begin to devour the clothing he'd removed from Jack Williams the night before. The clothes he'd removed from Fred Barnes had previously been destroyed in the same brazier.

He watched the fire, fascinated by the flames as they licked around the clothes. He stayed there for ten minutes, until he was satisfied that all traces of the garments had been totally destroyed. He then made his way back to the house to get a container of water.

His captives needed a drink.

There was no way he was going to waste his time feeding them, but they would need water if they were to survive long enough for him to extract the maximum pleasure out of them before they were killed.

He walked into the kitchen and stared out of the window back at the stone outhouse.

Two down, one to go.

There was one other person who needed to pay before he could execute his plan and escape over the water to Ireland.

He planned to empty the bank account of Melissa Braithwaite and then drive north to Scotland. Once in Scotland, he would drive to the west coast and pay one of the hundreds of small fishing boats that operated between the west coast of Scotland and the Republic of Ireland to ferry him across. There would be no questions asked for the right amount of cash. He then planned to lie low in Ireland for a month or two before establishing a new identity. He'd done it before, he could do it again.

As he stared out of the kitchen window he pondered over the problem of Melissa Braithwaite. The easy option would be to kill her and leave her buried in the nearby woods.

It made the most sense and was the solution he kept coming back to.

He was pulled out of his reverie by the voice of Braithwaite, 'Jimmy, I've made you a cup of tea, it's on the kitchen table. Do you want anything to eat?'

'A couple of fried eggs on toast would go down well.'

She came into the kitchen and he watched her as she got the eggs out of the fridge and walked towards the cooker. She was like a ghost, a shadow of the woman she was when she'd first met him.

She had lost weight, her once voluptuous, full figure had all but disappeared. Her skin was sallow and her eyes were sunken with deep black rings below them. He couldn't find one thing about her anymore, that he found attractive.

In that instant he made his mind up.

When the time was right, she would be left in the forest.

'I'm just going to give our guests a drink of water Mel, that cup of tea will be cold by the time I get back. Make me a fresh one with my fried eggs.'

'Okay Jimmy, no problem.'

Wade grabbed the water filled container and walked back to the outhouse.

Placing the container on the floor he unlocked the padlock, opened the door and stepped inside.

'Good morning gentlemen.'

Both men recoiled as he stepped inside.

Wade looked at the puffy, bruised face of Williams who stared back at him through the one eye that wasn't totally swollen shut.

He grinned and said, 'And how are you Jack?'

Williams said nothing.

The grin instantly left Wade's face and he growled menacingly, 'I asked you a fucking question! How are you, Jack?'

With an air of defiance Williams said, 'Why are you doing this?'

'Because I can, Jack, because I can. When you two wankers thought it was brilliant fun beating on that helpless nutter Jimmy Wade, you never dreamed you'd end up here like this, did you?'

Williams shook his head and said nothing.

'I think an apology is in order, don't you Jack?'

Through gritted teeth Williams replied, 'I'm sorry.'

'What? I didn't quite catch that.'

'I said, I'm sorry.'

'Too late Jack, way too late. I've got special plans for you and fat Fred over there. Now who would like a drink?'

Barnes who had remained silent until now, shouted out, 'Me, I need water Jimmy, I'm dying of thirst here.'

In a sarcastic, mocking tone Wade said, 'Oh dear Mr Barnes, we don't want you dying of thirst, that would be far too easy wouldn't it?'

Wade stepped out of the outhouse returning seconds later with the container full of cold water.

He held it to the mouth of Barnes, began to pour the water and said, 'Here you are fatso, drink!'

Barnes gulped the water as it was poured into his mouth. He managed to swallow five mouthfuls before he began to cough and splutter, choking on the cold liquid.

'You see Fred, I always knew you were a greedy bastard by how fat you are. You should have taken your time and sipped it.'

Wade laughed, then stepped over to Williams and repeated the process, allowing the other man to drink some water.

He looked at the two men, who were now both soaking wet and said, 'That's all for today, gents. Make yourselves comfortable and I'll see you tomorrow, that's when the fun will really start. Don't go away now.'

Laughing at his own joke, Wade stepped outside. He replaced the padlock on the door and made his way back to the house. He was ready for his eggs on toast and a cup of tea now.

Back in the outhouse Barnes whispered, 'Do you see what I mean now Jack? I'm telling you we're in deep shit.'

'He's going to have to unlock us at some stage Fred, when he does we've got to be ready to take him down. We might only get one chance.'

'Do you think we'll be able to take him?'

'Both of us, yeah. If we work together we can do him, we've just got to be ready.'

'Okay Jack.'

Barnes shook his head in the gloom. His captor wasn't stupid, he seriously doubted that Wade would make a mistake. Barnes thought their only chance of survival was if somebody missed them and began looking for them.

He said to Williams, 'Should you have been at work today, Jack?'

'Yeah, I was on a day shift, why?'

'Well I haven't turned up for work for two days and now you're missing as well, do you think anyone will start wondering why we're not at work?'

'I did mention it to Staff Nurse Atkins yesterday that you hadn't turned in.'

'What did he say?'

'He said to wait until tomorrow and see if you came to work then. I told him I would nip round to yours yesterday after work. I went but your house was all locked up and your car was outside.'

'Yeah, because Wade got me outside the pub.'

'Do you think Atkins will start asking questions when I don't turn in for work today as well as you not being there?'

'I fucking hope so Jack, because if nobody finds us here I think were done for. This nutter isn't going to let us go, we're dead men, mate.'

Williams let out an audible groan.

CHAPTER 37

25th June 1986
Mansfield Police Station, Nottinghamshire

The telephone on Danny Flint's desk was ringing.

Rob Buxton walked into the vacant office, picked up the telephone and said, 'DCI Flint's office, DI Buxton speaking.'

'Sir, it's Detective Sergeant MacLaine from Newark CID, I need to speak with the DCI, is he around?'

Rob Buxton knew all about Malky MacLaine and his unorthodox methods. He wondered why he wanted to talk to Danny

'He's not far away, what's the problem Malky?'

'There's no problem sir, I've just locked up a drug dealer with about five kilos of heroin in his possession. The dealer knows he's fucked big style and is offering up information about one of his punters.'

'That's great, a very good arrest Malky, but I don't get why you need to speak to the Chief Inspector?'

'Because the punter he wants to talk about is the matron of the kids home that dead boy was in care at before he was killed. That's not all; my boy has inferred that the matron uses the drugs to supply nonces.'

'She's involved with paedophiles?'

'That's definitely the inference.'

'Right, now I understand. Where are you now?'

'I'm downstairs in your cell block. We nicked this tosser at The Limes Café so we've had to bring him over to Mansfield because of this new PACE shit. Mansfield was the nearest designated police station'

'I'll find Danny and we'll come down to see you. What's your prisoner's name and have you interviewed him yet?'

'The prisoner is a bloke called Billy Monk and no, we haven't interviewed him yet. My Dc's just booking him into custody, while I get these drugs into the secure property store.'

'We'll be right down.'

With a growing sense of excitement Rob put the phone down and walked out of the office just as Danny walked back into the briefing room.

'You alright Rob, you look a bit flushed?'

'I think the Gods of detection may just be smiling on us, boss. We need to get downstairs to the cell block, I'll explain on the way down.'

CHAPTER 38

25th June 1986
Marsh Lane, Dunham, Nottinghamshire

Tina Prowse and Rachel Moore got out of the car and looked at the secluded cottage.

The police woman sitting in the police patrol car parked in front of them also got out and walked towards the two detectives.

'Are you from the MCIU?'

Rachel said, 'Yes, thanks for waiting for us. I'm Dc Rachel Moore and this is Sgt Tina Prowse. Are you Pc Jennings?'

'Yes, Sarah Jennings.'

'Okay Sarah, what have we got?'

'I was called here this morning by the local postman. While he was delivering the post, he'd found the cottage with the front door wide open, the telly on and all the lights still on. He thought it was strange so he called the police.'

Tina said, 'What's the postie's name?'

The young policewoman looked at her notebook, 'His name's Wally Hastings, he works out of the Retford depot. I took his initial account, but I haven't taken a statement from him because he had to finish his round. I've got all his contact details though.'

'That's fine Sarah, we'll go and see him later for a statement. What did he say to you when you first arrived here this morning?'

'He said that he'd noticed the door was wide open and the hall light was on. He called out but there was no reply so he left the post on the floor and then walked down the lane to deliver the mail to the last house. When he came back the letters hadn't been touched and were still on the floor in the hallway.'

'Why did he come back up to the cottage?'

'Marsh Lane's a dead end, he would have had to walk back this way.'

Rachel said, 'I bet he'd left his mailbag in the garden and walked down the lane without it, that's why he came back to the door.'

Sarah smiled, 'That's probably it. Wally's getting on a bit and his post bag did look bloody heavy. He'd never admit that though. I think he'd be in real bother with his bosses if they found out he'd done that.'

Tina said, 'Have you been inside the cottage yet?'

'Yes. I thought I'd better check that the owner wasn't inside somewhere lying injured and Wally had missed him.'

'And there's no sign of anyone?'

'No. The property's owned by the people who live at Redgates Farm, but the tenant of the cottage is Mr Williams. I've done some checking with the owners and apparently Mr Williams is a nurse at Rampton Hospital. He's lived here for just over two years now. According to the PNC, that's his car on the lane, the Ford Fiesta. When I got here, the bonnet was stone cold so he hasn't been anywhere in that. I've also made some enquiries with Rampton Hospital. I asked our control room to phone them. Apparently, he was expected to start work at nine o'clock today. He never turned up for work.'

Rachel said, 'That's good work Sarah. Do you know who your control room spoke to at Rampton?'

Sarah again looked at her notebook, 'I made a note of it, they spoke to Staff Nurse Brian Atkins, he's Mr Williams' immediate supervisor. Apparently, Mr Atkins did say something a little bit strange, when the control room spoke to him.'

'What was that?'

'He said, that was the second one of his nurses in two days, that hadn't shown up for work.'

'Who was the other one?'

'Sorry, they didn't ask that question.'

'Not to worry, we'll go and see Mr Atkins after we leave here. Shall we go and have a look inside?'

The three officers walked up the path to the open door.

Rachel asked, 'Are there any signs of a struggle anywhere, Sarah?'

'No, nothing, everything looks fine. It's as if he walked out of that door and never came back.'

'Have you found any house keys?'

'Yes, there's a set of keys still in the front door, on the inside. His keys for the Ford Fiesta are on the same fob.'

Leaving the policewoman standing in the hallway, the two detectives then made a cursory inspection of the cottage. Finding nothing obvious, they re-joined the policewoman in the hallway.

Tina said, 'Okay Sarah, make sure everything is switched off, lock the door, take the keys and enter them into the Other Than Found Property register at your station. Later today I'm going to request a visit by Scenes of Crime to the cottage. I want them to come and do an inspection of the hallway to see if we've missed anything. If we can't get back later, would you be available to meet them here with the keys and let them in?'

'No problem sarge, I'm on duty until six o'clock. If they contact me through our control room I can meet them here with the keys.'

'That's great Sarah, one last thing, have you ever met Mr Williams?'

'I can't say that I have, this is such a quiet lane. Nothing ever happens here.'

CHAPTER 39

25th June 1986
Bleasby, Nottinghamshire

The isolated grey stone cottage stood in its own grounds at the end of a very long tree lined lane. The windows of the cottage were all shuttered and there was a large brand new padlock on the heavy wooden front door.

The front and back gardens were untended and overgrown.

A rusting front gate was hanging on by a single hinge and several of the dark grey slates were missing from the steeply sloping roof of the abandoned farmhouse.

The decaying building was in an advanced state of disrepair.

The only thing new about the entire building was the large padlock on the front door. The padlock had been unlocked and was now dangling from the hasp.

The front door was slightly ajar and the raised voices of a man and a woman could be heard from one of the upstairs rooms.

'I don't know why you're panicking, they've got nothing.'

'That's all very well for you to say, you weren't here when it happened.'

'No, I wasn't, but it was me that cleared up your fucking mess, wasn't it?'

'Yes, it was and I'm grateful for what you did that night, but this is serious shit. I'm not going to lie to you, I'm starting to get scared.'

'Look councillor, nobody even knows this cottage exists, let alone what goes on here. You and the others pay me very well to make sure it stays that way. You've got to trust me, everything will be fine. Yes, it will be in the news for a little while and questions will be asked, but none of it will come back to you or the others. I'm effectively the barrier between the police and your little group of likeminded individuals. Trust me, it worked in Cornwall, it will work here too. So, stop worrying and please don't call me out here again.'

'Okay, I won't call again, I promise. I just needed some reassurance. Some of the others have already started to ask, how long before we can go again?'

'That's hard to say, we need to let things at the home settle down a bit. Maybe we should wait for someone new to be placed into care with us. None of the other boys at the home are suitable. The best thing about Jenkins, was the fact he would never say anything to anyone. We need another quiet, timid one like him.'

With a note of frustration, the man asked, 'But how long will that be?'

Her reply was filled with venom and anger, 'What the fuck's wrong with you? One minute you're shitting yourself that the police are going to catch you and the next you're pressuring me into supplying another kid. Tell the others from me, they'll have to be patient. Nothing's going to happen again until I say the time is right.'

'I'll tell them but they won't like it. There are some seriously influential people in our little group, they know how to apply pressure.'

167

'Well you go and tell them to back the fuck off! They'll only get another kid as and when I say. Not a second before, do you understand?'

'Okay, okay, I'll tell them.'

'Make sure you do. Tell them all to calm down and to stay away from this place. I need the people who live round here, to think this place is derelict and abandoned. Nobody comes here again until I say so, you got that?'

'That shouldn't be a problem, it's so far off the beaten track anyway. Nobody ever sees us coming here, don't worry about that.'

'If you do what I tell you councillor, everything will be fine. This isn't the first time I've sorted out a mess like this. We'll all be fine, as long as you and your friends can hold your nerve.'

CHAPTER 40

25th June 1986
Mansfield Police Station, Nottinghamshire

Danny Flint and Rob Buxton followed Malky MacLaine into the interview room at Mansfield Police Station custody suite.

Danny had just come off the telephone after speaking to Detective Chief Superintendent Wainwright. The conversation had centred on the information that may possibly be provided by the drug dealer Billy Monk and what the police would be prepared to offer in exchange for that information.

Bill Wainwright had been adamant that no deals should be struck in relation to the charges of possession of Class A drugs with intent to supply faced by Billy Monk.

The Home Office had recently made drug dealing a priority offence and therefore no deals could be contemplated. The best that Danny was going to be allowed to offer Monk was a hand-written letter to the judge at his trial.

Such a letter would mean that upon Monk's conviction, the judge presiding over his trial would have sight of the letter from the police explaining how the offender had assisted the police to clear up another crime.

Depending on the nature of the information provided and the merit the judge put upon that information, he would then have discretion to cut time off any custodial sentence.

It would be entirely up to the individual judge whether or not he decided to act on such a letter. It would be the judge's choice to reduce a custodial sentence or to totally ignore the content of the letter and not reduce it at all.

Danny knew he was going to have to work hard to sell this idea to Monk.

The dealer was a career criminal who was used to prison and wouldn't be fazed by the prospect of a long sentence. From what Danny had already heard from Detective Sergeant MacLaine, he knew he really needed to get Monk to agree to give up the information. It could be crucial, the breakthrough they were looking for.

Monk was sitting quietly in the interview room.

The detectives all sat down and MacLaine said, 'Billy, this is Detective Chief Inspector Flint and Detective Inspector Buxton of the Major Crime Investigation Unit. I want you to tell them what you told me earlier.'

Monk grinned and said, 'I'm sorry Mr MacLaine, I don't recall telling you a fucking thing!'

Danny had expected this and quickly interjected, 'Billy, you've been arrested today in possession of about five kilos of heroin. Fact. You need some help and I need some information from you, so why don't we both stop beating around the bush and talk sensibly?'

Billy Monk leaned forward, rested his elbows on the table and said in a confidential whisper, 'Alright Mr Flint, this is how I see it. Yes, as you say I'm well in the shit, I don't dispute that, but we both know that I can do a long stretch inside standing on my head. Prison doesn't bother me that much. Obviously, I'd much rather spend as little time as possible in there. I do have some information that I think you'll find very useful and because of the nature of the people involved, this is information that I'd have absolutely no qualms in passing onto you, but…'

'But what Billy?'

'But, Chief Inspector, I need certain reassurances, I need to know that it's in my best interest to tell you what I know.'

'Okay, here's what I can do for you. This isn't a negotiation by the way, this is a one off, take it or leave it deal. Are you interested?'

'I'm still listening Mr Flint.'

'What I can offer you is a handwritten note from me to the judge presiding at your trial.'

'What good will that do me?'

'If your information assists me in identifying and convicting the people responsible for the death of an eleven-year-old child, I promise you I'll write to the judge at your trial and identify that fact in the strongest terms possible and request that he shows suitable consideration for your actions in assisting the police before passing sentence.'

'And that's all you've got is it?'

'No Billy, that's all you've got. That handwritten note could be the difference between a double figure jail term and a single figure one. You said yourself, you've got no qualms about giving us this information because these people are nonces, evil bastards. This is a win, win situation for you. You get the chance of having significant time knocked off your sentence and you also ensure that these evil fuckers get sent down as well.'

Monk sat back in his chair, folded his arms and said, 'And that's it?'

'That's it Billy, take it or leave it. I'll find these bastards anyway, it might take me a bit longer without your help, but I'll get them eventually. Do yourself a favour, get ahead of this and give me the information. Trust me, I'll make sure it's worth your while.'

Monk unfolded his arms, clasped his hands behind his head and said, 'Fuck it. You're on Mr Flint. What do you want to know?'

Standing behind Billy Monk, Detective Sergeant MacLaine smiled.

Rob Buxton opened his notebook and said, 'Okay Billy, tell us about this special punter of yours.'

CHAPTER 41

25th June 1986
Rampton Hospital, Nottinghamshire

It had been a couple of months since Tina Prowse and Rachel Moore had last been inside Rampton High Security Hospital.

When Jimmy Wade had first escaped, a lot of manpower had been thrown into the enquiry to try and recapture a man considered by the press to be one of the most dangerous criminals of recent times.

Both Tina and Rachel had spent a lot of time at the hospital interviewing staff, trying to build up a picture of the escape and also the circumstances leading up to it.

As they walked along Fleming Drive towards the main entrance, they shared a sense of unease.

Tina voiced those feelings and said, 'Is it just me, or does this place give you the creeps as well Rachel?'

'It always has. For some reason it seems even more foreboding today than when we were last here.'

'I suppose those huge black clouds don't help, it's going to chuck it down.'

As if on cue, there was a white flash, as lightning streaked across the sky followed quickly by a loud roll of thunder.

The two detectives sprinted for the front door of the hospital as the heavens opened and huge raindrops began to fall heavily.

They only had twenty yards to run, but both women were drenched by the time they reached the door and burst into the foyer.

The hospital was in the process of a huge improvement in security.

Following the escape of Jimmy Wade and Clive Winstanley back in March, the public outcry had been enormous. Quite rightly, people wanted to know how two highly dangerous prisoners had been allowed to escape so easily.

The fact that the level of violence needed to carry out the escape was so high, appeared to be lost on the public. Four members of hospital staff had been very seriously injured, one of them critically.

The furore died down a little following the immediate recapture of the child rapist Winstanley, however, Wade was still at large and the public wanted reassurance that other escape attempts would be prevented.

A budget of almost twenty million pounds had been set aside by the Home Office to drastically upgrade security. Outside the hospital this was already evident. Smaller fences around the perimeter were now being changed to twenty-foot-high, specialist anti-climb fences.

The layout in reception, where the two detectives now stood, had also changed dramatically. There were now state of the art body scanners and metal detectors in front of the door that led inside the hospital.

Rachel said, 'Wow! This place has changed.'

The receptionist behind the huge counter smiled and said, 'Can I help you?'

The two detectives fumbled in wet coat pockets for their warrant cards, Tina smiled and said, 'We're here to see Staff

Nurse Brian Atkins. I phoned about an hour ago, I'm Sgt Prowse and this other drowned rat is Dc Moore.'

The receptionist looked down at her notepad, 'Ah yes. The detectives from the MCIU. Please take a seat, I'll let Staff Nurse Atkins know you're here. If you want to start emptying any pockets you have and checking in your bags, it will save a little time later. I'm afraid you'll both have to go through the scanners to be allowed into the hospital. Our instructions are very clear, there are to be no exceptions.'

Rachel began to empty the pockets of her coat into her handbag and said, 'No problem.'

Tina said, 'What about my jewellery?'

With a sympathetic smile the receptionist said, 'I'm sorry, it's easier if you place everything in your bag. Everything can then be placed into one of the secure lockers.'

'Okay.'

The receptionist then lowered her voice and in a voice little more than a whisper she said, 'I'd better warn you ladies, Brian won't be in a very good mood when you see him.'

'Why's that?'

'I'm surprised you haven't heard. Steve Thorne died earlier today.'

Rachel asked, 'Staff Nurse Steve Thorne, who was attacked by Jimmy Wade?'

'Yes. Brian and Steve were best mates, I think they joined this job together.'

Before she could say anything else, the door to the hospital entrance opened and a tall, thin man with a mop of bright ginger hair and horn-rimmed glasses walked in. He was wearing denim jeans and a light blue sweatshirt top.

He looked at the two detectives and said, 'Brian Adkins. I think you wanted to see me?'

Tina replied, 'Yes Brian. I'm Tina Prowse and this is Rachel Moore, we need to talk to you about one of your nurses, Jack Williams, if you've got a minute.'

'I've literally only got twenty minutes to spare. I don't know if you've heard this already, but Steve Thorne died this morning. I'm knocking off early to go and see his wife and young son.'

'I'm really sorry to hear that Brian, I promise we won't keep you. I just need to ask you a few questions about Jack Williams.'

'Yeah, you said before. I don't know what it is you want to know, all I can tell you is that he didn't turn up for work today. Fred Barnes the day before and then Jack today. It's all very strange, neither of them miss a shift in months and then both together, weird.'

Rachel said, 'I know this is the last name you want to hear today Brian, but were either Brian or Jack involved in looking after Jimmy Wade?'

'Jimmy 'fucking' Wade, I'd like to get my hands on that bastard. He wouldn't be coming back here that's for sure.'

Rachel ignored the emotive comment and repeated, 'Brian, did either Fred Barnes or Jack Williams have anything to do with Wade?'

'The short answer, is yes. Fred Barnes was tasked with getting Wade to comply when he first came here. Letting him know who was boss, if you know what I mean detective.'

Tina said, 'Spell it out for me, Brian.'

'Look, I know that Barnes can be a little heavy handed at times and Williams follows him like a sheep. Whatever

Barnes does, Williams will do the same in an effort to try and impress.'

'In what way is Barnes heavy handed?'

'Barnes likes to let the new boys know who's in charge. The bigger the name, the harder he goes in.'

'Was Barnes ever "heavy handed" with Jimmy Wade?'

'It's certainly possible. There were never any complaints from Wade as far as I know.'

'Have you got time to get me Fred Barnes' home address, please Brian?'

'Yes of course. You don't think Wade's got anything to do with the two of them not coming into work, do you?'

'I don't know Brian. Hopefully, when we get to Barnes' house he'll be there drinking beer with his best mate Jack Williams.'

Rachel asked, 'Did you ever see Jimmy Wade with any injuries, Brian?'

'No, I didn't. To be perfectly honest even if I had, I wouldn't have said a word. That bastard deserved everything he got. Don't expect me to have any sympathy for that piece of shit.'

A look of recognition suddenly flooded over Atkins face and he said, 'Hang on a minute, Dc Rachel Moore. You're the detective he tried to kill, aren't you? If anybody should understand how I feel about Jimmy Wade, it's you. Now if you don't mind I'll get you that address, I've got to be somewhere.'

Tina said, 'Thank you Brian, like I said before, we don't want to keep you.'

Ten minutes later and armed with the home address of Fred Barnes, the two detectives were walking back to their car.

Tina said quietly, 'Does it bother you, Rachel?'

'Does what bother me?'

'When people refer back to what happened, like Atkins did just then.'

'Not so much now. It used to bother me a lot. When I was recovering, just after it happened, I only had to hear Wade's name and I would go cold and clammy. I've started to get used to it now, it doesn't bother me so much. I must admit though, I would feel a whole lot better if that monster was back behind bars.'

CHAPTER 42

25th June 1986
Mansfield Police Station, Nottinghamshire

It was now almost eight o'clock at night, Danny had called a meeting of his supervisors to check that everything was now in place for the operation planned for the following morning.

'Brian, have we got the Special Operations Unit ready to carry out the searches at Tall Trees Childrens' Home?'

'Yes sir, the Chief Inspector on the Unit has tasked A and C Sections to assist us with the searches. A Section will concentrate on searching the property and C Section will concentrate on searching the grounds and recovering the Ford Transit, if it's there.'

'Excellent. Have you informed the Vehicle Examiners to be on standby in the morning, with a full lift?'

'They're going to be standing by at Central Police Station. I've also contacted Scenes of Crime and warned them we'll be needing the vehicle forensic examination bay at headquarters, sometime tomorrow.'

'Good work, Brian. In the morning, I want you to accompany the Special Ops lads when they're doing the searches. It's always useful to have one of our team on the ground with them, it helps to prioritise what needs seizing.'

'No problem. The raids are due to take place at six thirty tomorrow morning and the SOU teams are going to be here for the briefing at six o'clock. It was always my intention to brief them myself anyway. I'll just travel in with them to the premises.'

'Okay. Right Rob, how did you get on at the Magistrates Courts?'

'It was a lot easier getting the Misuse of Drugs Act warrant sworn out than it would have been trying to get a Section 8 PACE warrant that's for sure. I've stipulated that the warrant covers all the outbuildings and any vehicles found in the grounds of Tall Trees as well as the main house.'

'Excellent. Do we anticipate any problems fetching them both in?'

Detective Sergeant Wills spoke up, 'No problems boss. I've fired a call in this evening to Social Services so they can have someone on call, ready to temporarily take over running the home. The residents will be looked after as normal by the staff that are on duty. As it's a week day, a lot of the lads will be going out to school anyway.'

Danny acknowledged Andy's comments and then continued, 'Right Rob, I want you to arrest Caroline Short on suspicion of supplying Class A drugs. Andy, you nick Bill Short for the same thing. Let's hope we find some drugs in the place, it will make life a whole lot easier. Talking of finding drugs, has anybody spoken to the dog section?'

Brian said, 'I called them after speaking to Special Ops, they can let us have a drugs dog later in the morning, around eight thirty. That's the best they could do at such short notice. The handler of the specialist drugs dog doesn't go off duty until two in the morning, but he's willing to come back on duty at eight and be at Tall Trees for eight thirty.'

'I think that's everything, have the interview teams been notified?

Rob said, 'Yes boss, they have. I'll be supervising the interviews and I've no doubt you'll be around the cell block yourself for most of the day.'

'I'm sure I'll be down there at some stage Rob. Right, if there's nothing else, I'll see you all at six o'clock tomorrow morning for the briefing.'

Everybody left the office, leaving Danny alone with his thoughts. He began to mull over the various different outcomes of the scheduled arrests and searches planned for tomorrow.

The shrill ringing of the telephone on his desk snapped him back to the present. He grabbed the phone and said, 'DCI Flint.'

'Sir, it's Tina Prowse. I'm glad I caught you, I just wanted to give you an update on the Wade enquiry.'

'Okay Tina, fire away.'

'I'm afraid it's bad news sir. Steve Thorne died today. As soon as we heard the news I contacted the hospital and told them not to remove any of the life support systems that have been keeping him alive.'

'Why the hell weren't we informed of the situation?'

'I can't answer that sir, but I've managed to prevent any problems evidentially. We're on our way over to the hospital in Worksop to take possession of all the intubation equipment, tubes, cannulas etc. so we can exhibit them. The body is currently in the mortuary at Worksop Hospital.'

'Well done Tina, that could have caused us a right headache if all the medical equipment had just been binned. How did you find out?'

'We were at Rampton Hospital just after the news had come through there.'

'I'll contact Seamus Carter and see if he's going to be available to carry out the post mortem as soon as possible. Apart from that awful news Tina, how are things progressing up there? Did you find the missing male nurse?'

'No, we didn't and there's definitely something strange going on. We started by going to see the duty inspector as you suggested. He immediately directed us out to the cottage at Dunham, where we spoke to the officer who had initially been called to the property this morning. It's very bizarre. When she got there this morning the front door was wide open, the lights and the telly was on and the owners car still on the driveway. The tenant, Jack Williams was nowhere to be seen. There's no sign of any struggle, it's as though he's just disappeared into thin air.'

'Do you think his disappearance could be connected to Jimmy Wade?'

'I didn't at first, but then we went to Rampton and spoke to Staff Nurse Brian Atkins. He's Jack Williams' line manager and he informed us straightaway that another nurse had failed to turn up for work the day before. This was another male nurse, by the name of Fred Barnes. It subsequently turns out that both of these male nurses were directly involved in the supervision of Jimmy Wade. Atkins also let slip, that both men had a tendency to be somewhat heavy handed with the prisoners in their charge.'

'I don't like the sound of that, Tina. After you've finished at the hospital tonight, get over to Barnes' house and see if he's there. If it's late just do a check of the address and see if he's at home. If he isn't there, leave it for tonight but make sure you're both back there first thing tomorrow.'

'Do you think Wade's involved in their disappearance sir?'

'I wouldn't like to be either of those two nurses if he is. Revenge is never pretty and if Jimmy Wade's involved, it could be positively horrific.'

'In the meantime, I'll get Seamus Carter to contact you direct at Worksop Hospital. Good work today. I'll just give you a quick update from this end, we're arresting Caroline and Bill Short tomorrow morning at the same time as executing a Misuse of Drugs Act warrant on the property at Tall Trees.'

There was a measure of incredulity in her voice as she asked, 'A Drugs Act warrant?'

'It's a long story Tina, I'll update you fully sometime tomorrow. If Barnes is at home, safe and well, call me and let me know. It doesn't matter what the time is, I need to know asap if he's okay. If I don't hear from you tonight, I'll take it he's not there and that you'll be commencing further enquiries in the morning.'

'Okay sir, will do and good luck with the warrant tomorrow.'

CHAPTER 43

25th June 1986
Retford, Nottinghamshire

After meeting Seamus Carter at Worksop Hospital, Tina and Rachel had bagged up the life support items as they were removed from the body of Steve Thorne. All the items had been correctly exhibited and labelled and would now form part of the evidential chain that had come so close to being irreparably broken.

With the items safely placed in the correct store at Worksop Police Station, the two detectives had then driven to the home address of Fred Barnes.

Rachel Moore parked their car directly outside 74, Eastern Avenue.

Tina said, 'That's his car in front, the Mini Metro. I got the registration number from his file at Rampton.'

Rachel replied, 'That's good, maybe he's at home.'

The detectives got out of the car and approached the front door of the two up, two down, terraced house. The front yard was tiny; it was literally two steps from the gate to the front door. The yard was concreted and had a single, forlorn looking conifer in an earthenware tub to one side of the front door. The windows were covered by thick net curtain and the house was in darkness.

Rachel pressed the doorbell on the heavy, windowless door. She could hear the chimes inside the house.

There was no answer.

Rachel pressed the doorbell again, with the same result. In frustration, she bunched her fist and banged loudly on the front door.

There was still no response and no movement within the house.

The next-door neighbour opened her door and said, 'Who's doing all the banging?'

Rachel said, 'We're from the CID, we need to speak to Mr Barnes.'

The elderly woman squinted at Rachel and said, 'The CID? Is that the same as the police?'

'Yes, it is. We're detectives from the police and it's important we talk to Mr Barnes tonight. Is he in?'

'Doesn't look like it, does it sweetheart? If he hasn't answered the door after all that racket.'

'Have you seen him at all lately?'

'I haven't sweetheart, not seen him for a few days. You should try the pub at the end of the road, he's always in there. Goes in most nights, now he's on his own.'

'Okay thanks, we'll try the pub, at the end of this road you said?'

'Yes sweetheart, it's on the corner, the Crown and Anchor.'

Rachel started to say thank you but the woman had already slammed the front door shut.

Tina grinned and said, 'Shall we try the pub, sweetheart?'

Rachel smiled back and replied, 'What a good idea sweetheart, apparently he's always in there.'

'Now he's on his own, sweetheart.'

They both laughed and walked back up the dark street towards the pub.

The Crown and Anchor was a typical back street pub; it had one entrance door that was situated right on the corner of the building.

The pub sign swung precariously above the entrance and depicted the name of the establishment with a poor painting of the crown above a ships anchor. From the outside, it was obvious the pub had seen better days. The opaque glass windows were in desperate need of cleaning and the frames hadn't seen a coat of paint for years.

Rachel said, 'This looks like my kind of place.'

'Doesn't it just', replied Tina

Rachel opened the door and they both walked in.

The pub only had one room. The bar was on the left as they walked in. There were bench seats around the other three walls and a few tables and chairs scattered around the room. The toilets were situated to the right of the bar at the far end of the room, the signs clearly visible.

In front of the bar were half a dozen bar stools. Three of the stools were occupied by elderly men nursing half-drunk pints of beer. The only other people in the pub were two middle aged women sitting at a table in the far corner who were chatting animatedly in between sipping from two half-pint glasses of Mackeson stout.

There was a young barman standing alone behind the bar.

The air was smoke filled as the three men on the bar stools were all smoking cigarettes, the ash trays in front of them piling up. They weren't talking to each other, with sullen expressions they stared straight ahead, looking over the tops of their pint pots.

As the two detectives approached the bar, the somewhat surprised barman smiled and said, 'What can I get you ladies?'

He had a friendly open face and his smile revealed even white teeth. He had blonde hair that was quite long and parted down the middle. He wore a white Levi T-shirt and faded blue denim Levi jeans. Rachel thought to herself that he wouldn't have looked out of place serving cocktails in a trendy town centre bar. In here he looked like an intruder, he didn't belong in these surroundings.

As if reading the detective's mind, he said hastily, 'I'm on my summer holiday from Uni in Cornwall. I'm just helping my dad out for a few weeks.'

Rachel said, 'Cornwall eh! Well that would explain the surfer look then.'

She smiled and continued, 'My name's Detective Constable Rachel Moore, I'm trying to trace a man by the name of Fred Barnes. I've been told that this is his local and he's a regular in here. Do you know him?'

The barman returned her smile and said, 'Everyone in here knows the old soldier. In a previous life Fred was in the Army. He never gets tired of telling you what he got up to as an enlisted man. That's his stool right there.'

The barman indicated an empty stool at the end of the bar.

Tina asked, 'When did you last see Fred?'

'Let's see, he was in a couple of days ago, not seen him since.'

'What time was that?'

'He popped in for a couple of beers after work, I served him. He had his usual two pints of bitter then left.'

'How did he seem?'

The barman looked puzzled, 'How did he seem?'

'How was his demeanour? Did he seem okay?'

'He was just Fred. As usual he was enthralling us all with his tales of heroism in the army.'

Rachel said, 'Was it the usual crowd in that night?'

'I wouldn't exactly call it a crowd, but yeah, pretty much. I can't remember if Doris and Flo were in that night.'

His eyes flicked over to the two women sipping stout in the corner.

'No one unusual in the bar that night? Any strangers? They would definitely stand out in here, wouldn't they?'

'They would that. No. Wait a minute, there was something strange, that night.'

'What was that?' urged Rachel.

'I remember seeing a really fit young blonde walk in while Fred was still here. She looked around and then walked straight out again. I never even got a chance to ask her if she wanted a drink. I remember her though, she looked gorgeous.'

'After this blonde came in and left again, how soon did Fred leave?'

'Almost immediately. He finished his pint, didn't want another and left.'

'And you haven't seen him since?'

'No.'

'Do you have any cctv in the pub?'

'No, we haven't got anything like that, it's only a small back street boozer.'

'Has your dad or any of the other bar staff seen him?'

'There's only me at the moment, my dad's not been well. That's why I've come home for the summer, to help him out. I don't know what's going to happen to the pub when I have to go back to Uni next month. The joke you made about surfing, that was actually bang on. I usually spend all my holidays in Devon or Cornwall surfing.'

Rachel smiled at the young barman.

Tina asked, 'Do any of your customers know Fred?'

'They all know him, but as you can see none of them are what you would call talkative. That's why I always remember when Fred's been in, at least he has a conversation with you even if it's as boring as fuck. Sorry ladies, pardon my French.'

Rachel wrote her name and the telephone number of the MCIU onto a beer mat, handed it across the bar and said, 'Sorry, I didn't ask you before, what's your name?'

'My name's Ben, Ben Jackson.'

'Okay Ben, this is the number for the Major Crime Investigation Unit, if Fred Barnes comes in for a beer anytime soon, would you give me a call straight away please?'

Ben looked at the beermat, 'Of course, if he comes in. Is Fred in any trouble?'

'He's not in any trouble, but we are starting to get worried about him.'

'No problem. If I see him, I'll give you a call. Now would you like a drink? It's on the house.'

'That's very kind of you Ben, but we're on duty so better not, thanks anyway. Another time, maybe.'

'I'd like that.'

Rachel smiled and followed Tina as she walked out of the pub.

Outside, Tina smiled and said, 'How do you do that, Rachel?'

'How do I do what?'

'You can get men of all ages, shapes and sizes eating out of your hand in minutes.'

Rachel laughed and said, 'It's either all in these big baby brown eyes, or it's witchcraft, I'm not sure yet.'

Laughing, Tina turned to walk back to the car.

Something glinted in the gutter, catching her attention.

A metallic object had reflected the feeble street light. Tina walked over and bent down, retrieving the metal object from the dirty gutter.

'Look at this Rachel.'

She held up the polished stainless-steel cigarette lighter and said, 'It's engraved on the back.'

Holding it up to get the maximum light from the street lamp she said, 'It says "Guardsman Frederick Barnes" and there's some sort of regimental badge on it.'

'Hang on Tina, I've got an exhibit bag in here somewhere.'

After rooting through her handbag, Rachel finally found a self-sealing evidence bag. Tina dropped the lighter in the bag and said, 'Come on Rachel.'

She turned and walked straight back into the Crown and Anchor.

Ben smiled and said, 'Changed your mind about that drink?'

'No Ben we haven't, sorry. Have a look at this lighter. Do you recognise it?'

'Of course, I've seen it enough. That's Fred's, it's got his name on it. I've heard the story countless times. He was presented with that lighter by his mates in the army when he left. It's got to be one of his most prized possessions, where did you get it?'

'I found it in the gutter outside the pub, just now.'

'That's weird. He would never lose that, he loved that bloody lighter.'

'Thanks Ben, don't forget to call if you see Fred.'

'I won't forget. I hope he's okay.'

Once again, the two detectives walked out of the pub and back along Eastern Avenue towards their car.

Tina said, 'What are you thinking Rachel?'

'I think Barnes was abducted outside the pub.'

'And the blonde woman, where does she fit in?'

'We always thought that Wade had help getting away from the hospital after he escaped. Maybe he's still getting help. What if this blonde woman distracted Barnes, so that Wade could snatch him up?'

'Do you honestly think Wade would stay in this area? My money's on him being long gone from here. I reckon he's well out of this country by now.'

'I think you're wrong Tina. My gut instinct's telling me, that Jimmy Wade's still here, still around, still playing his deadly games.'

CHAPTER 44

26th June 1986
Tall Trees Children's Home, Bilsthorpe,
Nottinghamshire

The four Special Operations Unit Transit vans, rumbled down the long lane towards the Tall Trees Children's Home. In convoy behind them came two plain cars occupied by the detectives tasked with arresting Caroline and Bill Short.

Sitting in the rear of the first SOU Transits was Brian Hopkirk. He'd briefed the men of the SOU earlier and had informed the sergeants in charge that he would be accompanying them during the search of the property and any vehicles found within the grounds of Tall Trees.

Riding in the back of the van, listening to the banter flying between the men of A Section had rekindled happy memories for Brian. Prior to him joining the CID, he'd spent three years as an authorised firearms officer on the Special Operations Unit. He'd loved every minute.

He knew all about the harsh banter prevalent within groups of men that constantly work in stressful and sometimes very dangerous situations. He was also fully aware, how that banter would cease and be replaced by consummate professionalism as soon as the doors opened and they began their task.

The four Transits pulled up at their pre-allocated points within the grounds and the two CID cars pulled up outside the small, three bedroomed detached house that made up the residential quarters of Caroline and Bill Short.

The van that Brian Hopkirk was travelling in pulled up directly outside the Short's residence. Immediately the men inside got out of the vehicle and surrounded the house.

The detectives from the MCIU got out of their vehicles.

At exactly six thirty, Rob Buxton and Andy Wills stood to one side of the front door and gave the signal for two officers from the Special Operations Unit to force entry. Armed with a Misuse of Drugs Act warrant, entry was forced to prevent the loss or destruction of evidence. As soon as the front door was smashed open by the solid metal Enforcer door opener, other officers from the SOU streamed into the premises.

Within just a few seconds, the house was secure and the sergeant in charge of the forced entry invited Rob and Andy to enter the house. They were accompanied by Dc Fran Jefferies and Dc Nigel Singleton. Fran Jefferies made her way into the master bedroom of the house where Caroline Short was sitting on the bed wearing a dressing gown.

Rob Buxton stood beside Fran Jefferies and said, 'Caroline Short, I'm arresting you on suspicion of being concerned in the supply of controlled drugs. I have a warrant to search the property. This is Detective Constable Fran Jefferies, she's going to stay with you while you get dressed, then you will be taken to Mansfield Police Station for questioning.'

Rob then cautioned Short who said, 'This is a bloody farce, I've never heard anything so blatantly ridiculous. I want to speak with my solicitor right now.'

Rob said, 'Get dressed. A solicitor will be sorted out for you at the nick.'

Downstairs in the living room Andy Wills repeated the same process with Bill Short.

Bill Short said nothing at all following his arrest.

He stared impassively across the living room, sitting on the settee, dressed only in his light blue pyjama bottoms and a dressing gown.

As soon as Caroline had got dressed she was handcuffed, brought downstairs and taken by Rob Buxton and Fran Jefferies out of the house. As she passed by the living room, she shouted at her husband, 'Don't say a word at the police station until your solicitor gets there, understand?'

Bill said nothing and continued to stare straight ahead.

Nigel Singleton then accompanied Bill Short upstairs, so he too could get dressed. Once dressed, Bill Short was also handcuffed and then taken out of the house. He was conveyed to Mansfield Police Station by Andy Wills and Nigel Singleton.

As soon as the two prisoners had been removed from the house, the detailed search of Two Trees Children's Home began.

Brian Hopkirk spoke to the SOU sergeant in charge at the house, 'Just secure the property for now. Don't start the search until the drugs dog has been through the house.'

'Okay boss, what time's the dog handler arriving?'

'He's come on duty early and will be here in about an hour's time, so there's time, for at least some of your blokes, to get a quick brew. Task half of them to begin a rummage search of the grounds, while the other half grab a coffee and then change them over. I'm going to see how C Section are getting on inside those garages. It's vital that we locate and secure the Ford Transit that Caroline Short uses.'

'Okay boss.'

Brian then walked from the house to the two garages that had been identified earlier by Fran Jefferies. One of the garage doors was secured by a padlock.

The padlock was unceremoniously forced off the door by one of the men from C Section, wielding a heavy crowbar. The double doors were pulled open, revealing a dark blue, wide wheel base Ford Transit van.

Brian immediately stooped down and looked at the rear tyres on the vehicle. The tyres were Goodyear Cargo Ultragrip, the size was 215/65. They were identical to the make of tyres that had left the tracks at Haywood Oaks Lane.

It would take a full forensic examination to match the tread patterns that had been left in the mud at the deposition site, so an identification was still some way off.

Brian grinned broadly and turned to the SOU sergeant, 'This is the van, the tyres are right and they're still covered in mud. Can you organise the vehicle examiners to attend with a full lift? I'll contact Scenes of Crime and let them know that we've got the vehicle we were after and we'll be bringing it into the forensic bay at headquarters.'

'No problem boss, I'll get onto the control room and get the examiners to attend asap.'

'As soon as the Transit's been removed, I want this garage and the one next door turning upside down, okay?'

'You've got it boss.'

Brian walked back around to the small three bedroomed house where he sought out Sgt Archer. He found the SOU supervisor standing outside the front door of the house.

As he approached the sergeant he smiled and said, 'Good news sarge, the van we were looking for is in one of the garages. Have your lads recovered anything from the gardens and grounds yet?'

'Nothing yet boss. We need that drugs dog here as soon as possible, then we can crack on with a proper search.'

'The dog handler didn't go off duty until the early hours of this morning, he's doing us all a massive favour coming back in so early.'

The sergeant grinned and said playfully, 'I'd better get my fucking medals ready for him when he does arrive then boss.'

'You do that sarge! But don't pin any medals on him, until after his hound has found some gear!'

'You might as well get yourself a coffee off the van boss, you know where everything is.'

'Why not, we can't do anything until Lassie gets here!'

Half an hour later, the Dog Section van could be seen being driven slowly along the same lane the four white SOU vans had travelled down earlier.

The Dog Section van pulled up outside the house.

Waiting eagerly outside the open front door of the property were Brian Hopkirk and Sgt Archer. The dog handler got out of the vehicle, walked over to the two men and said, 'Pc Terry Jamieson, boss. Where do you want me to start?'

Brian replied, 'I need your dog to do a sweep of the house first and foremost. I've held off the search team to wait for you, so we didn't confuse the issue, but we need to get cracking.'

'That's great boss. It does make my life easier if every Tom, Dick and Harry hasn't been crawling all over the scene.'

Pc Jamieson walked back to his van and retrieved a beautiful, liver and white coloured Springer Spaniel from the rear compartment.

He slipped a lead on the excitable dog, made a fuss of her and said, 'Come on then Jess, go seek.'

Hearing those particular words, the dog knew she was now working and her tail began to wag furiously.

The dog handler walked into the house followed by Sgt Archer.

The SOU sergeant would make a note of any items that caused an indication from the dog. If the dog identified a general area, then that particular area would be searched thoroughly later by his team from Special Ops.

Bending down at the side of his dog Terry Jamieson said, 'Go seek.'

Almost immediately the dog began to show a classic indication sign over a small leather grip bag that was on the floor of the hallway.

The dog froze in front of the grip bag, lay down and began staring at the bag then looking up at her handler before staring at the bag again. The handler pointed to the grip bag and said, 'Can you do the honours sarge, I'm not wearing gloves.'

Sgt Archer, who was wearing gloves, unzipped the bag and looked inside.

'It's empty Terry.'

'From Jess's reaction, that bag, at some time, has contained drugs. It will need to be seized for a full forensic examination.'

'Got it.'

Systematically, the dog handler allowed Jess to go through the house until every room had been searched. The springer only made one other positive indication and that was towards a shoe box hidden beneath clothing at the rear of a wardrobe in the master bedroom. Again, the little dog displayed the classic freeze indication.

'The same with this shoe box sarge, it must have contained drugs at some time.'

'Okay Terry, we'll seize that too.'

Another twenty minutes had passed before the search was completed and Terry Jamieson had put Jess back into the back of his van. The handler turned to Brian Hopkirk and said, 'Sorry we haven't found any drugs boss. The dog has given a very strong indication towards a grip bag and an empty shoe box. I would be very surprised if there aren't traces of drugs in both of those. Good luck with the rest of the search.'

'The Ford Transit van has just been removed from the garages by the vehicle examiners. Would the dog be okay to have a quick check of the garages before the lads start a physical search?'

'I'll put her through them sir, but she's getting tired and there's a possibility she could miss something.'

Sgt Archer said, 'We'll be searching it anyway Terry, but the dog might give us an indication where we should concentrate our efforts.'

'No problem. I'll get her out again and put her through, nothing to lose is there?'

The handler got the dog out of the van again, then made his way around to the garages.

Ten minutes later he returned and said, 'Sorry sir, there were no obvious indications, but if I'm being brutally honest, the dog wasn't interested. It will need a proper search by the SOU lads.'

'Okay Terry, no problem, thanks for trying anyway. You need to get yourself off home for some sleep, thanks for coming back into work.'

'Cheers boss, I'm back on at five o'clock tonight and I'm ready for a kip.'

It took another two hours before the search teams from the Special Operations Unit were satisfied that the search of Tall Trees Children's Home was completed.

Sgt Archer sat in one of the SOU vans talking to Brian Hopkirk.

'Right boss, disappointingly we haven't recovered any drugs or drug paraphernalia. What we have recovered are a number of items that may prove useful. We've recovered Caroline Short's address book. On a page at the back of this book there are a list of numbers that are prefixed by two initials. It could be her punters list but it will need some work to identify them. The empty shoe box and the grip bag that the drugs dog went bananas over. A pair of size 5, green wellington boots that are covered in mud. Your briefing mentioned shoes or boots that were covered in mud that could possibly be linked to the deposition site. This is the only dirty footwear we've found in the house. There's also documentation and bank statements for a Nat West Bank account in Caroline Short's name. Finally, we've recovered the keys for the Ford Transit. They're on a large bunch of keys. All the other keys fit the property and buildings here, except for one that looks like it's the key for a padlock. We haven't found any such padlock here boss.'

'Okay. Have they all been bagged up and labelled correctly?'

'Of course, sir.'

'Good work sarge, I know your teams were hanging around a bit this morning, but it couldn't be helped.'

'It's just a bloody shame we didn't find any drugs.'

'If it ain't here you can't find it, can you?'

'Very true.'

'I need you to drop me off back at Mansfield on your way through to headquarters.'

'That's fine sir, we've got to drop off all the exhibits into your property store, or wherever your interview teams want them. The lads who recovered them also need to do their statements.'

CHAPTER 45

26th June 1986
Mansfield Police Station, Nottinghamshire

'It's been a bloody nightmare Danny. The first thing Caroline Short did was demand to have her solicitor present for all interviews.'

'Who's her solicitor?'

'She's got that supercilious arse Grenville Slater, from Hooper and Billings in Derby.'

'So, am I correct in thinking that both Caroline and Bill Short have answered "no comment" to all of your questions?'

'As there was a possible conflict of interest Bill Short's got Eric Buckle acting as his solicitor. Bill hasn't even bothered to answer "no comment," he's just stared at the wall, ignoring everyone. Caroline's answered with "no comment" to every single question.'

'Good, that's excellent.'

'How can it be good?'

'Listen, the object of the exercise today was to get them in custody on legitimate grounds so we could search the property and recover the Ford Transit. Have we done that?'

'Yes, we've done that, but wouldn't it have been better to at least have found some drugs so we could have charged them and gone for a remand in custody?'

'I don't want you to take your eye off the ball here, Rob. We're looking at these two for being involved with a paedophile ring, drug supply and the murder of an eleven-year-old child. Let's try and use the situation to our advantage. Ask Brian to come in, will you?'

Rob stuck his head out of the office and shouted over to Brian, 'Brian, you're wanted in here a minute.'

Brian walked in and said, 'Everything okay sir?'

'Brian, how confident are you that the van we've recovered today, will subsequently be identified as the vehicle that left the tyre marks at Haywood Oaks Lane.'

'The tyres are certainly the right make and they're still covered in mud so we may get a match from the soil samples as well as the tread patterns.'

'That's great. What else have we got from the search of the house used by the Shorts?'

'A pair of size 5 Wellington boots that are also covered in mud. Again, there's a chance we could get lucky and forensics are able to match the mud on the boots to the deposition site.'

'I don't want the recovery of these boots to be mentioned to either Caroline or Bill at this stage.'

'Okay boss.'

'What else, Brian?'

'Bank documents for a Natwest account in Caroline Short's name.'

'Have we got a Financial Investigation form signed by either of them?'

'They both refused to sign one at the beginning of the interviews.'

'Well we've got these documents for Caroline's account, so if we need to get a court order to look into their bank details later at least we've got a starting point. If we've got details of one account we'll be able to find all their other linked accounts.'

Brian continued, 'We've also recovered an interesting address book. On a page at the back there's a list of ten numbers. They look like telephone numbers. All the numbers are prefixed by two capital letters. I was thinking the letters could be initials. The problem is, when I've phoned the numbers they all come back as number not recognised.'

'Every single one?'

'Yes sir, but I'd put money on it that they're phone numbers.'

'Brian, I want you to stay with that address book. Get some advice and help from British Telecom. If they are phone numbers that have been jumbled up they may be able to help you identify them.'

'Okay sir.'

'Was that it for the search?'

'I've submitted the grip bag and the shoe box that the drugs dog indicated for forensic examination, the only other thing was the bunch of keys for the Transit. There's a single padlock key on the bunch that isn't accounted for.'

'Rob, I want you to go downstairs and organise the interview teams to have one more interview with Caroline and Bill. After that interview I want them released on bail pending the results of forensic examination of the bag, the shoe box and the van. Make sure you tell the interview teams to make it clear that the reason we're looking at the van forensically is to try and find traces of controlled drugs.'

'Okay, I'll get on it.'

'Hang fire a second. I need to make a phone call.'

Danny picked up the telephone and spoke to the switchboard, 'Could you put me through to Detective Chief

Inspector Mattie Carlisle of the Regional Crime Squad please?'

There was a delay and then Danny said, 'Hello Mattie, Danny Flint. It's been a long-time pal.'

The voice at the other end of the line said, 'Is that you Danny? I haven't seen you in years. I hear you're in charge of this new Major Crime Unit now. What do you want with the crime squad?'

'It must be at least seven years by now Mattie, we need to get out for a beer and a catch up properly soon. The reason I'm calling is because I need a huge favour. Are your team very busy at the moment? I may have an urgent surveillance job that needs doing.'

'This might be your lucky day then Danny. As it happens we haven't got that much on at the moment. A surveillance job might be just what the team needs to keep their skills up.'

'Can you get over to Mansfield in the next hour, with a team?'

'Blimey! You weren't kidding when you said its urgent. Yeah, I reckon I can do that. How many targets?'

'Two, but they're a couple.'

'Okay, how long before we need to be ready to drop on them?'

'They're both at Mansfield nick at the moment, I can probably delay their release for a couple of hours, but realistically no longer than that.'

'Okay Danny, I'll put a team together and be at Mansfield within the hour. Are you okay to pay the overtime bill on this job?'

'Overtime isn't a problem on this one Mattie, I'll tell you why when you get here for a briefing.'

'Now I'm well and truly intrigued Danny, see you soon.'

Rob was looking hopeful, having only heard half the conversation.

Danny smiled, 'Regional Crime Squad can put a surveillance team on the pair of them. That's what I meant by using the situation to our advantage. Hopefully we can give the pair of them just enough rope to hang themselves.'

'There's one other thing you need to know boss. Caroline's been informed by her solicitor that the Local Authority have suspended them both. They are not going to be allowed back at Tall Trees until after the drugs investigation has taken its course. Grenville Slater has been arguing with Bethany Jones at Social Services. They haven't budged though so Caroline and Bill aren't going back to Tall Trees when they're released.'

'Where are they going to go then?'

'Slater's somehow used his connections and arranged for them to have a council flat on the Oak Tree Lane Estate in Mansfield as temporary accommodation.'

'That's brilliant. Seriously, it couldn't have worked out better for us. Make sure we know the exact details of this address as soon as possible, that way we can get the Crime Squad plotted up on it. Try and delay the last interviews with them both for as long as you can Rob.

'Will do boss.'

Danny sat back in his chair, clasped his hands behind his head, smiled and said, 'I think we're getting there gents, we're definitely getting there.'

CHAPTER 46

26th June 1986
South Lodge, Retford

Wade crept into the stone outhouse, that had become a makeshift dungeon for the two abducted male nurses.

His captives were asleep.

Both men were naked, starving hungry and dehydrated.

Wade had allowed them only one drink of water since their abduction. He didn't plan on allowing them anymore. He needed the men to be weak and passive.

Having entered the building silently, he allowed his eyes to get accustomed to the gloomy half-light, before looking closely at his prisoners.

Fred Barnes was lying propped against the stone wall, his arms at a grotesque angle attached to the manacles. Wade wondered how he could sleep like that. The man was close to exhaustion, that much was obvious.

Wade smiled and turned to look down at Jack Williams. The younger man should have been faring better, but the savage beating he'd already taken, at the hands and feet of Wade, had obviously taken its toll.

The area around both sides of Williams head was caked in dried blood.

The open wounds, caused when Wade had bitten off both his ears in a fit of rage, were now crusty and pus filled. Both of the jagged wounds were already badly infected. Both of his eyes were black and swollen, his mouth and lips were pushed out of shape.

Looking closer, Wade smiled again as he realised that the younger man's jaw was in fact broken and displaced.

The stench coming off the two men was horrendous, both had dried faeces caked to their legs and backs and the smell of sweat and urine was strong.

He'd seen enough, it was time to wake the men up.

Wade aimed two brutal kicks into the ribcages of both men. Barnes first and then Williams.

Both men were instantly wide awake and shouted in pain.

Wade laughed and said, 'Come on gents, it's the middle of the day. Why are you sleeping?'

Barnes just groaned, but Williams said defiantly, 'Fuck off Wade!'

His defiance was instantly rewarded with another heavy kick, this time to the small of his back. The force of the blow caused him to yelp in pain, doubling over he began to dry retch.

There was no food left in his stomach to vomit.

In a menacing growl Wade said, 'I've been wondering what to do with you two. Well you'll both be pleased to know that I've finally come to a decision. I'm going to allow one of you to survive. Sadly, this does mean that unfortunately one of you will have to die.'

Both men sat in a wretched silence as Wade spelled out their fate to them.

'Gentlemen, this is what's going to happen. At some point over the next couple of days I'm going to unlock your manacles. Then I will leave the decision as to who survives and who dies completely down to you. It will be a straight fight. I'll be watching through the small window above you. I'm intrigued to know which one of you needs to survive the most. I'll leave you two alone to think about it, and I'll see you in a couple of days.'

Barnes said, 'If you want to see us fight, we need water and food.'

'I think there's still plenty of fat on you Fred. I reckon you've still got a bit of fight in you, without me wasting any more food and water on you. What about you Jack, do you want any food and water?'

'I'm alright. I don't want anything from you.'

'That's settled then, I'll see you soon. I can't wait to find out who needs to survive the most.'

Wade left the outhouse and replaced the padlock on the door.

He stamped away from the door, then tiptoed silently back and put his ear to the wooden door.

He could hear the two men talking, discussing their options.

Surprisingly, Williams was mentally much stronger than the old soldier Barnes.

With a real tone of defiance and anger in his voice he said, 'This is our chance Fred. When he unlocks our manacles, we've got to be ready to fight for our lives. If the two of us work together, we'll have a real chance to overpower him.'

Barnes said in a pathetic whine, 'I don't know Jack, we're both very weak, you're badly injured already and I'm knackered, I've got no energy. Why didn't you back me up for some water?'

'Fuck the food and water Fred. I'm telling you this will probably be our only chance, we've got to try. Do you really think he's going to let one of us live? Of course, he isn't. If we don't fight, we're both dead men. Are you at least going to try Fred?'

'Yes Jack, I'll try. As soon as he releases us from these fucking manacles we'll both go for him.'

'Good man, we can do this Fred, trust me.'

Outside the door Jimmy Wade had heard everything. He smiled and crept quietly away.

CHAPTER 47

26th June 1986
Mansfield Police Station, Nottinghamshire

Danny Flint sat in his office with Detective Chief Inspector Mattie Carlisle, Rob Buxton and Brian Hopkirk.

Rob Buxton said, 'They'll both be leaving in ten minutes boss, bail's been arranged for them to return to the police station in three weeks' time.'

Danny turned to Mattie Carlisle and said, 'Are your team in place?'

'They're in place ready to pick them up when they leave. Rob's given me the details of the solicitor's motor they'll be leaving in. I've also got the observation point set up on their temporary address at 4, Edale Close, Oak Tree Lane Estate. We've been dead lucky there, it's a cul de sac and there's a communal entrance to the block of flats they're in. Number four is one of the two top floor flats, so we can clock them in and out dead easy. I've set up the static observation point in a nursing home that overlooks both the end of the cul de sac and also the entrance into the block of flats. It really couldn't be better for us.'

'Were there any problems getting into the nursing home?'

'None at all.'

'Great stuff.'

'How often will your team check in with us?'

'Unless there's something drastic happening, like another abduction or something of that nature, they won't. They'll maintain an evidential log of the targets movements and will give that to you on the day they're due to answer bail. If anything significant happens, such as a meeting with someone or a visit to an address, the team will inform me so I can then pass it on to you. Every member of my team is in possession of a radio that links into your control room in case of an emergency.'

'That's okay Mattie, but I'd like us to talk everyday please. I need to know Caroline and Bill Short's movements. I might think something's very significant that your team, with all due respect, don't.'

'No problem Danny. I'll be in touch with you at six o'clock each evening to discuss the day's events.'

'That's perfect Mattie, thanks.'

'I've told my team that both Caroline and Bill Short are extremely surveillance conscious. From what you've told me I don't think they are, but it helps to keep the team on their toes. After your briefing to them about the job, they're all totally switched on to it anyway. They want to nail the evil bastards.'

'Well, let's hope they do something while they're under surveillance that gives us the opportunity.'

'I've got to go now Danny. I'll talk to you tomorrow at six as planned. Goodnight gents.'

'Goodnight Mattie and thanks again.'

As soon as the crime squad man had left the office, Danny turned to Rob and said, 'I take it nothing was said on the final interview?'

'No boss. Caroline continued her mantra of no comment and Bill said nothing at all.'

'Did Grenville Slater say anything to you?'

'Only that he thought the arrests were a scandal and following the couple's release without charge in three weeks' time he would be making an official complaint to the Chief Constable.'

'Did he now? Well we all wish him good luck with that, the snide bastard. Did you manage to find out who he spoke to when he arranged the temporary council flat for the Shorts?'

'It was a one-way phone conversation I was listening to, so it was tricky. All I can say for sure is that he called Mansfield District Council and asked to be put through to the Housing Department. I heard him say the name Lenny on a couple of occasions. I've done some checking and there's only two men named Lenny or Leonard at the council. One's a bloke called Lenny Briers, who's a licensing enforcement officer. The other's Councillor Leonard Mellor who works in the Housing Department. I'm not pretending to be a genius here Danny but my guess is that the Councillor's the only one with enough clout to arrange temporary accommodation in council properties.'

'Good work Rob. Let's do a few discreet enquiries into Councillor Leonard Mellor, with the emphasis on discreet.'

'Discretion's my middle name boss.'

'Brian, I want you to firm up on what we've got from the searches, notably the van. Get your team back down to Tall Trees and re interview all the staff. I want to know exactly who has access to the van and who drives it. I want to know when it was last used, where it went etc. I also want you to chase up Scenes of Crime and the Forensic Science Service so we can get a definitive word on the soil sample match and the tyre tread impressions. Chase them about the wellington boots we've recovered as well. Lastly, get the results of the forensic analysis on the grip bag and the shoe box whenever you can. To be honest, I really don't want to know the results of the examination on those items until the day before the Shorts are due to answer their bail, if you get my drift. I don't want to give Grenville Slater any more reason why we should arrange for his client and her husband to answer their bail early.'

'If you don't mind sir, I'll pass on the address book enquiry to Andy Wills, I'm going to be tucked up organising the enquiries you've just outlined.'

'That's a good idea Brian. Tell Andy I want that address book cracked. Tell him the same as I told you, get him to arrange for a British Telecom engineer to work on it with him.'

'Will do sir.'

'Is there anything I've missed gents?'

Both inspectors shook their heads.

'Okay, go and brief your teams as to what's required tomorrow, then get off home. I want everyone back here tomorrow at six thirty, for morning briefing.'

CHAPTER 48

26th June 1986
4, Edale Close, Oak Tree Lane Estate, Mansfield

Caroline Short leaned through the open driver's door window into the black BMW three series saloon and pecked Grenville Slater on the cheek, 'Thanks for everything today Grenville, you've been amazing.'

'We've got to help each other Caroline, just remember what I told you. Keep your head down, do nothing. The police are on a massive fishing expedition, they've got nothing. At the end of all this, I'll sue the arse off them for wrongful arrest, defamation of character, the works. With a bit of luck, you'll get a massive pay-out and you won't have to bother about working for a while.'

'That would suit me Grenville, you're a star.'

'Trust me, the pleasure will be all mine. I've never liked that jumped up cocky bastard Flint. Don't forget, I'll pick Bill up at ten o'clock in the morning to drive over to Tall Trees. We'll pick up enough of your personal belongings to last for the three weeks.'

'Thanks, Granville.'

Caroline stepped back from the car. She stood next to her husband and watched as the solicitor drove away. She held the keys to the flat in her left hand. She tossed the keys in the air, caught them and said, 'Come on Bill, let's go and check out our little palace.'

Bill nodded and they both walked into the block of flats, unaware that they had just become the subject of the first entry on the regional crime squad observation log.

The two-bedroomed flat was fully furnished but very basic, the food cupboards and the fridge were empty but there were plenty of pots, pans, plates and cutlery. There was also a kettle, toaster and a microwave in the kitchen. In the bedrooms the bedding on the two beds smelled fresh but needed airing. The whole place felt a little damp. Caroline switched on the heating that was serviced by a communal boiler. Very quickly the radiators were red hot and the flat began to warm through.

In the lounge was a dark brown leather three-piece suite, that had seen better days. There was also a coffee table and a small colour television in the far corner. There were no pictures on the wall. No personal touches at all.

It was basic.

They both sat down on the leather sofa and Caroline said through gritted teeth, 'The lousy rotten bastards.'

'You alright sweetheart?'

'No, I'm bloody not! I'm seething. I can't believe they've gone after us for drugs. Somebody's grassed us up Bill.'

'Who?'

'You idiot! Who do you think? It can only be that arsehole Billy Monk, nobody else knew about any drugs.'

Bill nodded, 'You're right, as usual.'

Caroline continued angrily, 'I hope you washed that fucking van out properly.'

'Of course, I have. I disinfected the back with bleach like you said.'

'We can't afford for the cops to find anything in the van,'

'They won't and even if they did, we can say that it's a van that's used by the home to take the kids out. We can always say he'd been taken out in it on a few trips.'

'You're right Bill, we could say that, but it would be much better if they don't find anything.'

'Are you sure you got rid of all the drugs out of the house?'

'I got rid of them that first night. After the two police-women came to tell us that they'd found the kid. I took all the drugs and buried them near the gateposts. They won't find them right out there and if they do they can't be connected back to us.'

'So we're sorted then sweetheart, they can't touch us.'

'I'm still worried about the cottage.'

'I've cleaned the cottage. They don't know about it anyway, nobody does.'

'Bill, I need you to go back out there and clean everywhere.'

'I've already done it. I've burnt the mattress and cleaned the room, like you told me.'

'I want the whole cottage cleaned, not just that room.'

'How am I supposed to get out there to do that?'

'I'll phone Lenny, he can take you. He's the only one that's got a spare key for the padlock anyway.'

'I've got no stuff to clean with.'

'Fucking well buy some tomorrow! Stop bloody arguing with me, this is important Bill. Unless you want to go back inside?'

'Alright, alright, there's no need to shout. I'll get the stuff tomorrow morning when I get some food in. I'll go to the shops before Grenville comes to take me to Tall Trees.'

'You see, that wasn't so hard to work out was it? It fucking exhausts me at times having to think for both of us. For fucks sake Bill, get a grip.'

'When are you going to call Lenny?'

'I'll call him tomorrow, while you're out with Grenville picking up our stuff. I'll arrange for Lenny to pick you up in a couple of days' time, when things have settled down a little. I'll get him to pick you up after seven o'clock at night. If you go over in the evening there's less chance of anyone seeing you at the cottage.'

'Okay Caroline, you're the boss.'

'There's one other thing Bill, I've binned all your videos.'

'You've done what?'

When I got rid of the drugs, I destroyed all your porn.'

'Why the fuck did you do that?'

'It was homemade porn you idiot! The stars of the movies were all kids from the homes. Jesus, you really are a fucking moron aren't you? Do you think we'd be sitting here now, if the police had found any of that shit!'

'I still don't see why you had to destroy it, you could've just hidden it so I could watch it after this has all blown over.'

'I don't know why you watch it anyway, it's fucking sick. You're sick. It's all gone, get over it! I'm going to bed and you're in the other bedroom. I can't be dealing with your shit tonight.'

'Yeah, you go and sleep on your own', he sneered, 'No doubt you'll be dreaming of the handsome Grenville!'

'Fuck off Bill, you moron!'

'You fuck off, you slag!'

CHAPTER 49

27th June 1986
Retford, Nottinghamshire

It had just turned eight o'clock in the morning.

Eastern Avenue in Retford was deathly quiet.

The rumble of a diesel engine shattered the silence as the instantly recognisable white Transit van of the Special Operations Unit drove down the road and parked up behind the CID car occupied by Tina Prowse and Rachel Moore.

Rachel glanced into the rear-view mirror and said, 'Bang on time, as usual.'

Both detectives got out of their vehicle and walked towards the van. Sgt Archer got out of the front seat of the van, smiled and said, 'Good morning detectives, what have you got for us today?'

Tina replied, 'Like I said to you on the phone last night sarge. We need to gain entry and search this house to look for evidence of a possible abduction.'

'And you think the owner of the house is the person who's been abducted?'

'Yes.'

'And you want us to force entry and search it? For what exactly?'

'I'm not sure really. If he was abducted from inside the house, there could be signs of a struggle.'

'Is there no spare key anywhere?'

'Trust me sarge, we've been down that road and exhausted every possibility. Can you pop the bloody door please, so we can have a look inside, we'll be here all day at this rate?'

'Alright, keep your hair on, it's just a bit unusual that's all.'

The sergeant walked back to the van and barked some instructions to the men in the back.

Tina and Rachel walked to the front door of 74 Eastern Avenue, Tina whispered, 'Bloody man, just get the fucking door open.'

Rachel grinned, 'Sgt Archer's a good guy, but he's a stickler for the rules.'

'It's all above board. He should know that we can force entry and search property if we fear a person's life may be in danger. For all we know, Fred Barnes could be lying injured inside.'

'We both know what the odds on that are Tina. I like the fact that you're starting to think more like a detective every day.'

Sgt Archer returned carrying the red Enforcer door opener, followed by three other SOU officers.

The burly sergeant said, 'Stand back ladies, let the dog see the rabbit!'

Rachel and Tina took a step back just as the Enforcer smashed through the door lock of the front door. The door flew open and Sgt Archer walked in followed by his men and then by the two detectives.

The house was definitely unoccupied, no sign of Barnes, dead, dying or otherwise. It was obvious straight away that there were no signs of a struggle anywhere in the house.

Tina turned to Sgt Archer and said, 'Thank you sergeant, I don't think we need detain you or your men any longer, we can take it from here.'

'Right you are, if you're sure you don't need us for anything else we'll resume. Have you got the boarding up sorted for the front door?'

'Yes, we have, thanks again.'

The SOU men left, leaving the two detectives' alone in the house.'

Rachel said, 'I love it when you come over all Upstairs Downstairs, Tina.'

'What do you mean?'

'You just then, "I don't think we need detain you or your men any longer" you sounded like the Queen talking to her footmen.'

Tina chuckled, 'Was it really that bad?'

'Yep.'

She chuckled and said, 'Oh well, he deserved it. Let's have a look around and see if we can find anything useful, before I arrange for the boarder uppers to come and secure the door.'

The two detectives began a cursory search of the property.

The only thing they found, that was of any use, was the up to date passport of Fred Barnes, which meant he hadn't gone abroad and taken an impromptu holiday.

Tina made arrangements for the house to be secured through the local control room.

Fred Barnes' house was exactly the same as the house rented by Jack Williams at Dunham; there were absolutely no clues in either property to help explain the disappearance of the two men.

Two men from Victory Glass arrived and began the task of boarding up, hammering a sheet of hardboard onto the front door to secure it.

As they finished their work, Rachel turned to Tina and said, 'I think we should go back to Rampton. The answer to all this has got to be there somewhere.'

Tina nodded, 'Let's finish the follow up enquiries on these two first, I want to see everyone on this street just to be sure we haven't missed anything here. We should be done in a day or two maximum. Then we'll go back to Rampton.'

'Okay, I don't think we're going to find anything else here though.'

CHAPTER 50

28th June 1986
South Lodge, Retford

Jimmy Wade had been patient, but now he felt he'd waited long enough.

It was falling from daylight into dusk. The air was still, the sun beginning to set below the thick woodland that surrounded the stone lodge.

'It's time, Mel.'

'Are you sure, Jimmy?'

'The sooner this is done, the sooner we can leave and start a new life in Ireland.'

'Do you need me to do anything?'

'No. Stay here and start preparing our evening meal, I won't be long. Unless you want to come and watch the fun?'

'You don't need me down there sweetheart, I'll make a start on the food. Would you like a cold lager pouring ready for when you come back?'

'That would be lovely Mel.'

He walked over and kissed her hard on the mouth.

In her mind she was thinking, why can't he be like this all the time? At times their relationship seemed perfectly normal, he displayed tenderness, affection and even love.

Most of the time, however, Melissa Braithwaite was literally in fear for her life.

Over a period of three months her spirit had been broken to such an extent that even when presented with opportunities to escape from Wade's clutches, she dare not take them.

She was now totally subservient and watched impassively as he walked off towards the outhouse. She felt nothing when she saw him slip the heavy lump hammer into the thick leather belt around his waist.

Wade unlocked the padlock on the door of the outhouse and stepped inside. Now that the sun had dropped below the horizon and the stone building was cast in shadow, the temperature inside had dropped markedly.

He paused in the doorway, allowing his eyes to adjust and his nose to get accustomed to the stench from inside.

Both of his prisoners were sat up. Fully attentive, eyes wide staring at their captor. He glanced at their hands to check they were still secured by the steel manacles attached to the wall.

With a superior air in his voice Wade addressed both men, 'Gentlemen, have you decided? Which one of you wants to live and who wants to die?'

The question was left hanging in the air, both men looked down at the floor and remained silent.

Wade looked at Fred Barnes, 'What about you Fred? You're old and fat, are you prepared to let Jack live instead of you?'

Again, it was a heavy silence that greeted the impossible question.

Wade turned to Williams, 'Jack, do you feel like sacrificing yourself, disfigured as you now are, so that Fred can survive?'

Silence.

'Thought not. There's only one way we can settle this, I'll have to unlock your manacles, shut the door and let the strongest survive. I'll leave you alone for one night. If you're both still alive in the morning, I'll kill you both myself. Do you understand the rules of the game?'

Without looking up, both men nodded.

'There's one last thing I need to do, to make this a fair contest.'

Removing the lump hammer from the belt around his waist, Wade stepped forward and smashed the heavy hammer into the lower leg of Barnes. The force of the blow shattered the shin bone just below the knee. He instantly turned and repeated the same action, this time smashing the shin bone in Williams' left leg.

Both men had been powerless to stop Wade. He had effectively crippled them in seconds. They were now screaming in agony. Wade stepped forward, unlocked and removed the manacles from their wrists.

Any thoughts of resistance had been smashed from their minds, by two sadistic blows from the lump hammer.

Leaving both men writhing on the dirt floor, Wade grinned and said loudly above the noise of the screams, 'I'll see you in the morning and one of you bastards had better be dead!'

Laughing loudly, he stepped out of the building, closed the door and locked the padlock.

He stalked away back to the lodge.

He stepped inside the kitchen where Melissa was waiting with a glass of cold lager.

'That's perfect Mel, thanks.'

CHAPTER 51

29th June 1986
Mansfield Police Station, Nottinghamshire

It was almost six thirty in the morning and Danny was being briefed by Rob Buxton and Brian Hopkirk.

Brian said, 'We've finally finished speaking to all the staff at the home and have re-interviewed them, this time specifically about the van. I've collated all the information from the statements taken, the findings are very interesting. It seems that the only person who ever drives that Ford Transit is Caroline Short. The vehicle is only insured for her to drive.'

Danny asked, 'Doesn't her husband drive it?'

'He doesn't drive at all; Bill Short was disqualified from driving a year ago. He was banned for three years following his second drink drive conviction. He actually served a six-week custodial sentence in HMP Lincoln for the same offence.'

'And none of the other staff drive it?'

'No, it's only ever Caroline.'

'Do we know what it's used for?'

'Because Caroline has insured the vehicle herself, she uses it for her own personal use as well as for trips run by the home.'

'But the vehicle is still registered to the local authority. Is that right?'

'That's right. It seems some sort of deal has been struck between the local authority and Caroline, which allows her use of the vehicle for her own personal use provided she insures it and maintains it.'

'When was it last used on a trip for the residents of the home?'

'The last time anyone remembered it being used on a trip was at the beginning of May. Some of the boys were taken to the local swimming pool. The trip to the pool used to be a regular weekly event, but after two of the boys absconded while on the swimming trip, Caroline's banned any further trips there.'

'That's very useful Brian. Rob, how are you getting on with Councillor Mellor?'

'The councillor appears to be a pillar of the community. He's heavily involved in the rotary club and other charities. He's been a councillor for over five years, he stood as an independent and won the seat easily. He's a builder by trade and still runs the family business along with his brother, Richard Mellor. He's been married for twenty years but has no children. His wife Vera, works as a secretary in the family business. It's early days, but so far there are no areas of concern.'

'Thanks Rob. Brian, how's Andy getting on with the address book?'

'He hasn't fared very well so far, but he's seeing a British Telecom engineer later today. This engineer's travelling up from Swansea and apparently if anybody can crack it, it's this Welshman.'

'I suppose it's too early to expect anything back from the van?'

Rob replied, 'I spoke with Tim Donnelly on the telephone late last night, he was quite excited. Apparently, they've recovered a single human hair from the rear of the van. '

'From where in the van exactly?'

'Where the back doors of the van are, there's a small recess between the floor of the van and the rear bumpers. Its like a small crevice that runs across the van directly below the rear doors. The hair was recovered from there. They plan on doing comparison tests on it today, we should know if it's a positive match for Evan Jenkins by the end of the day.'

'Wow! that's brilliant news.'

'Tim Donnelly said they often find useful debris in this area. If someone swills the van out, it's where the water runs. If it's not washed away immediately, stuff can get trapped in this little crevice.'

'It's still brilliant work. Is there any news on the tyres?'

'First reports are that the tread analysis is looking promising, but they need to find more identical markings to call it a positive match. It's still a work in progress, boss. The soil from the tyres has been sent off to the lab for comparison but that will take a little longer to process. The same goes for the mud sent from the pair of Wellington boots.'

'Thanks Rob. This is for yours and Brian's information only and isn't to be shared outside these walls. The crime squad surveillance team have maintained observations on Caroline and Bill Short. Caroline hasn't strayed from the flat. Bill, on the other hand has been out a few times. He went with Grenville Slater to Tall Trees to collect clothing and other articles as arranged. He then went on foot to the local Tescos and purchased food, toiletries and interestingly quite a lot of cleaning products.'

'Maybe the flat's a bit of a shit hole sir', said Brian.

'Could be Brian. What's really interesting though, yesterday Bill went out in the morning. Crime squad followed him into Mansfield, where he went to the bank and drew out a large sum of money; he spent the next three hours in the betting shop on the market square.'

'So, he's got a gambling habit', said Rob.

'Maybe Rob, but the interesting bit is what happened back at the flat while he was out at the bookies. Fifteen minutes after Bill had gone out, Grenville Slater arrived and was let in to the flat by Caroline, who was wearing a negligee. Two hours later, Slater left the flat looking red in the face and dishevelled. Make of that what you will, but it would appear that Caroline could be paying for her legal advice in kind.'

Rob shrugged and said, 'Like you said boss, it's interesting, but not really surprising. Grenville Slater isn't exactly a candidate for the Law Society's solicitor of the year, is he?'

'No, he isn't, but that unprofessional conduct may prove useful later if we can drip feed some of this affair into Bill's ear at some stage.'

'What do you mean? Try and turn them against each other?'

'That's it, Rob.'

'Well, I hope they slip up a bit more than that boss. It's going to take a bit more than an extra marital affair to convict these two shits of murder.'

'You're absolutely right Rob, but every little helps. We've just got to make sure we're there when they do slip up.'

CHAPTER 52

29th June 1986
South Lodge, Retford

Fred Barnes tried to ignore the excruciating pain from his shattered right leg. The shinbone had been smashed by a single blow from the lump hammer wielded by Jimmy Wade.

He hadn't been able to sleep all night because of the pain.

The slightest movement, sent a lightning bolt of agony from his leg to the rest of his body. He'd remained awake in the darkness, listening to the agonised moans of his fellow captive. The damage Wade had done to Jack Williams' left leg appeared to be even worse than his own. Coupled with the injuries already suffered by Williams, the younger man was now in a very poor state.

Throughout the long night Barnes had thought about the offer made by Jimmy Wade after he unlocked the manacles.

He could still survive, he could carry on living.

All he had to do was put Williams out of his misery.

As the morning light started to filter through the window above him he could see that Williams was now asleep. It was a fitful sleep, the pain that racked his young body wouldn't allow a deep sleep.

Barnes knew this was his chance.

Being careful not to aggravate his damaged lower leg, he began to ease himself towards Williams. He was no longer restrained by the manacles, but he was weak from a lack of food and felt dizzy because of dehydration and the shock of his own injury.

He steeled himself and crawled alongside Williams.

Getting himself into position he slipped both hands around the younger man's throat and began to squeeze with all the strength left in his body. Williams immediately awoke and realised what was happening. Feebly, he grabbed at Barnes' wrists and tried in vain to pull them away from his throat.

Barnes was struggling to maintain the effort needed to strangle Williams.

His forearms were burning, trying to keep his grip on the mans windpipe.

Ignoring his own pain, Williams began to thrash around the floor as the oxygen in his body began to run out. Somehow, Barnes continued to squeeze until the thrashing became twitching and eventually nothing, no movement at all.

Suddenly, everything in the small confined space was still.

A single beam of early morning sunlight streamed through the small window and illuminated Williams' face. The man's eyes were still wide open, but had already taken on a glassy stare.

Jack Williams was dead, killed by his friend and colleague.

Observing this struggle of life and death was a smiling Jimmy Wade.

He and Melissa Braithwaite were watching keenly through the small window, as Barnes strangled Williams to death.

As Fred Barnes crawled back across the dirt floor away from his dead friend, above him a very self-satisfied Jimmy

Wade said, 'There you are Mel, I told you one of them would do it, eventually.'

He laughed and continued, 'I've got to say though, I always thought it would be fat Fred who died.'

Mel said nothing and just nodded quietly.

The two of them had been coming out to the stone building at frequent intervals throughout the night. As soon as Wade noticed Williams had dropped off to sleep, he'd fetched Braithwaite. He knew Barnes would attempt to make the most of the opportunity.

Wade grinned, turned to Braithwaite and said, 'It's your turn now Mel.'

'What do you mean, Jimmy?'

'I want you to experience that special moment for yourself.'

'What moment?'

'That moment you only get as you see someone's life force leave their body. It's so beautiful Mel, you need to experience it at least once in your life. Come on.'

It was the moment she'd been dreading.

She had always known that sooner or later Wade would insist on her taking an active role in killing. Inside she shuddered at the prospect, but she also knew there was no choice.

She knew if she didn't carry out Wade's instructions immediately, without argument, it would mean her own death at the hands of the psychopath.

Barnes would be killed anyway and she would have died for nothing.

Meekly, she followed Wade to the door of the outbuilding.

Wade unlocked the padlock and they both walked in to the small cramped space.

As soon as they walked in Barnes said triumphantly, 'I've done it Jimmy, he's dead.'

'Good for you Fred, I knew you had it in you. I don't think it's fair that Jack is on his own on the other side though. I think you should join him.'

Before the injured man had a chance to speak, Wade grabbed him and pinned him down on the ground. He sat astride Barnes facing the open door and said, 'Come on Mel, it's time. Sit facing me and put your hands around his throat like I told you.'

Almost trancelike, Melissa Braithwaite did as she was instructed.

Kneeling down she faced Wade, her knees almost touching the back of Barnes head. Reaching down she slid her small hands around the fat neck of the struggling man.

'My hands are too small Jimmy.'

'Just squeeze his windpipe! You don't need to put them right around his neck. Do it now!'

Stunned by the anger and urgency in Wade's voice, she instantly adjusted her grip and began to squeeze the windpipe of Barnes.

Immediately, Barnes began to struggle harder as his airway was blocked and he couldn't breathe. His eyes bulged and he began to make strange gurgling sounds as he was slowly throttled.

Suddenly, there was a loud bang and Wade was knocked forward into Braithwaite. She fell back, losing her grip on Barnes throat, the man stayed on his back gasping for air.

Jack Williams had punched Wade on the back of the head and was now trying to follow up the attack. He shouted, 'Come on Fred, you've got to help me!'

Barnes still lay on his back desperately trying to draw air into his lungs passed his damaged windpipe. He could barely breathe and was in no position to help Williams.

Initially shocked and stunned by the attack from Williams, Wade quickly regained his composure, he turned and punched Williams hard in the face.

Barnes remained on his back gasping for breath.

Wade now quickly overpowered the man he had wrongly assumed was dead. He landed a flurry of further heavy blows to Williams' face.

In desperation, Williams made one more frantic plea to Barnes, 'Fred. Come on I can't do this on my own. You've got to help me.'

It was no use, Barnes couldn't move.

Williams had waited too long to launch the initial attack.

The damage already done to Barnes windpipe, prevented him from joining in the planned attack on Wade.

In their desperation, the two injured men had concocted a plan overnight to fake Williams death, believing it would give them one last opportunity to try and escape.

The plan had failed miserably.

Wade delivered a thunderous final punch to the side of Williams' head which effectively ended any resistance. Williams slumped to the ground unconscious, falling next to the still gasping Barnes.

In a fit of uncontrollable rage, Wade screamed, 'You pair of bastards!'

He grabbed Barnes and dragged him over to the wall, where he attached the manacles back onto his wrists.

He then dragged the unconscious Williams over to the manacles on the other wall and secured his wrists.

As the two men had made their futile bid for freedom, Melissa Braithwaite had fled out of the open door.

Wade now shouted, 'Get back in here Mel, you haven't finished.'

Melissa as usual did as she was ordered. Slowly she stepped back inside the makeshift dungeon.

'Get in here, you need to see this Melissa.'

Wade began to slap Williams hard across the face. Eventually, he came around, the first thing he saw was the face of Jimmy Wade inches from his own.

As he stared into those unblinking, blue eyes Williams knew he was a dead man.

Incandescent with rage, Wade screamed at him, 'Thought you could outwit old Jimmy did you Jacky boy? I'm sorry to disappoint you, but I've got to tell you my old Granny could punch harder than you.'

He glanced over at Braithwaite and noticed that the terrified woman had her eyes tightly closed. He grabbed her and pulled her closer, 'I've just told you that you need to see this. Now open your fucking eyes and watch!'

Terrorised, she opened her eyes and stared into Williams face as Wade placed his hands around the man's throat.

He began to squeeze and said in a quiet almost soft voice, 'Watch the eyes Mel, the beauty is all in the eyes.'

Wade slowly squeezed the life from Williams.

He allowed the dead man to slump from his grip, turned to a horrified Melissa and said, 'Your turn Mel.'

He forced the terrified woman over to Barnes who was still gasping for breath, his windpipe already damaged beyond repair.

Wade whispered menacingly, 'Finish him Mel. This is your last chance.'

Once again, she gripped the damaged windpipe with two hands and began to squeeze.

This time she continued to squeeze long after Barnes had stopped breathing, her hands throbbed and ached with the effort.

Still she squeezed.

'It's done Mel, you can stop he's dead. Did you see it? Wasn't it beautiful? I knew you could do it sweetheart. I need you Mel, I want to make love with you right now.'

She moved and spoke like an automaton.

She stepped forward, kissed Wade on the lips and said, 'Not here, Jimmy. Not in front of these two. Take me to the lodge, I want you in my bed not here. This time needs to be special.'

They left the outhouse door unlocked and walked quickly back to the lodge hand in hand.

Neither of them spared a thought for the two murdered men whose lifeless forms remained inside the outhouse, with frozen, unblinking eyes.

CHAPTER 53

29th June 1986
4, Edale Close, Oak Tree Lane Estate, Mansfield

Councillor Lenny Mellor parked his gun metal grey Range Rover directly outside the block of flats on Edale Close. He glanced up at the first floor flat now occupied by Caroline and Bill Short. There was no movement he could see within the flat.

He had hoped that Bill would be waiting outside for him when he arrived.

When Caroline had called to make the arrangements, he had insisted that Bill should be ready and waiting for him.

Typically, Bill was nowhere to be seen.

Councillor Mellor hated the Oak Tree Lane estate with a passion, as far as he was concerned the less time he spent there the better.

Unbuckling his seat belt, he swore under his breath, 'For fucks sake!'

He hauled his large, fat frame out of the car and waddled over to the communal door. He pressed the intercom for flat number four.

Caroline answered, 'Come up Lenny!'

As the door lock buzzed to allow him access he swore for a second time, 'For fucks sake!'

Now he had two flights of stairs to negotiate as well. What was wrong with these people?

Breathless, he reached the top of the stairs and saw that the flat door was open. He tapped on the open door, then walked in.

'Anyone around?'

Caroline answered, 'We're in here Lenny.'

Councillor Mellor followed her voice and walked along the hallway of the flat emerging into the small living room.

Seeing Caroline and Bill sitting on the settee he moaned, 'I thought we agreed that Bill would be ready to go when I got here?'

She pointed at the television and said, 'Sorry Lenny, Bill wanted to see his horse run, before he went.'

For the third time that morning the councillor swore, 'For fucks sake Caroline, I'm not your fucking chauffeur!'

'Bill's ready now so stop your whining. Just remember who calls the shots around here Lenny.'

Ignoring the barbed remark, Lenny said, 'Come on Bill, I haven't got all fucking day!'

Bill Short stood up and said, 'I'm coming, the bloody horse finished last anyway. I'll just grab the cleaning gear.'

He walked into the kitchen and retrieved a cardboard box full of cleaning products, cloths and a mop and bucket set.

As soon as Bill left the room and without looking away from the television, Caroline said under her breath, 'Make sure that idiot does a good job, I want that place spotless. We can't afford to have any trace of that kid left there.'

Lenny replied, 'I will, I will', before shouting impatiently, 'Come on Bill, what's the bloody hold up now?'

Bill shouted from the kitchen, 'I can't find the fucking bleach!'

Glancing at her watch Caroline shouted angrily, 'Look under the sink, you moron!'

'Oh yeah. I've got it!'

'Get a move on Bill, Lenny hasn't got all day!'

Nervously she glanced at her watch again.

Grenville Slater was due to arrive in ten minutes. The last thing she needed was for her lover to arrive while her husband was still at the flat.

Getting off the settee, she walked into the kitchen followed by Lenny, 'Come on Bill, get moving for Christ's sake and make sure you leave that place spotless, do you hear?'

She virtually shooed them out of the flat and closed the door. She then watched nervously from the window as they loaded the cleaning products into the Range Rover.

Two minutes later, she breathed a sigh of relief as the Range Rover was driven away.

She still had time for a quick freshen up before Slater arrived.

In her haste to be ready, Caroline never spotted the dark blue Ford Sierra that pulled out from behind the nursing home opposite and slotted in behind the Range Rover as it was driven away from Edale Close.

The surveillance team from the Regional Crime Squad had been on full alert after the Range Rover had pulled up outside the target premises.

Now that vehicle had left with one of the targets on board, a full team of detectives, driving several different vehicles, would keep it under constant observation until it returned.

CHAPTER 54

29th June 1986
South Lodge, Retford

Jimmy Wade and Melissa Braithwaite had spent the entire morning making love, they were now sitting up in bed enjoying a post coital cigarette.

The lovemaking had been both frantic and intense.

Braithwaite had been surprised at just how turned on she'd been, by witnessing and taking part in the deaths of the two nurses. It was as though Jimmy had seen a different side to her after she had killed Barnes. He'd reverted to being gentle and caring again. It felt like the lovemaking they had both enjoyed when Wade had first escaped from Rampton.

Taking the last drag on her cigarette, she reached over to the ash tray on the bedside cabinet and pressed down on the stub until it was out.

She looked back over her shoulder at Wade, who had his head back on the headboard, blowing smoke rings towards the ceiling.

'Would you like something to eat Jimmy?'

'Not yet, I've got to get rid of those two twats out there first. I wouldn't mind a fry up after I've buried them.'

'Of course, Jimmy, that was amazing. We haven't been that good together for ages.'

'It was fantastic Mel. It's such a turn on isn't it?'

Braithwaite continued to play her survival strategy and said, 'Isn't it just. I couldn't wait to have you after I'd finished off Barnes.'

'I always knew you'd appreciate it in the end Mel. I've always known there was a killer lurking inside you waiting to break free. I could see it the very first time I looked into your eyes at Leicester Crown Court.'

She snuggled into him and said quietly, 'Can we leave for Ireland now Jimmy?'

'As soon as we've finished what has to be done here. I've been thinking about it this morning and I've thought of a way to get hold of that dopey social worker, Stewart 'bloody' Ainsworth.'

'Do we have to bother with him?

'Yes, we bloody do.'

'What have you got planned?'

'Do you remember that time he visited you here, when he was checking you out because you were visiting me inside? You told me he couldn't take his eyes off your tits that day.'

'I remember, he gave me the creeps, the lecherous little shit.'

'We can use that to our advantage Mel. I want you to phone Rampton and ask to speak to Ainsworth. Tell him you want to see him out here.'

'What reason can I give?'

'I don't know, tell him you're feeling a little insecure as Jimmy Wade still hasn't been found and that the last time you visited him in Rampton he made threats against you because you'd walked out of the visit.'

'Do you think that'll work? Would that be enough to get him all the way out here?'

'You'll have to embellish it a little. Tell him you'll open a bottle of wine and cook him some dinner as a thank you. I'm telling you Mel, he won't be able to resist. He'll think he's being invited on some hot date with a chance of getting into your knickers.'

She continued her survival strategy and said, 'You know I'd never let that happen Jimmy.'

'I know that, but he's got to believe that's what's going to happen. When you talk to him on the phone, you've got to really lay it on thick. Do you think you can do it?'

'What are you going to do with him if I get him out here?'

'I think we should both have some fun with him, don't you?'

'That would be great Jimmy, then can we go to Ireland?'

'Once we've had our fun and he's dead then we'll go to Ireland.'

CHAPTER 55

29th June 1986
Bleasby, Nottinghamshire

The last part of the surveillance on the Range Rover had been the trickiest.

There was no way the detectives from the Regional Crime Squad could follow in their vehicles once the Range Rover had turned onto the single-track lane that led into thick woodland.

Dc Tony Armstrong and Dc Pete Burgin got out of their vehicle and began to jog along the side of the track.

Pete Burgin was clutching a loaded Nikon camera. He carried two more spare films in his jacket pockets. After one hundred yards the detectives saw the cottage and the Range Rover parked up outside.

Immediately, they ducked off the track and approached through the trees, keeping well hidden from the driver and passenger who were still sitting in the target vehicle.

Having got to within twenty yards of the vehicle, the two detectives squatted down in the thick bracken and watched.

The cottage appeared to be derelict. Most of the windows were boarded up and it looked ready to fall down.

Tony Armstrong whispered, 'What the fuck's all this about? This place looks ready for demolition.'

Pete Burgin shrugged then said, 'Quiet mate, they're getting out.'

They watched as Bill Short got out of the passenger seat and an unknown fat man got out of the driver's door.

Pete Burgin lifted the Nikon and began to take photographs.

As soon as he got out of the driver's door of the vehicle, the fat man walked towards the cottage, fumbling for something in his jacket pocket. Bill Short went to the boot and retrieved armfuls of cleaning products. He began to struggle as he carried them all towards the cottage.

Once again, the Nikon camera was recording everything.

Finally, the fat man found what he was looking for. From his jacket pocket he produced a small key, stepped forward and unlocked the padlock that secured the front door of the cottage.

Bill Short shouted after him, 'Lenny, get back here and give me a hand with this lot!'

The fat man walked slowly back to the vehicle and grabbed the mop and bucket from Short.

The detectives continued to observe as both men disappeared inside the derelict cottage. They contacted the rest of the surveillance team by radio and informed them what was happening, issuing an instruction to stand by.

They knew they would be out of the surveillance as soon as the Range Rover was driven off, but it was important that they remained where they were to give the rest of the team updates about what was happening and most important of all to give the surveillance team notice when the target vehicle was leaving.

That way the rest of the team could be ready to resume and maintain the surveillance on the Range Rover.

Bill Short and the fat man were inside the cottage for the best part of an hour.

When they finally emerged, Short walked over to the Range Rover and put the cleaning products back into the boot. The fat man followed him outside and immediately lit up a cigarette.

He replaced the padlock on the front door and slipped the key into his jacket pocket. Bill Short walked back over to the cottage and the fat man offered him a cigarette and a light.

The two detectives in the woodland couldn't quite make out what was being said by the two men as they smoked their cigarettes, but they could see that they were both laughing and joking.

Pete Burgin used the Nikon to capture their jovial mood.

They finished smoking their cigarettes, flipped the butts into the trees, walked towards the vehicle and climbed in.

The unknown fat man was driving again.

As soon as the engine started Pete Burgin picked up his radio and spoke to the rest of the surveillance team, 'Stand by, stand by. Target vehicle is leaving the plot, Target 2 plus unidentified driver on board. Vehicle leaving now, direction back towards the main road. Out.'

His message was acknowledged by a series of clicks.

In their covert ear pieces, the detectives heard the clicks and then a voice saying, 'Maintain your position until after target vehicle has left the plot. You will be picked up at the main road in fifteen minutes. Out.'

The Range Rover engine was revved loudly, it belched out a cloud of black diesel smoke from the twin exhausts, then seconds later it was on the move, being driven back along the single-track lane towards the main road.

After it had been gone five minutes the two crime squad detectives broke cover and walked over to the cottage.

Tony Armstrong made a note of the make of the padlock on the front door while Pete Burgin took photographs of the cottage and the padlock.

He looked at Pete and said, 'What the fuck was all that about? What the hell have they been cleaning up in there?'

'I don't know Tony, but we need to let the guvnor know about this right away. I think Danny Flint is going to be well interested in this place.'

As they walked back along the track towards the main road, Tony Armstrong used his radio to inform DCI Carlisle what they had seen and the make of the padlock being used to secure the cottage.

CHAPTER 56

29th June 1986
Mansfield Police Station, Nottinghamshire

Danny Flint opened the door of his office and scanned the large open plan room for Brian Hopkirk and Rob Buxton. He spotted the two men in conversation at the far end of the room.

'Rob, Brian I need you in here straight away.'

Danny turned, walked back into his office and sat down. Almost immediately, the two detective inspectors walked into the office.

Danny said, 'Close the door and sit down.'

As soon as the door was closed, Danny said, 'I've just had a very interesting telephone call from Mattie Carlisle. The crime squad surveillance operation on Caroline and Bill Short has finally turned something up. Bill Short was picked up from the flat on Edale Close earlier today by an unknown male driving a Range Rover. Short was then driven to a secluded, derelict cottage just outside the village of Bleasby. Both men were then observed taking a load of cleaning items into this cottage. They spent an hour inside the cottage before coming back out. The unknown male then drove Bill Short back to the flat at Edale Close. Meanwhile, during the two hours Bill was out of the way, Caroline was busy entertaining Grenville Slater again.'

Rob said, 'Who's the unknown male driving the Range Rover?'

The surveillance team carried out a PNC owner enquiry as standard and it turns out that the vehicle's registered to none other than Leonard Mellor.'

An incredulous Rob said, 'Councillor Leonard Mellor?'

'The very same.'

'Bloody hell.'

Danny continued, 'Apparently, the good councillor was in possession of the key that opened the padlock being used to secure the cottage.'

Brian was thoughtful then said, 'Danny, there's a padlock key on the bunch of keys used by Caroline Short for her Ford Transit. If you remember, that key couldn't be attributed to any of the locks at Tall Trees.

'That's right. Get hold of those keys out of the property store. The three of us are going to drive over to Bleasby and have a look at this cottage for ourselves. Rob, give Tim Donnelly at Scenes of Crime a quick call. If it's at all possible, I'd like him to join us.'

CHAPTER 57

29th June 1986
South Lodge, Retford

The sun was high in the sky and Jimmy Wade was sweating profusely.

His hands and forearms were covered in grime that clung to his wet skin.

One last time, he pushed the spade into the heap of freshly dug soil and piled dirt onto the top of the shallow grave.

It had taken him over an hour of hard slog to dig the two shallow graves.

They were only three feet deep and four feet long, but tree roots from the surrounding woodland had been a real pain to chop through. He'd picked a spot between the stream at the back of the lodge and the woods.

It was an area where the soil was quite soft and he thought it would be easy digging, he hadn't factored in the myriad of roots.

After digging the graves, he'd moved the dead men from the outhouse across the small bridge over the stream, before dropping them into their final resting places.

He'd moved Fred Barnes first.

The older man was the heaviest and it was a real effort to drag him out of the outhouse. Once outside, he'd used a wheelbarrow to take him over to the grave.

Wade had then unceremoniously tipped the nurse from the wheelbarrow into the shallow grave. Barnes had landed in an unusual way, face down with his backside in the air, his arms and legs tucked beneath him.

Wade grinned, picked the spade up and began to hurl the freshly dug soil over the body. He placed the grass sods, he'd removed when he first started digging, back onto the top of the fresh soil and stamped it down.

Apart from a small, almost imperceptible rise in the ground, the shallow grave was virtually invisible.

He'd then repeated the process, dragging Jack Williams from the outhouse, wheelbarrowing him over to the grave site and burying him.

Now as he began to replace the last of the grass sods onto the top of Williams grave, he suddenly craved an ice-cold beer. He shouted up to the lodge, 'Mel!'

Immediately Braithwaite emerged from the lodge and shouted back, 'Did you call me?'

'I've almost done here, get me a cold beer ready. It's nearly time for you to make that phone call.'

'Okay.'

Wade stamped down the last grass sod then placed the spade into the wheel barrow and pushed it back over the bridge. He stopped half way across the bridge and looked back. Unless you knew exactly where the graves were located, you couldn't see them.

He smiled, satisfied at his work, then made his way up to the lodge.

Sitting in the kitchen, he stared at the ice-cold beer in front of him.

He could feel beads of sweat trickling down his face as he stared at the small bubbles rising slowly through the amber liquid and the condensation forming on the outside of the glass.

He lifted the pint glass and gulped the beer down greedily.

The ice-cold fluid burned the back of his throat as he swallowed. He drank the pint in one go, slammed the glass down onto the table and let out a loud belch.

'Get me another Mel, that one didn't touch the sides!'

Instantly, she placed another beer in front of him, this time he sipped it slowly.

'Right Mel, it's time for you to make that telephone call. Are you sure you know what you're going to say?'

'I'm sure Jimmy.'

They walked from the kitchen to the hallway where the telephone sat on a small table near the front door. The number for Rampton Hospital was in the address book that sat on the table next to the telephone.

She flicked through the book until she found it.

Lifting the receiver, she dialled the number.

When the hospital switchboard answered she said, 'I'd like to speak to Mr Stewart Ainsworth, he's one of your social workers.'

The switchboard confirmed that they were putting the call through to his office.

She replied, 'Thank you.'

There was a pause before Stewart Ainsworth came on the line, 'Hello, this is Stewart Ainsworth, can I help you?'

In a soft, almost seductive voice Mel said, 'Hi Stewart, it's Melanie Braithwaite. I don't know if you'll remember me? You came to see me at my house some time ago.'

'Hello Melanie, of course I remember you. I came to see you about your visits to Jimmy Wade, didn't I?'

'That's right, you did. Wade's the reason I'm calling today. I'm terrified that he still hasn't been caught and is still out there somewhere. Would it be possible to see you later today? I need to have a chat about what I should do. I'm so worried and you were the only person I could think of who might be able to help me.'

Ainsworth had remembered Braithwaite straight away, how could he forget her, she was gorgeous. The poor woman sounded terrified. If he played this situation right he might be able to use her fear to his own advantage.

A sly grin formed across his mouth and he said, 'Of course Melanie, I'd be more than happy to come and see you, but I don't finish work until later.'

'Please Stewart, I'm desperate. I need to talk to someone as soon as possible. I've got an idea, why don't I cook for you? You could come over after work, I'd make us a nice meal and we can have a chat over a bottle of wine.'

Stewart Ainsworth's sly grin turned into a full blown lecherous smile, this was going to be easier than he'd first thought.

'That sounds perfect Melanie, are you still at the same house?'

'Yes, I'm still at South Lodge.'

'The place in the woods?'

She giggled and said, 'That's right, but don't worry, if you drink too much wine, there's a spare room, you can always sleep over.'

'I finish work at six o'clock, I can be at yours for six thirty if that's ok?'

Mel purred, 'Thank you so much Stewart, that's wonderful. Look forward to seeing you later.'

Stewart Ainsworth put the telephone down, let out a whoop and said aloud, 'Result!'

As Mel replaced the handset Jimmy Wade looked at her and said, 'That was fucking brilliant, come here sweetheart!'

He grabbed her and pulled her to him, 'I'm filthy, I need a hot shower. Get up those stairs. You're coming in with me to help wash all this grime off.'

She smiled but said nothing as she followed Wade up the stairs.

She knew in her heart that she had just sealed the fate of Stewart Ainsworth.

CHAPTER 58

29th June 1986
Bleasby, Nottinghamshire

The small derelict cottage hadn't been easy to find.

The three detectives and the scenes of crime officer sat crammed into the small CID car. They had followed the detailed directions given by the crime squad surveillance team and they had still struggled to locate it.

It really was off the beaten track.

As Rob Buxton turned off the country lane and onto the single track that led into dense woodland he said, 'Are you sure this is right Danny?'

'According to the directions, apparently the cottage is about a hundred yards down this lane.'

Rob continued to drive slowly, trying to avoid the potholes on the unmade track.

After negotiating a bend in the track, they got their first glimpse of the cottage.

The property had originally been built for use by farm workers employed at the nearby Beech Tree Farm, but it hadn't been occupied for years.

Beech Tree Farm itself was no longer functioning as a working farm and most of the land associated with the business had been sold off to the Forestry Commission.

The majority of the land sold off was now planted with ten-year-old conifers. The conifer growth made the surrounding area seem dark and uninviting; that, coupled with its remote location made the cottage a forgotten building.

The occupants of the car got out and stared at the grey stone cottage.

It was a small property, that had two boarded up windows downstairs either side of the heavy front door and two windows on the first floor that were also boarded. A weed covered garden path led from the front gate to the front door.

On the rusting gate was a small sign that read, 'Mayflower Cottage'.

The gate itself had at one time been decorative and ornate. Now it was hanging by one hinge and was in keeping with the rest of the decaying building.

The gardens were overgrown and unkempt.

The detectives walked around the perimeter of the cottage and found an outside privy and a couple of other stone outbuildings at the rear of the property.

The only sign of any recent human involvement with the cottage, was the shiny new padlock that had been used to secure the front door. Even the boards that now protected the windows, were covered in a dark green mould caused by years of untreated rain damage.

Danny turned to Brian and said, 'Have you got the keys?'

Brian produced the bunch of keys that had been seized from the home address of Caroline Short. The keys were for her Ford Transit, but they also contained a key for a padlock.

He stepped forward and tried that key in the new padlock.

The well-greased arm of the padlock sprang open with a turn of the key. Brian removed the lock from the hasp and opened the heavy door.

'I think we're going to need some torches boss, it's pretty dark inside.'

Tim Donnelly said, 'I've put a couple of Dragon lights in the boot, I'll fetch them.'

He turned and walked back to the car.

Danny said to Rob, 'Is it possible for a building to feel evil?'

'I don't know Danny, but this place gives me the creeps.'

Tim returned carrying two of the heavy-duty Dragon lamps that when switched on, provided a light as bright as day. He was also carrying a large rucksack over his shoulder.

Putting the bag on the floor he said, 'I've brought suits, gloves, overshoes and exhibit bags. I suggest we all get suited and booted before we have a look inside.'

Without saying a word, the men put the protective clothing on.

Danny then picked up a Dragon light and led the way into the cottage.

He stepped from bright sunlight, into the dark unlit cottage. He paused to allow his eyes time to adjust, but still unable to see clearly, he flicked on the Dragon light.

The inside space was instantly flooded with bright white light.

Danny could see that he was standing in the entrance hallway of the cottage. Directly ahead was a wooden, uncarpeted staircase. To the right was a doorway that led to what had once been the lounge. The door was no longer there and the lounge itself was uncarpeted and unfurnished. There was a strong smell of damp and decay emanating from the room.

Danny turned to the left and saw another open doorway minus the door. This room had once been the sitting room and was also bare and damp.

To the immediate left of the staircase was a passageway that led to the rear of the property.

Stepping forward slowly, being careful where he placed his feet, Danny walked along the passageway.

He saw a small utility cupboard beneath the stairs. Opening the door, he could see a dust covered electricity meter. There were a few old tools strewn on the floor, the space inside was thick with cobwebs and reeked of mould. The door looked as though it had been recently opened though, the cobwebs around the door had been brushed to one side.

Danny closed the cupboard door and moved forward again.

He stepped through another open doorway and into what had once been the kitchen.

There was no smell of damp or mould in this room, the overpowering smell was one of bleach. Looking around the room he could see a sink unit and four cupboards. There was a space where the cooker had once stood. It was a space that would have been filled by a huge oil powered Aga. There was no gas connected to the cottage.

The kitchen was completely devoid of any cups, pots or pans of any description. There was a ramshackle wooden table and four chairs in the centre of the room.

Rob wrinkled his nose and said, 'Bloody hell, can you smell that?'

Danny replied, 'It's bleach. This room's been thoroughly cleaned but I don't think anyone's been in the two rooms at the front of the building in years. Tim, you and Brian have a good look down here. Rob come with me, we'll go and take a look upstairs.'

Tim Donnelly switched on the Dragon light he was carrying and together with Brian, began an examination of the downstairs rooms. Danny and Rob retraced their steps along the hallway then began to climb the wooden staircase.

Pausing at the top of the stairs, Danny was confronted by three doorways. The doors to the rooms upstairs were all still in place. Once again there was the overpowering, cloying stench of bleach.

Danny pushed open the first door.

It led into a small bathroom that contained a white toilet, a hand basin and a bathtub.

Everything in the bathroom was absolutely spotless.

The cottage was in such a state of disrepair everywhere else, it was strange to be confronted with such a pristine, bleach cleaned bathroom.

Rob said in a low voice, 'Somebody's certainly given this room the spring clean of the century.'

'I'm getting a bad feeling about this place Rob, let's look in the bedrooms.

Stepping out of the bathroom, Danny turned right, opened the door and stepped inside the first bedroom. Again, there was the strong smell of bleach and disinfectant. There wasn't a speck of grime or dust to be seen. No cobwebs in this room.

Danny noticed a light bulb hanging from the ceiling.

'Flick the light switch, Rob.'

Rob flicked down the light switch near the door. The lightbulb flickered into life.

'If the property's derelict and unoccupied, why's the electricity still connected?'

'Good question, Danny. What it does mean, is there'll be a utility bill somewhere that's being paid by somebody.'

'When we get back to the office, I want you to find out everything you can about Mayflower Cottage. Check with the Land Registry and find out who's listed as the current owners. Make enquiries with the utility companies and find out who's paying for the electricity. Somebody's gone to a lot of effort to obliterate all trace of anyone being here. Do you know if the crime squad lads got any photographs during the surveillance?'

'They did. When they followed the targets down here on foot, one of the lads had the presence of mind to grab a camera.'

'So, have they got shots of Short and Mellor carrying cleaning gear into the cottage?'

'As far as I know, yes. I haven't seen any of the photographs yet, but I'm told they made full use of the camera they had with them.'

'That's bloody brilliant! Remind me to buy that detective a beer.'

Danny stepped into the other upstairs room. It was the same as the first, slightly smaller but the layout was the same. Again, there was a single lightbulb hanging from the ceiling. Danny flicked the switch and again the light came on.

Danny switched off his Dragon light and shouted, 'Tim, can you come upstairs please?'

Tim Donnelly came up to the first floor and was surprised to see the lights on.

'That's interesting. Somebody forgot to remove the lightbulbs. Once they've cooled down I'll get them printed. It's not very often people remember to put gloves on to change a lightbulb, we might get lucky there.'

Danny said, 'Tim, this place has obviously been bleached to death. Is it possible to take samples that would identify the type of bleach used to sterilise the place?'

'It's a good question Danny, I can find out. We'll definitely be able to get the samples and I'm guessing the lab would be able to identify the separate chemical components that make up the bleach used. Whether that chemical make-up differs between brands of bleach, I don't know. It's something we can certainly try.'

'It's important Tim, if the crime squad have got photos showing Bill Short and Councillor Mellor carrying in the bleach that's then found all over the cottage, they're going to have some difficulty explaining their reasons for cleaning up a derelict property.'

'I'll get on it straightaway Danny. I'll arrange for a team to join me here and we'll do a full forensic examination of the cottage.'

Danny turned to Brian, 'Brian, stay here with Tim and his team and keep me informed of the progress please. I'll get Fran Jefferies to bring a car out for you.'

'No problem sir.'

'Rob, you come back to the office with me, I want you to start doing the enquiries into Mayflower Cottage. My instincts are telling me, this is the place where Evan Jenkins was abused and killed. There'll be a connection between this property and Caroline Short somewhere, we just need to find it.'

CHAPTER 59

29th June 1986
Rampton Hospital, Nottinghamshire

It had been another long day in what had already been a long week for Tina Prowse and Rachel Moore.

With little else to go on, they had returned to Rampton Hospital and began to re-interview the staff that had been involved in the care and supervision of Jimmy Wade in any way.

The hospital had allocated them a room that contained a table, four chairs and a telephone.

If they wanted to interview a staff member, they had to contact the hospital admin department on the phone and request that staff member be sent to their room. This arrangement allowed the two detectives to carry out their enquiries and also alleviated the need for the hospital to provide a staff member to accompany them around the various departments of the maximum-security hospital.

It wasn't ideal, but it was practical and it worked.

Rachel glanced at her watch, it was now almost five thirty in the evening.

She said to Tina, 'What's the name of Wade's social worker?'

Tina flicked through her notes and replied, 'Stewart Ainsworth, why?'

'It's only half past five, we've still got time for one more, let's see if Mr Ainsworth's at work today.'

Tina nodded and phoned the hospital admin department.

Having made the call she said, 'He's at work, but he finishes his shift in thirty minutes. Admin are sending him over to us now.'

Five minutes later there was a quiet tap on the door.

Tina said, 'Come in!'

The door opened and the tall, skinny social worker stepped inside.

He said nervously, 'I'm Stewart Ainsworth, Admin said you wanted to see me?'

Rachel smiled and said, 'Come in and take a seat Stewart, this won't take long. I'm Detective Constable Rachel Moore and this is Sergeant Tina Prowse, we're currently investigating the escape of Jimmy Wade. We're talking to everyone who had any involvement with Wade while he was incarcerated here. Our understanding is that you were his allocated social worker. What were your duties in relation to Wade?'

Ainsworth, having sat down opposite the detectives, flicked back his lank brown hair, grinned affably and said, 'It was my role to look after his general welfare. Any issues he had, he could talk to me. It's a role designed to assist the patients to settle into the regime of imprisonment. Most of the patients here have been sentenced to life imprisonment. If not a whole life sentence then most of them are here detained at Her Majesty's pleasure. Either way, they're destined to be detained here for most of their lives, if not all their life. This can be a very frightening and daunting prospect for most of the patients.'

Tina said, 'How did you get on with Jimmy Wade?'

'Wade was okay, he settled into the routine of incarceration very quickly.'

'Did he have any issues at all? When he first arrived, maybe?'

'Not that I recall. He very much kept himself to himself. He didn't mix with the other patients much.'

Rachel said, 'Stewart, we've been here a couple of days now. We've spoken to quite a few members of staff and we've heard reports that some of the staff were quite heavy handed in their approach to Wade.'

'What do you mean, heavy handed?'

'The inference being, that Wade was physically assaulted on several occasions. It's also inferred that these assaults were carried out by two male nurses in particular. Did Wade ever make a complaint of assault to you?'

'Not that I remember.'

Rachel continued, 'Specifically, did Jimmy Wade ever complain to you about being assaulted by either Fred Barnes or Jack Williams?'

'No, he did not. I never took any reports of assault from Jimmy Wade.'

'If you had received such a report, what would you have done?'

'If any patient reports an assault to me, I'm obliged to make a written report of the allegation, detailing the assault, then raise the matter with the line manager of the member of staff the allegation relates to.'

'But Jimmy Wade never made any such allegations, specifically against Barnes and Williams?'

'No, he didn't, and I never saw Wade with any injuries.'

'How well do you know Fred Barnes and Jack Williams?'

'Obviously I know them both from working here. I do, on the odd occasion, sometimes see Jack Williams outside of the work environment. We're of a similar age and have been out for a beer together, why?'

'Are they your mates?'

'Not particularly, why?'

'Would you cover for them Stewart?'

'No, I wouldn't.'

'Would you ever turn a blind eye to an assault on a patient?'

'No, never and I resent the insinuation.'

'Okay Stewart, I want to take a written statement from you outlining exactly what you've told us.'

'I've no problem about making a statement detective, but would it be possible to make the statement tomorrow morning? I'm on a day shift again tomorrow. The only reason I ask, is because I've got a first date with a new girlfriend this evening. I really don't want to stand Melissa up, especially not on the first date. It would be so rude and there's no way I could get a message to her.'

Tina said, 'That's okay Stewart, we won't keep you. It's our day off tomorrow, but we're back on duty the day after. Are you working then?'

'I'm on the same shift all week. The day after tomorrow, I'll be starting work at nine o clock in the morning as usual.'

'Okay, we'll see you the day after tomorrow at nine thirty sharp. I don't want you to miss your date with Melissa whatever her name is.'

Stewart interjected and said, 'Braithwaite, Melissa Braithwaite.'

Tina continued, 'Whatever. Stewart, please take the time to have a good think about what we've discussed this afternoon. I would hate for you to say something that was later proved to be a lie. Do you understand me?'

'Yes, I understand you sergeant. I won't be changing anything I've told you. I've told you the truth, I wouldn't cover for anybody, I'd lose my job.'

Rachel said, 'No problem Stewart, we'll see you soon.'

Ainsworth stood up and hurried out of the room before the detectives had the chance to change their minds.

For one horrible moment, he thought he was going to miss out on his hot date with the very sexy Melissa Braithwaite. As he hurried along the corridor he found himself smiling just thinking about her.

Back in the interview room Tina said, 'What do you think of Stewart Ainsworth?'

'He's a liar. He knows Barnes and Williams have assaulted Wade, he just hasn't taken the report. Basically, he's covered it up.'

'Do you think he'll say that the next time we see him?'

'Not a chance. Like he said earlier, if he had covered for them he'd lose his job. While ever there's no sign of Barnes and Williams to contradict his account, Ainsworth will stick to the bullshit story. He won't change his mind.'

'I think you're right Rachel, but it won't do him any harm to have a couple of days to think about it. Come on Rach, we're off tomorrow, let's call it a day.'

CHAPTER 60

29th June 1986
Mansfield Police Station, Nottinghamshire

Danny felt nauseous.

Ever since he'd arrived back at the police station and sat alone in his office, thoughts of the derelict cottage flooded his mind.

All he could see were images of Evan Jenkins being abused by faceless men.

The boy's face was contorted in agony, his mouth wide open letting out a silent scream.

A knock on his office door banished the horrifying image to the back of his mind, for the moment. The detective knew it was a nightmare that would reoccur.

'Come in!'

The door opened and a beaming Andy Wills came in.

'Boss, I've cracked the telephone numbers! Well, to be honest my new best mate Gareth has cracked the numbers.'

For a split-second Danny looked blank, 'Numbers?'

'The list of numbers in the address book recovered from Caroline Short. You remember, they looked like phone numbers, but were all showing as a dead line.'

'Right. Those numbers. Come on then Andy, you're looking suitably pleased with yourself. Tell me what's happened.'

'I took your advice and contacted British Telecom for assistance. They sent up their top engineer from Swansea, to have a look at them. I've got to tell you boss, Gareth Church, is a bloody genius. He spent four hours trying different permutations before he cracked it. It was like watching one of them code breakers at Bletchley Park in the second world war. Bloody amazing!'

'That's all well and good Andy, but do the numbers mean anything now?'

'Right boss. This is how Gareth did it, he swapped the last digit of each of the numbers with the third digit, then the first digit with the second from last digit and hey presto! Each number then related to a telephone number that is listed on the network. A couple of them are ex-directory numbers but they're all live lines. It was an ingenious code, but at the same time very simple.'

'Do the telephone numbers relate to people we know?'

'Two of them leap off the page at you. Councillor Lenny Mellor and Grenville Slater are both on the list.'

'What?'

'Yes boss, you heard me right.'

'Why would you need your solicitor in a coded list? Why not just have his office number?'

'My thoughts exactly, boss.'

'What about Councillor Mellor's? Is that his office number?'

'No, it's an ex-directory private number that is registered to his home address.'

'What about the other numbers?'

'I'm still researching them, but so far I've got ten people including Slater and Mellor. Within that group of ten, there's a vicar from a Methodist church just over the border in Derbyshire, an anaesthetist from a hospital in Chesterfield, a pit deputy, two factory workers and three local businessmen, one of whom is an estate agent in Mansfield.'

'Did you say there's an anaesthetist on that list?'

'Yes Danny. The initials W.B. relate to a man called William Baxter. His home address is just outside South Normanton in Derbyshire, he works as an anaesthetist at Chesterfield General Hospital.'

'Do you remember the toxicology from the post mortem? The drugs that were found?'

As if to answer his own question, Danny quickly scanned through his enquiries log and said, 'Here they are, Thiopentone and Suxamethonium.'

'I remember, yes.'

'What's the betting that William Baxter has access to these drugs in his work?'

'I'd say the odds would be pretty good boss, I'll look into it as a priority.'

'Thanks Andy, are the rest of the names on the list all men?'

'Every single name on the list is a man.'

'Our paedophile ring?'

'Could be boss.'

'That's brilliant work Andy. Have BT charged us for their engineer?'

'No, they haven't. Gareth was good enough to come up here on his day off.'

'I want to meet him before he goes back to Swansea, to say a massive thank you.'

'Sorry boss, he left straight away, he needed to get home.'

'Okay, if this all pans out how it's looking, remind me to draft a letter of thanks to his bosses. In the meantime, grab Phil Baxter and Simon Paine and start researching the names on that list. I want to know everything about these men by tomorrow morning please.'

'Will do boss.'

Andy hurried out of the office leaving Danny alone with his thoughts.

Just maybe those anonymous, faceless men in his nightmare would soon have names, identities and more importantly, faces.

Danny was deep in thought.

Things were moving on quickly, depending on the enquiries on the cottage and now Andy's enquiries on the names from the numbers list, he may have to consider an early arrest for Caroline and Bill Short.

CHAPTER 61

29th June 1986
South Lodge, Retford

As Stewart Ainsworth drove his small rusting Fiat Uno along the secluded, tree lined lane that led to Melissa Braithwaite's pretty little cottage, his mind drifted to the time three months ago, when he'd first met the pretty student, studying for her Masters in Psychology.

It had been a routine visit to ascertain the reasons why she was regularly visiting Jimmy Wade at Rampton.

He'd been instantly taken by the petite blonde with the wonderful curves and had often racked his brains trying to think up an excuse to revisit her.

Melissa Braithwaite absolutely oozed sex appeal.

He'd been shocked, amazed and excited in equal measure when he received the phone call from her. It was completely out of the blue. Now as he drove along the lane he could feel a sense of anxiety stirring within himself.

He desperately wanted this to go right, he felt a strong attraction towards her that he wanted to continue. He didn't want the date tonight to be a one off.

As soon as he finished work he'd rushed home, showered and had a quick shave. He had maybe used a little too much Paco Rabanne aftershave and deodorant spray. Better too much than not enough, he thought.

He had quickly put on a freshly laundered, light blue Lacoste polo shirt, faded Levi jeans and a pair of brown loafer shoes. He'd then checked himself out in the full-length mirror at his flat, he thought he looked pretty good.

He completed the look with a pair of pilot style, Ray Ban sunglasses.

She had promised a home cooked meal with wine, that's got to be a good start, he thought. He had felt excited about the evening ahead

As he continued to drive along the pot holed lane, his mind turned back to work. His thoughts turned to the two, busy body detectives who had spoken to him at Rampton and nearly screwed everything up.

He couldn't understand why they were so bothered. So, what if Jimmy Wade had received a few slaps from a couple of the male nurses when he first came into Rampton? Surely, the serial killer deserved that and much more. He thought the police would be happy that Wade had at least received some summary justice.

He put the two detectives firmly to the back of his mind.

He didn't want to think about them or Jimmy Wade tonight.

This evening it was all about him and Melissa.

The trees started to thin out a little and just as the sun was starting to dip below the tree line, he got his first glimpse of the pretty stone cottage where she lived.

He parked his Fiat behind the Ford Transit van that was already parked directly outside the cottage. There was no sign of the dark blue Ford Sierra she used to have.

People do change their cars, he thought.

As he got out of the car he noticed that the front garden, that had been so neat on his last visit, was looking a little untidy and scruffy. The lawn hadn't been cut and there were weeds all over the flower beds.

He walked from the cinder parking area, up the garden path and to the front door of the cottage.

He was about to press the ornate doorbell when he noticed the front door was slightly ajar.

He pushed the door open a little wider and shouted, 'Melissa!'

There was no reply, but he could hear the television playing in the lounge.

He opened the front door fully, stepped inside and shouted again, 'Melissa, it's me Stewart. Are you home?'

He strained to listen above the music that was blaring from the television. There was still no reply, but now he got the faintest whiff of a delightful perfume. He breathed in deeply. He remembered the smell of the perfume from his last visit, she was definitely in the cottage somewhere.

He walked through the lounge and into the kitchen at the rear of the cottage. In here the perfume smell had been replaced by the beautiful aroma of a chicken casserole being slowly cooked in the oven. He could see a saucepan full of peeled potatoes and another pan of peeled carrots sitting on the hob of the cooker, waiting to be turned on.

The kitchen table was laid for two places. In the centre of the table stood a large white church candle and a bottle of Pinot Grigio white wine, next to two crystal wine glasses.

Reaching out he slid his finger along the neck of the wine bottle. The glass felt chilled as though it had just been removed from the fridge

The back door that led from the kitchen out into the garden was wide open.

That explains it, he thought, she must have stepped outside for a second.

He stepped outside and noticed immediately that the lawn at the back was really overgrown and hadn't been cut for weeks.

Looking down the garden, he saw that the nearest outhouse had been fully renovated. The door to that outhouse was wide open, he shouted, 'Melissa, it's Stewart. Are you out here?'

Finally, he got a response. He heard her voice from within the recently renovated outhouse, 'I'm in here, Stewart.'

He walked from the back door down the garden to the outhouse. He stopped outside and peered into the gloom.

'What are you doing in there?'

She moved forward out of the shadows and purred, 'I'm in here, waiting for you. What took you so long?'

Stewart Ainsworth couldn't believe his eyes. Melissa stood totally naked just inside the outhouse. In the half-light he could see every delicious curve of her body.

She tousled her blonde hair and said seductively, 'It's so nice and cool in here after that hot kitchen. I've been waiting for you to arrive Stewart, are you coming in?'

Ainsworth was stung into action by her words and began to pull off his polo shirt. Bare chested he kicked off his loafer shoes and stepped forward towards the open door of the outhouse.

He was so engrossed in what he was seeing, that his other senses totally betrayed him. He never heard a sound as Jimmy Wade crept out from behind the bush where he had hidden, waiting for Ainsworth.

Wade covered the few yards swiftly and silently, before smashing a ball pein hammer onto the back of the young social workers head.

As soon as Ainsworth fell to the ground, Melissa stepped out of the shadows of the outhouse and walked slowly over to Wade.

'Is he dead, Jimmy?'

'No, he's not dead Mel, just unconscious.'

'Can I do it Jimmy? Can I finish him?'

'Listen to you, have you got a taste for it now sweetheart?'

She smiled up at the serial killer and nodded.

He pulled her towards him and kissed her hard on the mouth. Her warm body felt good to the touch and she smelt wonderful, 'Go up to the house, wait for me upstairs, I just need to secure this idiot. I'm going to enjoy watching you play with him later, but right now I need to have you.'

Without a word, she walked back towards the kitchen door swinging her hips as she went. She knew Jimmy was watching her every move.

When she had asked Wade if she could kill Ainsworth, she'd been deadly serious. She wanted to experience that sense of mastery over another human being again.

The abuse and manipulation, the months of brutality and degradation had finally taken its dreadful toll.

Melissa Braithwaite had lost her mind.

CHAPTER 62

29th June 1986
Mansfield, Nottinghamshire

It was the first evening meal they had eaten together for over a week.

Sue Flint placed the freshly baked lasagne in the centre of the table, next to a plate of hot garlic bread and a bowl of fresh green salad. She took out a match from a matchbox and lit the candle in the centre of the table.

She shouted, 'Danny, dinner's on the table!'

Danny walked into the cosy dining room, carrying a corkscrew in one hand and a bottle of Chianti in the other.

He asked playfully, 'Would madam like a glass of wine with her dinner?'

'Madam would like that very much. Oh, it's so nice to be able to sit and have a meal together, like normal people for once. Just lately, we've been like ships that pass in the night.'

'I know, I'm sorry. It's been pretty full on since we got back, but at least we're getting somewhere on the Jenkins case now.'

Sue sunk the serving spoon into the piping hot lasagne and served an enormous portion onto Danny's plate.

She said, 'That's great news, help yourself to the garlic bread and salad.'

Danny poured two glasses of Chianti and heaped salad on his plate next to the pasta.

They both ate in silence.

At the end of the meal Danny said, 'That was bloody lovely, thanks. I'll make a start on the dishes.'

As he started to stand, Sue touched his arm and said, 'Don't rush off Danny, have another glass of wine and tell me about the progress on the case.'

Danny topped up his own glass, Sue's was still full. He picked them both up and said, 'Okay, but let's sit in the lounge where it's a bit more comfortable. I'll clear the dinner things away later.'

Sue stood up and followed Danny into the lounge.

He placed the wine glasses on the coffee table and they both sat on the large leather sofa.

Automatically, Sue cuddled right in next to him drawing her feet up below her bottom. When she had made herself comfortable she squeezed Danny's hand and said, 'So, you're making progress are you?'

'I think we are. I think we're really close. The evidence is beginning to stack up against our main suspect. Over the next couple of days, if the enquiries we're doing prove positive, I'll be ordering more arrests.'

'That's brilliant news sweetheart. I've felt you tossing and turning in the night. I know this case has affected you more than some of the others you've worked on.'

'Because it's a child, Sue. Whenever kids are involved it really gets to me. Don't get me wrong, all murders are awful, the fallout caused to relations of the victims is always devastating. I think this one really hit home, after I'd been to see Evan's mum. Every day, I can still hear her saying to me, that Evan was supposed to be safe by going into the care system. If things do pan out the way it's looking, Evan Jenkins was anything but safe going into care.'

'I know, it's awful Danny. It's the vulnerability of children that makes any attack on them so upsetting.'

'That's exactly it, they're the weakest, the most vulnerable in our society.'

'I'm so glad you're making progress.'

'Thanks sweetheart. You've not touched your wine.'

'Danny, I've got some news as well.'

'What's that Sue?'

'There's a good reason I haven't touched my wine. I've been waiting to confirm everything before I told you. I had my suspicions when we first got back from Madeira.'

Danny interrupted, 'Suspicions about what exactly?'

'I've been to see the doctor today, he's confirmed what I already thought. I'm pregnant Danny.'

Danny was stunned.

Sue said, 'Well say something.'

Danny's face creased into a wide smile, 'That's fantastic news, when?'

'When did it happen? Or when's the baby due?'

'When's the baby due?'

'If the dates are right, and they'll be confirmed once I've had my first scan, the baby's due to arrive at the end of February.'

Danny could feel a surge of emotion coursing through him. He was overjoyed at the news, he'd always wanted a family and had thought that maybe the opportunity to become a father had passed him by. He was also experiencing a tinge of sadness, that neither of his parents were still here to see their grandchild.

Picking up on his mood Sue said softly, 'Are you okay Danny?'

'I'm so happy Sue, you wouldn't believe how happy I am!'

'Is there a but in there somewhere?'

'Definitely not! It's what I've always wanted Sue, you know that. I just wish my parents were still here to enjoy their grandson.'

'Just a minute mister, who said anything about a son?'

'Definitely a boy Mrs Flint, we only ever produce male offspring in the Flint family, it's all in the genes.'

Sue laughed and said, 'Well unfortunately for you, this baby like all babies will inherit HER genes from the mother. So, we'll definitely be having a little girl, as girls run in my family.'

'Twins!' Danny exclaimed, 'One of each, then there'll be no arguments.'

He reached forward and picked up the two glasses of red wine. He handed one to Sue, but then paused and said, 'Is it okay? Are you still allowed to drink?'

'This will probably be my last sip for a while, why?'

'I wanted to propose a toast. To the three of us!'

Danny raised his glass, Sue clinked her glass into his and said, 'Or the four of us!'

They both took a sip of the velvety, red wine and felt the warmth as the alcohol added to the feeling of their burgeoning love for one another.

Danny slipped his arms protectively around his wife and said softly, 'You've made me the happiest person on the planet.'

Sue snuggled in his embrace and whispered, 'That makes two of us Danny.'

CHAPTER 63

1st July 1986
South Lodge, Retford

This was the second day Stewart Ainsworth had woken up in the outhouse.

His head had stopped aching now, but he could still feel the caked on dried blood that had run from the wound on the top of his head down his bare torso.

Nobody had come to check on him, his arms ached from the unnatural way they were twisted.

Whoever had knocked him unconscious, had also chained him up. His wrists were now clamped in a set of steel manacles, that were bolted to the stone wall. He had tried manfully to dislodge the bolt that held the manacles, but to no avail.

He still didn't fully understand what had happened, one minute he was staring at the gorgeous, naked body of Melissa, then blackness.

Although conscious for most of yesterday, he had drifted in and out of a groggy sleep. He hadn't had the chance to take in any of his surroundings. Today, as the bright morning sun began to stream in through the small elevated window, he began to appreciate his predicament better.

He'd been chained up, in what was, to all intents and purposes, a makeshift dungeon.

He could see a further set of manacles bolted to the bare stone wall opposite. The floor of his prison was dry, dusty dirt. He could see rake marks in the dirt where it had recently been cleaned, but he knew someone else had already been held here.

The stench of excrement and stale urine was still very strong and he knew that before much longer he would be adding to the stink. He could feel his bladder was fit to burst and the pains in his stomach were getting worse.

There was a dark stain on the opposite wall, near to the bolt that held the manacles.

It looked like dried blood.

Questions raced through his head.

Why would anybody want to do this to him?

What was Melissa's involvement?

The answer rushed into his brain like an express train.

Jimmy Wade.

Surely, Melissa hadn't deliberately enticed him out here so Wade could capture him? Had she?

Other disturbing thoughts rushed into his brain at an alarming speed now.

What if the other people held here had been the two missing male nurses?

If it was, where were they now?

The fear and panic began to rise inside him and in desperation he shouted at the top of his voice, 'Help me, please! Somebody help me!'

He carried on screaming and shouting out for another ten minutes before the futility of his efforts dawned on him. There was nobody to hear him out here. He already knew just how remote Braithwaite's house in the middle of the forest was.

His throat hurt from the screaming, he was already parched and thirsty.

With little more than a whimper, he slumped back against the wall. If it was Jimmy Wade who was behind his incarceration he knew he was a dead man already.

He closed his eyes, unwilling to fight against his fate.

As all hope left his body, so did the contents of his full bladder and bowel.

Stewart Ainsworth began to sob pitifully.

CHAPTER 64

1st July 1986
Mansfield Police Station, Nottinghamshire

It was six o clock in the morning, Danny had gathered almost the entire MCIU team for an early morning briefing. The only people missing from the briefing were Rachel Moore and Tina Prowse.

It was the day Danny had waited for.

The final pieces of evidence had been confirmed late last night.

Firstly, Andy Wills had confirmed that Mayflower Cottage had been sold to Caroline Short a year ago.

Secondly, Tim Donnelly had contacted him to say that he'd managed to lift two sets of fingerprints from the light bulbs at the cottage.

The evidence was beginning to pile up against both Caroline and Bill Short.

There was now evidence that the Ford Transit van owned and driven solely by Caroline, had been at the deposition site on Haywood Oaks Lane prior to the discovery of the body of Evan Jenkins. The tyre cast taken had been proven forensically to be an exact match for the tyres fitted to the vehicle.

Soil samples taken from the deposition site also matched the soil found underneath the vehicle's wheel arches.

A single hair that had been found inside the vehicle was an exact match to the dead child.

On the bunch of keys used for that vehicle, a key had been found that opened the padlock that was used to secure the secluded Mayflower Cottage at Bleasby. The same cottage that had been purchased through Gordon and Chisholm estate agents in Mansfield for next to nothing. The agent dealing with the sale was Derek Chisholm. His initials D.C. were one of the ten sets of initials found alongside encoded telephone numbers in an address book found at Caroline Shorts home address.

One of the other names on that list was William Baxter, an anaesthetist at Chesterfield General Hospital. Discreet enquiries made at the hospital revealed that Baxter had access to the drugs Thiopentone and Suxamethonium, the substances found in the toxicology reports from the post mortem of Evan Jenkins.

Bill Short had been driven out to Mayflower Cottage by Councillor Leonard Mellor whilst he was under surveillance by the Regional Crime Squad.

Both men had been photographed carrying in cleaning equipment including bottles of Exoclean Bleach. The forensic science service had matched the samples of bleach taken from the cottage to that particular brand.

The RCS surveillance team had also noted that it had been Councillor Mellor that opened up the cottage, using a key in his possession.

The forensic evidence was strong and was backed up by other good evidence.

A full investigation into the finances of both Bill and Caroline had shown a constant stream of individual payments of one thousand pounds, being paid at regular intervals into a Building Society account opened by Caroline Short.

Further investigation into these unusual payments showed that the payments had all come from accounts run by the ten names found on the list of initials in her address book.

The links were there.

It would now be down to Danny and his team to prove exactly what the payments being made to Caroline were for.

'Okay people listen in. We're being supported by members of the Special Operations Unit from both Nottinghamshire and Derbyshire in today's operation. You've already been split into your teams and you all have a package identifying your target, the reason for their arrest and what you should be looking for evidence wise, in the subsequent searches of their addresses.

I've arranged for extra staff to be on duty in the cellblocks at Hucknall and at Worksop. Under no circumstances, should any of the nine men identified be brought to Mansfield Police Station.

The arrest teams designated to detain Caroline and Bill Short are to bring their prisoners direct to Mansfield, they're to be told that our enquiries are now complete and that the bail has been cancelled. I'm fully expecting Caroline Short to request the services of Grenville Slater to act as her legal representative and that is the reason no arrest team has been designated for him.

I would like Slater to be present throughout at least the first interview with Caroline so that the interviewing officers are able to gauge his responses as the interview unfolds and some of the evidence we've gathered is revealed.

Slater will be subsequently arrested when the time is right. If this all goes to plan, our best chance of obtaining admissions, is to try and play one detainee off against the other. I'll brief the interview teams for Caroline and Bill about strategy and tactics separately. First and foremost, let's get out there and get these bastards under lock and key.

It's vital that all the address are visited at the same time, seven o'clock. There are to be no telephone calls from the addresses. Tell your prisoners they will be allowed a phone call at the station. Hopefully, we'll have them all under arrest by then.'

'Are there any questions?'

'Shouldn't we be taking the arrests made in Derbyshire into one of their designated police stations, as they are closer?'

'I made enquiries about this with the Force lawyers last night. As it is a joint operation and the arrests being made are all for the same offence of conspiracy to commit murder, it will be fine to take them to the nearest designated police station within the force area in which they are sought. In this case the nearest of our stations is Hucknall, so that's where you take them. Any other questions?'

'Just one sir, are we expecting any violence or resistance at the addresses?'

'No, we're not expecting it. The arrests should come as a total shock to them. However, that doesn't mean you might not encounter some resistance. You have teams of Special Operations Unit officers with you and I expect them to deal quickly and effectively with any resistance you meet. Right, everyone let's get on the road. Don't forget, do not knock on your doors until dead on seven o'clock. This operation will only work, if the arrests are all made simultaneously. As soon as your respective prisoners have been detained, fire a call back into this office immediately. Good luck everyone.'

The office erupted into a cacophony of sound, chairs were scraped back and voices all began to talk at the same time.

Danny, Rob and Brian walked back into Danny's office and sat down.

Brian said, 'Do you think we've got enough Danny?'

'We've certainly got enough to get them all in. What we really need is for one of them to turn and start talking. If we can get one doing that, then we'll get them all.'

'Rob, it's going to be down to you and Glen Lorimar to interview Caroline, hopefully with Grenville Slater representing her initially. My guess is that he will instruct her to go no comment, as per usual. At this stage, I don't want you to disclose anything about Mayflower Cottage or the address book. For that first interview, stick solely to the evidence from the van. Towards the end of the interview, start asking her about the address book and what the initials refer to. I want you to see his reaction when you read out the initials G.S. I think he'll immediately attempt to close the interview down. He'll demand more disclosure if we want to question her further. When he does that, I want you to agree to close down the interview. Ask him to accompany you to the custody desk. It's at that point I want you to arrest him on suspicion of being involved in a conspiracy to murder. I'm not bothered if Caroline hears you do it.'

'Got it Danny.'

'Then we take it from there. We really need them to turn against each other. Brian, you're interviewing Bill Short with Lyn Harris. Bill normally says absolutely nothing. He doesn't even bother to say no comment. I think you may be able to shock him into talking by revealing that he's been under surveillance at Edale Close. Drop it out to him who's been visiting his address every time he leaves the flat. I bet he already has his suspicions, it won't hurt to confirm them for him. I don't really give a shit if it's unethical. It's legal and we need to turn these bastards against each other. Okay?'

'I've got no problem with any of that boss.'

'Okay, let's get amongst them and get this thing cracked. Keep me posted on progress.'

Both the inspectors left the office.

From being absolute mayhem, the office was now deathly quiet.

Danny walked into the small kitchen that serviced the office and made himself a coffee.

He returned to his office, sat down, opened his notebook, took a sip of coffee, sat back and waited for the telephone to start ringing.

CHAPTER 65

1st July 1986
South Lodge, Retford

Stewart Ainsworth woke with a start.

He had no idea what the time was, but he could hear voices outside the building he was imprisoned in. It was a man and a woman, they were laughing and joking.

The voices were getting closer.

Suddenly, he could hear the padlock on the door being opened. The door was flung open and bright sunlight streamed into the gloom, temporarily blinding him.

'You see Mel, I told you our guest would be wide awake by now.'

'You're always right Jimmy, I should have known.'

Ainsworth cringed, just the name Jimmy was enough to make his heart race. As his eyes became more accustomed to the bright light, he could now make out the features on the faces of his captors.

He instantly recognised Melissa Braithwaite.

What he didn't recognise was the cruel smirk on her face, or the evil glint in her eye.

The man standing beside her looked familiar.

Was it Jimmy Wade? The hair was different, the face slightly fatter. Then he saw the cold, piercing blue eyes and he knew immediately that he was staring into the face of the psychopath.

Ainsworth finally found his voice and quietly asked, 'Why are you doing this to me?'

Wade replied, 'Mr Ainsworth, surely you know the answer to that already. You thought it was highly hilarious and perfectly okay to allow those two thugs to beat me up with impunity. Then to make matters worse, you also thought it was alright to turn a blind eye to their savagery.'

'I never realised what was happening to you Jimmy, I swear it.'

'Don't lie to me, of course you did. I told you myself what was happening, you grovelling piece of shit.'

'It's not too late, I can report them now. I can make them pay for what they did to you.'

Wade roared with laughter, 'Oh! You can make them pay, can you? I think it's probably a little late for that Stewart. Have you seen them around lately?'

'No, I haven't, nobody has.'

'I'll let you into a little secret, I've seen them Stewart. Fred and Jack have also been our guests here. They loved their stay so much, they both told me they never want to leave the place.'

'What have you done to them?'

'Who am I Stewart?'

Ainsworth shook his head, the enormity of his situation sinking in.

'I asked you a question Ainsworth. What's my name?'

'Jimmy Wade.'

'And what exactly does Jimmy Wade do?'

Again, he didn't answer but shook his head and shrunk back towards the wall.

'Tell him Mel, tell the social worker what Jimmy Wade does better than anybody else.'

'Jimmy likes to kill people Stewart.'

Ainsworth spluttered, 'They know I'm here, they'll be looking for me.'

'Who knows you're here?'

'The police. Two women have been poking their noses in around the hospital, asking about Barnes and Williams. I told them I was coming to see Melissa.'

Wade was now intrigued and said evenly, 'Were they detectives, Stewart?'

'Yes, CID.'

'You're making it up, I don't believe you. What were their names?'

'It's the truth, one of them was a sergeant. Her name was Prowse, I think.'

'And the other one?'

'Rachel something or other.'

'Detective Constable Rachel Moore?'

'Yes, that's her. They both knew I was coming here.'

'Never mind about all that Stewart. It's immaterial whether or not they knew you were coming, the bottom line is we both know you won't be leaving here alive, don't we? Now as much as I'd love to stop here and chat with you longer, Mel and I are going for a lie down now. We should only be gone for an hour, so don't go away will you. Melissa wants to say goodbye to you properly, don't you Mel?'

'I can't wait, Jimmy.'

She stared at Ainsworth and smiled.

Her cruel, manic smile sent a cold shiver down the spine of the social worker. In that instant Stewart Ainsworth knew Braithwaite would be the one to kill him and not Wade.

CHAPTER 66

1st July 1986
Mansfield Police Station, Nottinghamshire

Danny looked at the clock on the wall of his office.

It was now almost eight o'clock in the morning.

For the past hour, the telephone in his office hadn't stopped ringing. All but one of the targets for the mornings operation had been detained and were now in custody.

He was feeling very disappointed that the only person they hadn't been able to arrest was William Baxter. The anaesthetist at Chesterfield Hospital was high on the list of people that Danny wanted to interview.

When detectives had drawn a blank at Baxter's home address in the small village of Heath, close to the M1 motorway, they had immediately moved on to his place of work. It was during these enquiries at Chesterfield Hospital that they discovered Baxter was on holiday in the Maldives for another week.

Caroline Short and her husband Bill had both been detained at their temporary home address without fuss and were currently being booked into the custody suite downstairs.

Rob had just telephoned Danny and informed him that, as expected, Caroline Short had requested Grenville Slater to be her legal representative and to be present for any interviews.

As usual, Bill Short had requested the services of Eric Buckle to legally represent him.

Danny knew there would now be a delay while the interview teams waited for the solicitors to arrive. The detectives would then have to provide the legal representatives with disclosure, informing them exactly what matters they wanted to talk to their clients about. Then the solicitors would have a consultation with their respective clients where advice could be offered in private.

The whole process would take at least a couple of hours.

It was frustrating.

The new rules had been in place ever since the introduction of the Police and Criminal Evidence Act. The fact of the matter was they were in force now and that was that. As usual the police would have to adapt, to make the new system work they would need to become far more professional.

Danny paced his office like a caged tiger.

He really wanted to be downstairs in the custody suite, preparing to interview the suspects. It was what he enjoyed most, actually talking to offenders, presenting them with overwhelming evidence until the point where they cracked and admitted their guilt.

Since his promotion there had been a few days where he had felt this urge. For some reason today, he felt it even more keenly.

He desperately wanted to interview the people he believed were responsible for the death of Evan Jenkins and personally bring them to justice.

He walked back behind his desk, sat down heavily in his chair and muttered out loud, 'Patience Danny, patience.'

CHAPTER 67

1st July 1986
Rampton Hospital, Nottinghamshire

Rachel parked the car in the visitor's car park on Fleming Drive.

The two detectives had returned to Rampton Hospital to interview and take a statement from the social worker Stewart Ainsworth.

As they walked towards the front entrance of the hospital Tina asked, 'What do you think Ainsworth will say today?'

'Do you mean, do I think he will have changed his version of events from what he told us the other day?'

'I suppose I do mean that, yeah.'

'Not a chance Tina, Ainsworth won't change his mind, he'll just try and brazen it out.'

'We're still a bit early, he doesn't start work until half past nine, it's only just gone eight.'

'Not to worry. Let's get inside, sort out a brew and set our office up ready, before we contact the hospital admin department.'

'Do we have any other interviews today?'

'There are three other staff members to see after Ainsworth, then we're done here Tina.'

'I'll need to contact Danny tomorrow and give him an update on our progress, or rather our lack of it.'

'Sounds like they'll all have their hands full today. I was chatting to Fran yesterday. The entire Unit are in today making arrests on the Jenkins case.'

'Bloody hell, that sounds like a proper job and we're still stuck up here chasing our tails on this enquiry!'

'Tina, you can't think like that. Don't forget this is also a murder enquiry now. We're not just chasing Jimmy Wade the escaper, don't forget that Steve Thorne is now dead. He died as a direct result of the injuries inflicted by Wade. This enquiry is just as important as the murder of that young boy.'

'You're right Rachel, sorry. I'm just frustrated because we don't seem to be getting anywhere.'

'I know what you mean, let's talk to Ainsworth and the others today and then we can fully assess where we're at.'

'I can't wait to talk to Ainsworth this morning. I'm not going to put up with any of his bullshit today. There'll be no softly softly approach with him today, he can bloody well start talking.'

'That's more like it, Tina. Come on, let's get inside and sort that brew out before we get Ainsworth in.'

CHAPTER 68

1st July 1986
South Lodge, Retford

'Is everything ready, Jimmy?'

'Ready for what Mel?'

'For Ireland of course. As soon as Ainsworth has been dealt with, we can leave here and start our new life together.'

Wade remained silent.

'You're not changing your mind, are you Jimmy?'

'It's what Ainsworth said before. You heard him yourself. One of the detectives he spoke to was Rachel Moore.'

'So, what?'

'So, what! Don't you get it Mel, it's her fault I was ever put in that bloody place. It was her lies that convicted me.'

'Forget her Jimmy. You've had your revenge with these three, leave it at that.'

'I can't. If there's even the smallest chance I can get even with Rachel Moore, I have to take it.'

'Do you still want her Jimmy, is that it?'

'No, I don't want her. I just have unfinished business with her, that's all.'

'If you promise we can go to Ireland afterwards, I'll help you get her.'

'How can you do that?'

'The same way I got Ainsworth here, that worked didn't it?'

'Trust me, Rachel isn't as stupid as that imbecile Ainsworth.'

'I know that Jimmy, but I can tell you still want her.'

'What are you rabbiting on about Mel, I don't fancy her like that. I just need to get even. I have to win, I have to come out on top.'

'I wouldn't mind, Jimmy. If you wanted to use her before you kill her, I wouldn't care. I think I'd enjoy watching.'

Wade looked into Braithwaite's demonic eyes staring at him and smiled.

She really was on the edge of madness.

'Let me think about it Mel. Shall we go and sort out the little problem of Stewart Ainsworth first?'

He wanted to test just how far into his own depraved world she had slipped

'Let's do it Jimmy. I can't wait.'

'Do you remember how I said to do it?'

'Yes Jimmy, I've got it.'

Hand in hand they walked from the kitchen down to the outhouse.

As the padlock was removed, Ainsworth shrank back away from the door and started to beg, 'Please, you don't have to do this. I won't tell a soul about what's happened. Can't you just let me go? Please!'

Wade growled, 'Do it Mel, use the rope like I showed you.'

Braithwaite grinned and unfurled a length of white nylon cord. She wrapped the cord around her small hands until she gripped both ends, leaving a foot length between her clenched fists.

She slipped behind Ainsworth.

He began to bob his head backwards and forwards, trying in vain to prevent her from slipping the cord over his head.

He failed.

Suddenly, he felt the cord bite into his windpipe. She stood behind him and pulled her fists together pulling the cord ever tighter.

Ainsworth began to struggle violently, flailing his arms, that were restrained by the manacles, until his wrists bled. His legs and feet thrashed about in the dirt as Braithwaite continued to pull the cord ever tighter.

The last thing he saw before he slipped into unconsciousness and death, were the cruel, staring eyes of Jimmy Wade.

She continued to squeeze until Wade said, 'That's it Mel, he's done.'

Her arms ached from the effort and she gasped, 'I did it like you said Jimmy!'

'You certainly did sweetheart, it was amazing.'

She laughed and said, 'I'm knackered.'

Wade smiled knowingly, 'Go and get yourself a cup of tea and relax. As soon as I've buried this piece of shit next to his best mates, we can get a nice shower together.'

'That sounds wonderful Jimmy, do you need any help?'

'No. It won't take me long. After the shower we can go to bed, make love and then discuss what we're going to do about Detective Rachel Moore.'

'Okay Jimmy, don't be long. I want you in my bed.'

CHAPTER 69

1st July 1986
Mansfield Police Station, Nottinghamshire

The first interview with Caroline Short was coming to a natural conclusion.

As expected she had answered every question with a surly, 'No comment!'

Glen Lorimar had meticulously questioned her about the use of the Ford Transit van. Every question he'd put to her had been met with the same stony stare and non-committal response.

Like the excellent interrogator he was, Glen had maintained a slow pace throughout, allowing a long, deliberate pause between Short's no comment response and the next question.

He'd now exhausted all the questions he needed to ask about the van, subtly he made eye contact with Rob Buxton.

Rob gave him an almost imperceptible signal.

Lorimar paused, then said, 'Caroline, when a search was made of your living accommodation at Tall Trees, a number of items were recovered. One of them was this address book.'

The detective reached into the briefcase on the desk in front of him and removed a plastic exhibit bag that contained the address book recovered from Tall Trees.

Glen held out the address book and said, 'For the tape, I'm now showing you the address book we recovered. Do you recognise this address book, Caroline?'

There was a pause and she looked towards her solicitor, who ignored her attempt at non verbal communication.

She said, 'No comment.'

Glen continued, 'It contains your personal details on the front page of the book, these have been handwritten.'

From the briefcase he took out a photocopy of the first page of the book and held it in front of Short so she could clearly see it.

'Is that your handwriting?'

She paused again before answering, 'No comment.'

This time Grenville Slater did interject, 'I'm sorry detective, but I don't recall any mention of this exhibit in your disclosure. Is it at all relevant to the van?'

Glen answered, 'It will become clear, Mr Slater.'

The solicitor shook his head dismissively and sat back.

The detective then took out another photocopied sheet of paper from his brief case. This sheet contained a list of initials and numbers.

He showed the photocopied page to Short and said, 'This is a photocopy of the back page of that address book. What can you tell me about this list of initials and numbers Caroline?'

'No comment.'

'What do they mean?'

'No comment.'

'Are they telephone numbers?'

Short smirked and said, 'No comment.'

'Do the initials that prefix the numbers refer to names?'

'No comment.'

'Are they names of people you know?'

'No comment.'

'Let me read the initials out to you Caroline, it might jog your memory. The first initials on the list are G.S. Do those initials relate to anyone you know?'

'No comment.'

Instantly, there was a response from Slater, 'Look detective, I really must protest, if you're going to continue to question my client along these lines I would like to have a few minutes to advise her accordingly.'

It was the interruption Rob Buxton had been waiting for, he immediately interjected, 'Very well Mr Slater, the time is now eleven fifteen and we'll close down the interview.'

Rob switched off the tape recorder and said, 'Dc Lorimar please escort Mrs Short back to her cell, I need to have a word with Mr Slater at the custody desk.'

The two detectives stood up and waited for Short and Slater to also stand. The four of them then walked from the interview room, back to the custody desk.

Caroline Short was booked out of interview and Glen Lorimar delayed returning her to her cell just long enough for her to overhear Rob Buxton say loudly to Slater, 'Grenville Slater, I'm arresting you on suspicion of conspiracy to commit murder.'

Rob cautioned the solicitor who replied angrily, 'What do you think you're playing at Inspector? Have you lost your mind? In case you hadn't noticed I'm here to represent my client.'

'Not anymore Mr Slater, you're under arrest. Don't worry about Mrs Short, arrangements will be made for alternative legal representation for your client. At this moment in time there appears to be a rather large conflict of interest preventing you from doing it.'

As Caroline was escorted down the corridor, Slater shouted after her, 'Just keep saying no comment, Caroline. This is nothing but a big fishing expedition!'

Rob Gripped the solicitors arm and said, 'That's enough Slater, be quiet.'

Slater squirmed out of the detective's grip and said through gritted teeth, 'This is ridiculous, I demand to see your senior officer immediately. I wish to make a formal complaint.'

'That's your choice Slater and an opportunity to speak to my boss to make that complaint will be given to you later. Right now, you need to listen to what the custody sergeant is going to say to you.'

The custody sergeant then went through the process of booking Grenville Slater into custody.

Slater was subsequently searched and placed in a cell.

Rob Buxton and Glen Lorimar left the custody suite.

As they walked up the stairs to the MCIU offices Rob said, 'Was there any reaction from Caroline?'

'Oh yes, her head was on a fucking swivel trying to see what was happening.'

'Did she say anything, Glen?'

'Not a peep, but she's well and truly rattled. Just after we ask her about the initials G.S., Slater gets nicked. She's not stupid boss, her brain will be going into overdrive now wondering exactly what else we know. The next interview will be very interesting.'

'Come on Glen, let's go and have a brew with Danny and tell him how his plan went down.'

As Rob and Glen made their way upstairs to the MCIU offices, in the interview room next door to the one they had occupied in the cell block, Brian Hopkirk and Fran Jefferies were also coming to the end of their first interview with Bill Short.

Again, this interview had centred on the Ford Transit van owned by Caroline.

Fran had questioned Bill Short at length and had been met with his traditional response to police questioning. Bill Short sat with his chair half turned away from the interviewer and stared into the middle distance.

He never made any eye contact with the detective and refused to say a word. He never even acknowledged a question with a no comment reply.

At the conclusion of her planned questions, Fran switched off the tapes.

As Fran dealt with the completion of the labels for the tapes, Brian sat forward towards Bill and said quietly, 'You do know we've had you two under surveillance, don't you?'

Bill Short never moved a muscle.

Brian leaned in a little closer, 'It's amazing the comings and goings at your new flat, Bill. Every time you go out the place becomes a hive of activity.'

Still Short didn't move.

His solicitor Eric Buckle, seemed totally disinterested by what the detective was either doing or saying.

Brian pressed on and whispered near Short's ear, 'Yeah Bill, one visitor in particular. Funny though he only ever arrived after you'd already gone out.'

Finally, Bill turned and stared at the detective, his face becoming flushed.

Brian whispered, 'He looks different when he leaves the flat though.'

Under his breath and barely concealing his rage Bill Short said, 'Who?'

Brian grinned and said, 'I'm sure he's only coming around to give legal advice. Nothing at all for you to worry about. It must be exhausting work though Bill, he always looks totally fucked when he leaves a couple of hours later.'

Short said through gritted teeth, 'If you're on about that bastard Slater, you'd better tell me what you know detective.'

'Or what?'

'Just fucking tell me!'

'Yes, it's Grenville Slater, so what?'

Bill Short flew into a rage, lunging across the desk at the detective.

Eric Buckle was shocked and almost fell backwards off his chair, he hadn't heard the whispered conversation between the detective and his client.

Brian restrained Short, taking him to the floor, as Fran Jefferies hit the panic strip.

As he gripped the raging Short, Brian whispered in his ear, 'Listen you idiot, don't take it out on me because that slime ball Slater is taking you for a mug.'

'I'll sort the bastard out detective! I know things about him!'

'Keep talking Bill, what do you know about him?'

'Go fuck yourself detective.'

'I'm going to put you back in your cell Bill. You need to calm yourself down and get ahead of the game here. Certain people are taking you for a mug. Come on, up you get!'

Brian hauled the irate man back to his feet, just as two uniformed officers burst into the interview room responding to the panic strip alarm. They grabbed Short and frogmarched him back to his cell.

Brian shouted after him, 'Talk to me Bill, I can help you.'

'Go fuck yourself detective!'

Brian turned to the elderly solicitor and said, 'I think we'll take a break there Mr Buckle, what do you think?'

'It won't hurt detective, let him calm down a bit. I've never seen Bill behave like that before.'

'I know Mr Buckle, me neither. Something upset him, I didn't really understand what he was saying. Very strange behaviour.'

Fran Jefferies smiled and said, 'Shall we go and have a word with the boss upstairs sir?'

'I think we should Fran. Mr Buckle, the custody sergeant will get you a cup of tea, if you ask her nicely.'

'Oh, I don't drink tea Inspector. I'll just wait upstairs at the front counter until you're ready for the next interview. I can't stand it down here, this place gives me a headache.'

The two detectives walked in silence with Mr Buckle and showed him to the front counter, where he took a seat in the waiting area.

Brian said, 'I don't think we'll be too long Mr Buckle, we'll let your client calm down and then have another interview, see if he wants to talk to us properly this time.'

'Okay detective, see you soon.'

As they walked back to the MCIU offices Fran said, 'Bloody hell boss, I thought he was going to have you in there.'

'Yeah, I know. He obviously already suspects that Slater's shagging his wife. I just hope I've riled him up enough to drop them both in the shit.'

CHAPTER 70

1st July 1986
Mansfield Police Station, Nottinghamshire

As the heavy, metal cell door slammed shut behind her, Caroline Short slumped down onto the hard-wooden bench that was covered by a one-inch thick plastic covered mattress.

Her mind was racing.

The solicitor representing her had just been arrested for conspiracy to commit murder, by the same officers who were interviewing her.

The arrest had come minutes after she'd been asked about the list of telephone numbers in her address book.

Caroline Short was stunned. Both by the questions and the subsequent arrest of her solicitor Grenville Slater. As her mind raced for answers, she concluded it could only mean one thing; the police already knew the answer to the question they had posed.

The G.S. initials in the address book, obviously related to Grenville Slater, her solicitor, her confidant, her lover.

What she didn't understand was how the police now knew it was Slater.

Did they know? Or were they just putting two and two together?

She had heard Grenville shout after her, telling her to continue saying no comment. Was he saying that to try and help her or to save his own skin?

If the police were getting close maybe it was in his interest to implicate her deeper in the boy's death than was actually the case. Caroline had played no part in the boy's actual death and had only helped to clear up the mess caused by Slater and his moronic friends.

It was Slater who organised the parties.

Slater who pocketed the lions share of the money that was paid into her bank account and Slater who found the clientele.

Her only involvement had been to supply the boys and the recreational drugs for the parties.

She knew that Slater wasn't a paedophile, he couldn't be. The way he made love to her at every opportunity, there was no way he was turned on by kids.

As she sat on her own in the cell, the four walls closing in, doubts began to surface.

Why was it always her vehicle that had to be used to convey the boys to and from the cottage? Why had Slater insisted that her name be on the cottage when in actual fact it had been his money used to purchase the property? Why did the clients always pay the money directly into her bank account?

Little things she had buried now started to come to the surface again. The fact that he always become more attentive towards her when the shit had hit the fan. He would ignore her for weeks, then whenever he needed a boy for a party, suddenly he would become her biggest admirer and lavish her with attention.

Sat in the cold stark cell with only her thoughts for company, she began to see some very unpalatable truths emerge.

Suddenly, it became clear that Slater had only ever used her, he didn't really care about her.

Why should she now take the rap for the boy's death? She wasn't even there when he'd died, for Christ's sake.

Caroline knew she had some tough decisions to make, she needed to start looking out for herself.

Thinking things through, she realised that she could wait and see exactly what the police knew. If they truly had cracked the code that Slater had dreamed up when he wrote the list of client's numbers in her address book, then she would have to look after herself.

There was no way she intended spending the rest of her life in prison.

Her only other alternative, was not to wait at all and talk to the police straight away. Tell them exactly what her involvement had been, that she was in no way responsible for the boy's death.

Caroline Short had a decision to make.

On another corridor of the cell block, Bill Short was also in a cell alone with his thoughts. He'd finally calmed down, but continued to pace the floor of the small cell.

The big detective had deliberately goaded him until he got a reaction.

Bill wasn't stupid.

He knew exactly what the detective was trying to do, but it had still got to him and he cursed himself for allowing that to happen.

He already knew Grenville Slater was fucking his wife, whenever and wherever he got the opportunity.

Bill had made up his mind a while ago that he didn't care, as long as the slimy toad didn't rub his face in it, he wasn't bothered. He'd fallen out of love with his wife many years ago and at least Slater was a good stream of income, organising the parties.

What really worried him, was the detective's insinuation that he'd been under surveillance.

If that was true and the police had been watching them day and night, then he was in big shit.

He'd been the one that had gone to the cottage with the fat councillor to clean up the mess after the last party.

He would be well and truly in the frame for murder, even though he'd been at home in bed when the kid was actually killed.

Fuck that.

No way was he going down for murder, especially one he had nothing to do with.

Bill made his decision there and then.

He would sack off his useless solicitor and ask to speak to the big, lairy cop that had wound him up.

His instincts were telling him that he needed to get ahead of this mess, before Slater and his cronies tried to stich him up and drop him deeper in the shit than he already was.

He pressed the alarm button in the cell and with his balled-up fist started to bang repeatedly on the metal door.

CHAPTER 71

1st July 1986
Mansfield Police Station, Nottinghamshire

The door to Danny's office was closed.

Inside, deep in conversation with Danny were Rob, Brian, Fran and Glen. The two interview teams were bringing Danny up to speed on the first round of interviews.

Rob said, 'It's gone as well as can be expected, Danny. As we thought, Slater advised Caroline to go no comment throughout, which she did unwaveringly.'

'What was the reaction when Glen started talking about the address book?'

'There was a muted protest from Slater that we hadn't disclosed it prior to interview, but surprisingly he let it continue.'

'And when you mentioned the specific list at the back of the book?'

'Panic! Big style, he couldn't shut the interview down quick enough.'

'Did you make sure Caroline witnessed Slater being arrested?'

'I did boss. I virtually shouted what he was under arrest for, just to make sure she heard it.'

'Good work. What was her reaction when you took her to the cell, Glen?'

'She said nothing, but she was definitely rattled. You could almost hear the cogs in her brain turning.'

'And she said nothing?'

'Nothing at all, but she suddenly went from being very assured, to looking like a rabbit caught in headlights.'

'I don't think we need to mess about any more. I'm of the opinion that we start piling on the pressure by letting her know exactly how much evidence we've got. What do you think Glen?'

'I'd say drip feed it into her boss, let her realise there's no wriggle room. We need her to start identifying who did what, as well as admitting her own part in all this. We need her to understand that co-operation is her only and best option.'

'That sounds good to me, Glen. Let's concentrate on getting her talking and take it from there. Do you think she'll persevere with the no comment strategy given to her by Slater, now he's under arrest?'

'It's hard to say. I think if she refuses further legal advice, then we're in business and she'll start talking.'

'Don't wait too long Rob, I want you both back down there, get her a new brief if she wants one and get her talking. Let's try and keep the pressure on.'

'Okay boss. What do you want doing with Slater?'

'Nothing yet, let him stew for a bit. Concentrate on Caroline, I still think she holds the key to unlocking this case.'

Danny turned to Brian, 'How did it go with Bill?'

Brian was just about to answer when the telephone on the desk started to ring.

Danny quickly snatched it off the hook, 'DCI Flint!'

'Sir, it's Pc Mayhew in the custody suite, Bill Short is asking to speak to Detective Inspector Hopkirk, without his solicitor being present.'

'Thanks.'

Danny put the phone down and said, 'I don't know what you did down there Brian, but Bill Short has sacked his solicitor and wants to talk to you urgently. Get down there sharpish and see what he's got to say. It would appear that the cracks are beginning to show.'

CHAPTER 72

1st July 1986
Rampton Hospital, Nottinghamshire

'What do you mean he's not at work yet, he should have been here at half past nine. Has he phoned in sick?'

Tina Prowse glanced at her watch, it was now approaching ten thirty.

'He should've been here an hour ago and you've had no phone call explaining his absence?'

There was a pause.

'Great, so now you're telling me he wasn't at work yesterday, either?'

Another pause.

'No that's fine, it's not your fault. Can you get me his home address please? We'll go and check on him there later, thanks.'

Tina put the phone down and looked at Rachel.

Rachel said, 'I take it the elusive Stewart Ainsworth has decided against talking to us today.'

'Bloody too right, apparently he didn't make it into work yesterday either. Let's crack on with the other three members of staff we've got to speak to today, then we'll take a trip out to Ainsworth's home address. I've got to admit Rach, I'm starting to get a little pissed off with Mr Ainsworth.'

1st July 1986
Mansfield Police Station, Nottinghamshire

Brian and Fran sat opposite Bill Short in the interview room.

Fran placed the tapes in the recorder and switched it on. She quickly went through the introductions on tape before finally reminding Bill Short that he was still under caution.

Bill Short waved his hand at the young detective gesturing for her to hurry up, then nodded his head saying, 'Yeah, yeah.'

Brian said, 'Are you happy for this interview to continue without your solicitor being present?'

'Yeah, I'm sure.'

'Is there any reason you don't want your solicitor present?'

'I don't need one, I've got things I want to say.'

'Go on then Bill, what is it you want to say?'

'For a start, I've been arrested for conspiracy to commit murder. What the fuck is all that about? When that kid died I was miles away in my own bed.'

'Just for the record Bill and so we're both clear, exactly what child are you referring to?'

'That Jenkins boy.'

'Do you mean Evan Jenkins, who up until the time of his death was a resident at Tall Trees Children's Home, where your wife is the matron in charge?'

'Yeah, that's him.'

'How do you know exactly when Evan Jenkins died?'

'Because I was at home in bed with Caroline when she took the phone call to say he was dead.'

'When was that?'

'It was the night of the 3rd of June.'

'What had happened?'

'I don't know exactly what had happened. All I know is that Caroline took the phone call. She then tells me that the kid has died at the party they were having and they wanted Caroline to go over and clear up their mess.'

'What sort of party are you talking about?'

'A fucking nonces party.'

'What do you mean, Bill?'

'Nonces! Blokes that like young boys, it was that sort of party.'

'Who made the phone call to your wife about the boy?'

'That smarmy bastard, Grenville Slater.'

'I realise that Caroline took the call, but do you know exactly what was said to her?'

'I only got the gist from her. She told me to get out of bed and to get dressed straight away as the kid had died at the party and we had to go over and clear up the mess.'

'So, what did you do Bill?'

'I didn't have a lot of choice, detective. I went with Caroline to the cottage to pick up the kid.'

'What cottage?'

'Don't mess me about detective, I'm being straight with you here. You know where I mean, Mayflower Cottage, you must've followed me and fatso out there the other day.'

'Okay Bill. When you got out there that night, who else was at the cottage?'

'Just Slater, everybody else had gone.'

'How many had been there?'

'I'm not sure, but Caroline will know and so will Slater.'

'What did Slater say when you got there?'

'He was talking in whispers to Caroline, so I only heard bits. I did hear him say something about a drugs overdose. Apparently, the stuff from the doctor was too strong or something.'

'What stuff?'

'I don't know.'

'What doctor?'

'I don't know his name.'

'Where was Evan Jenkins?'

'He was upstairs on a mattress.'

'What was he like?'

'What the fuck do you mean, what was he like? He was dead.'

'Was he dressed?'

'No, the kid was naked. The fucking nonces had been there, hadn't they?'

'What exactly did you do, Bill?'

'Caroline told me to carry the kid down to the van and put him in the back.'

'And did you?'

'Yeah.'

'Then what did you do?'

'Caroline drove the van to some woods and I carried the kid from the van to the woods and buried him under some loose soil and leaves.'

'Why didn't you come to the police?'

'How could I? I couldn't grass on my own wife. She was the one who'd taken the kid out there as usual. She was the one who'd supplied the drugs to the nonces for money. I had no choice detective, I had to do what she asked.'

'Did you have any involvement, other than what you've already said, in the events that led to the death of Evan Jenkins?'

'No, I did not, not a chance. I'm not a fucking nonce! I kept telling Caroline that what she was doing was wrong and that eventually it would come back to bite her on the arse, but she wouldn't listen. She was led by that piece of shit Slater and wouldn't turn down the money.'

'How many of these, "parties" has your wife provided boys and drugs for?'

'God only knows. She did a couple down in Cornwall using kids from the other home we worked at, but as soon as she hooked up with Slater, there were loads, at least a couple every month.'

'How many times was Evan Jenkins taken to the parties?'

'Quite a few times, the nonces kept asking for him.'

'Were the parties always at the cottage?'

'As far as I know, yeah.'

'Who owns the cottage?'

'It's in Caroline's name, but she couldn't afford to buy it. I think Slater and fatso gave her the money to buy it.'

'You mentioned fatso earlier, who's fatso?'

'Fatso is what I call Councillor Lenny Mellor. He's the biggest nonce of the lot. I can't stand that piece of shit.'

'What else have you done to try and conceal this crime, Bill?'

'Caroline asked me to clean the van and the cottage afterwards.'

'And did you?'

'Yeah, what choice did I have?'

'Is there anything else you want to say, Bill?'

'Yeah, what's going to happen to me now? You can't charge me with murder, I never killed that kid.'

Brian closed down the interview and returned Short to his cell.

Rob Buxton and Glen Lorimar were standing in the cell block alongside Caroline Short and her new solicitor, waiting to go for a further interview.

Brian said, 'Rob, you need to put her back in the cell and have a listen to what Bill's just told us.'

Caroline's eyes widened as she heard the big detective's comment.

Glen Lorimar immediately took Caroline back to her cell.

At the door to her cell Caroline stopped, looked at the detective and said, 'What's Bill said, I need to know?'

'I don't know yet Caroline. I'll come and get you for that interview in a while. I'll sit your solicitor down upstairs until we're ready.'

Caroline finally made her decision.

She couldn't afford to wait any longer.

She grabbed the detectives' arm and said, 'Look, I don't want a new solicitor, I need to talk to you right now.'

'Ten minutes Caroline, I'll be back. If you still don't want a solicitor then, we'll go and have a chat straight away.'

CHAPTER 74

1st July 1986
Mansfield Police Station, Nottinghamshire

Twenty minutes after she'd been returned to her cell, Caroline was relieved to see the cell door swing open.

Standing in the doorway were Rob Buxton and Glen Lorimar.

Caroline immediately stood up, a panicked expression on her face, 'What's Bill said?'

Rob replied, 'Caroline, we can't talk to you unless your solicitor is present.'

'Bollocks to that! I don't want a solicitor, I need to talk to you. Bill doesn't know the whole truth, I do.'

'Okay Caroline, we need to go and see the custody sergeant first so that you can give him your reasons for not wanting a solicitor present for your interviews. Once that's all done, then we can go and have a chat.'

After the legal requirements with the custody sergeant, Caroline was shown into an interview room with Rob and Glen.

Glen inserted the tapes and started the recorder. He made the introductions and clarified the fact on tape that Caroline no longer wanted to be legally represented during her interview.

'Caroline, as we took you from your cell earlier, you made a comment to me saying that your husband Bill didn't know the truth but you did. Is that an accurate account of what you said?'

'Yes, it is.'

'What did you mean by that comment? What truth?'

'The truth about how Evan Jenkins died.'

'Okay Caroline, what can you tell me about the death of Evan Jenkins?'

'At the request of certain powerful people, I took Evan Jenkins to a party.'

'When was this?'

'The 3rd of June, this year.'

'How did you get Evan to the party?'

'I drove him in my van.'

'Where was the party?'

'In the cottage.'

'Does the cottage have a name?'

'Mayflower Cottage.'

'Where's Mayflower Cottage, Caroline?'

'Out near a village called Bleasby.'

'Who owns the cottage?'

'It's in my name, but I didn't buy it.'

'Why is it in your name, if you didn't buy it?'

'I don't know, you'll have to ask him.'

'Ask who?'

'Grenville Slater, he gave me the money to buy it, so we could have the parties there.'

'You said parties, plural, how many have there been?'

'I'm not sure, quite a few.'

'You keep referring to them as parties, what happened at these parties?'

'Men and boys.'

'What do you mean?'

'They were parties organised for men who like boys. The men paid so they could have sex with the boys.'

'What was your involvement, Caroline?'

'I was asked to provide some of the boys from the home.'

'When you say the home, where do you mean specifically?'

'Tall Trees Children's Home.'

'Did the boys have a choice?'

'Sort of. They were given presents and money from the men at the parties to keep quiet about it.'

'How many boys went to the party on the 3rd of June?'

'Just one, I was asked to bring Evan Jenkins on his own. A lot of the men only ever wanted Evan.'

'Why was that?'

Caroline shrugged her shoulders and said, 'No idea.'

'Who asked you to bring Evan?'

'The person who organised the parties.'

'And who was that, Caroline?'

'Grenville Slater.'

'So, when you arrived at the cottage with Evan, how many men were there?'

'Everyone was there. The list of initials you asked me about in my address book, they are the people who were there.'

'Who are they?'

'I only know some of them by name, Grenville wrote the list in my address book. He just put their initials and swapped the telephone numbers around somehow, I think he did that so I couldn't call them myself.'

'Didn't you think it was slightly odd that so many men were there and just one child?'

'I suppose it was looking back, but I didn't think about it like that at the time.'

'Did you stay at the cottage?'

'No, I drove home.'

'So, let me get this right Caroline. You dropped an eleven-year-old boy off at a cottage with a dozen or so men, who you knew were all paedophiles?'

Caroline looked at the floor and said quietly, 'Yes, I did.'

'What else did you take to Mayflower Cottage that night Caroline?'

'Nothing else.'

'Do you recall we did a drug warrant at your home address some time ago? Forensic tests on certain items recovered from your property, came back as positive for controlled drugs. Are you a drug user, Caroline?'

'No.'

'Is your husband Bill a drug user?'

'No.'

'I'll ask you again Caroline, did you take anything else to the cottage that night?'

'It sounds to me like you already know the answer to your own question detective.'

'Well?'

'Yes, I took recreational drugs to the parties as well.'

'Why did you take drugs to the parties?'

'So, I could sell them to the clients and make a bit of cash.'

'What drugs did you supply?'

'I used to take Cocaine, Amphetamine and Cannabis.'

'Caroline, you've described how you took Evan Jenkins to the cottage and then left. What do you know about the events that led to the boy's death?'

'I got a phone call just before midnight from Grenville, saying something terrible had happened and that I needed to get straight back to the cottage.'

'What did you say?'

'Obviously, I asked him what had happened to the boy. He told me that the kid was dead and that I needed to get to the cottage. He told me that I had to come and get the boy and deal with the mess.'

'What did you do?'

'I woke Bill up and we drove to the cottage.'

'Who was there when you arrived?'

'Grenville was the only one still there, the others had all gone.'

'Where was Evan Jenkins?'

'He was upstairs, lying dead on a mattress.'

'Did Slater say what had happened?'

'He told me that the boy had come around while someone was having sex with him. The men in the room panicked and somebody injected him again. It was the second injection that killed him. The dirty bastards didn't realise until the end, that the poor kid was dead.'

'What do you mean, "until the end"?'

'Until they'd all had their turn, until they'd all had sex with him.'

Glen remained composed and through tight lips said, 'You said the boy came around. Had he been drugged?'

'Yes, the kids were always drugged. One of Slater's friends brought this stuff he used at work. The kids would be out of it but not unconscious. They hadn't got a clue what was happening to them, but they were still conscious.'

'What was the drug?'

'It was some fancy sounding name. It wasn't street bought crap, it was a proper drug that doctors use.'

'Do you know who that friend is?'

'I don't know his name, but he's in the book. His initials are WB.'

'What did you do with Evan Jenkins?'

'I got Bill to carry him out to the van.'

'Then what?'

'Then I drove to the nearest woods I could find. I drove off the main road and told Bill to get the kid out and bury him.'

For the first time Rob Buxton spoke, 'Why did you do this Caroline?'

'I just panicked, I had to get rid of the kid.'

'I meant, why did you take boys to these men to be abused?'

'I don't know really. All I did was turn a blind eye to what was going on at the cottage. Most of the kids never complained and Slater paid me well. It seemed like easy money.'

'What about the children?'

She shrugged.

'They were supposed to be in your care, Caroline.'

'What do you want me to say, detective?'

'When we go and question Grenville Slater, what do you think he's going to say about your allegations?'

'This is what I meant at the beginning when I said about the real truth. Slater will definitely try and lay the blame for all this on me. I'm not stupid, I can see how it looks. Mayflower Cottage is in my name, the names are all in my address book, the money goes into my account, I supplied the boys, I supplied Evan Jenkins, I supplied the drugs. That's why I'm talking to you now detective. I need you to understand that I wasn't the main instigator of all this, it was Slater. I don't know what my husband has already said to you, but I'm sure he'll back me up about Slater. If you can find all the men on that list, they'll tell you it was Slater who organised everything and that it was him who contacted them about the parties, not me.'

'Is there anything else you want to tell me, Caroline?'

'Yes, there is. The only other person who I know by name from that list is Councillor Leonard Mellor. I recognised him at one of the first parties I went to, I'd seen his face in the local paper. He helped me to buy the cottage and was always at every party. He was the one who always told Slater to make sure I took Evan Jenkins to the parties.'

Rob Buxton then closed the interview.

CHAPTER 75

1st July 1986
Grosvenor Road, Retford

It was getting dark as Rachel Moore parked the CID car directly outside 23, Grosvenor Road, Retford, the home address of Stewart Ainsworth.

She turned to Tina Prowse and said, 'Well, that doesn't look too promising does it?'

The small terraced house was in total darkness.

The hardwood door had a small window three quarters of the way up. Rachel pressed her nose to the glass and peered inside. The door would have opened on to a hallway with the stairs going off to the right. She could see the door into the living room was wide open.

There were no sounds coming from inside.

No television, no radio.

Nothing

Taking the car key in her right hand, Rachel used it to bang loudly on the glass of the front door. It made a shrill knock that would have been clearly heard throughout the house.

There was no reply.

Rachel began knocking on the neighbour's door.

Eventually, a light came on and the door was answered by a young woman who opened the door with her index finger pressed to her lips. She said quietly, 'Shhhh, I've only just managed to get the little one asleep.

Rachel got out her warrant card, introduced herself and said, 'I'm really sorry to disturb you when it's so late. I hope we haven't woken your little one, but we really need to speak to your neighbour, Mr Ainsworth.'

The young woman said, 'I haven't seen Stewart for a couple of days now. Generally, if his car isn't on the street, he's out.'

'What sort of car does he have?'

'I'm sorry, I'm not very good at cars, it's only a small one, Italian I think.'

'Okay. Thanks for your help and sorry to disturb you.'

The young woman closed her front door softly.

Rachel turned to Tina and said, 'Is it me or are you getting a sense of déjà vu here too?'

'I know what you mean, Rachel, its' like Fred Barnes and Jack Williams all over again.'

'The mystery blonde at the pub when Barnes went missing, Williams disappearing into thin air and now Ainsworth doing a vanishing trick too.'

'Don't forget Ainsworth was supposedly going on a hot date. That's twice a woman has been involved in the vanishing trick.'

'Well, he's obviously not here.'

'No, he isn't and I've got to phone the boss in the morning with an update on our enquiries so far. I'll be standing there saying, sorry sir, but we've achieved a big fat zero.'

'Good luck with that Tina. Don't worry, I'll be standing there next to you, we can share the bollocking.'

1st July 1986
Mansfield Police Station, Nottinghamshire

It was getting late.

Danny sat alone in his office slowly taking stock of the day's events.

After the admissions made by Caroline and Bill Short, things had progressed at a lightning pace. The interview teams dealing with the men from the list had all been informed of the sinister events at the cottage near Bleasby.

Every one of the men arrested that morning, initially either made no comment when questioned, or made total denials.

As the day progressed and they were interviewed further, it became apparent to the men, after they were slowly drip fed the evidence that tied them to Caroline Short and Grenville Slater, that they could no longer deny their involvement in the terrible events at the cottage.

Slowly, one by one, the men began to tell the detectives the sordid truth.

Every single one of them claimed to have only taken a minor part in the prolonged abuse of Evan Jenkins.

No one admitted to administering the second injection of the drug, supplied by William Baxter, to quieten the boy. Several of the men hinted that the injection had been clumsily administered in haste by a panicking Lenny Mellor.

The only person who had maintained a stony silence throughout his interviews was Grenville Slater. The evidence provided by the other people involved in the paedophile ring he'd organised, purely for profit, would see him sent to prison for a long time.

Danny didn't care if the solicitor never uttered a word, he was fucked.

There was a knock on the office door.

Bill Wainwright stuck his head around the door and said, 'I wondered if you'd still be here, Danny. Sounds like congratulations are in order.'

'Come in Bill, do you want a brew?'

'I think something a little stronger would be more appropriate, if you've got any Danny?'

Danny pulled open the bottom drawer of his desk and took out the bottle of Bushmills Irish whiskey and two tumblers.

He placed the glasses on his desk, unscrewed the cap of the bottle and poured two generous drinks.

He handed one of the glasses to Bill Wainwright and said, 'Here's to the result, not the job.'

'Definitely. I'll drink to that Danny.'

Both men took a sip of the fiery liquor and sat down.

Bill said, 'Have you got them all, Danny?'

'There's just the good doctor William Baxter still to arrest. The anaesthetist, who supplied the drugs to stupefy the kids as they were abused, is currently out of the country on holiday in the Maldives. His flight is scheduled to arrive at Manchester Airport at eight o'clock tomorrow morning. I've got Andy Wills and Jeff Williams travelling up to Manchester tonight, so they can be at the airport ready to arrest him as soon as he gets through passport control. I've already informed Special Branch at the airport and they've agreed to take the doctor into a side room when he goes through, so our boys can do the business out of sight of the public.'

'It's all come together very fast, Danny.'

'We had a bit of luck, Bill. It was the arrest of a low-level drug dealer that first got us looking seriously at Caroline Short. Then we dropped lucky when we were able to get the Regional Crime Squad to carry out round the clock surveillance on both her and her husband Bill. It was that surveillance that subsequently identified Mayflower Cottage at Bleasby. We just had that bit of luck you need to get everything falling into place on an enquiry like this.'

'You're being far too modest, Danny. It came together quickly because it was managed right and those opportunities that did present themselves were taken advantage of in the correct way. I've just popped in to let you know that the Chief Constable is very much looking forward to the press release tomorrow morning outlining the success of the operation. He's a very happy man, Danny.'

'Well that makes a nice change Bill.'

'What time is the press conference in the morning?'

'It's scheduled for eleven o'clock, why?'

'I want to go and see Tania Jenkins before the press conference is shown on air. I want to tell her personally what happened to her boy and to let her know the people responsible for his death are going to be behind bars for a very long time.'

'Not a pleasant task Danny, but I suppose with rank comes responsibility.'

'I know what you mean Bill, but it's the least I can do. I told her I would keep her informed, so I will.'

'How's everything else Danny? How's married life treating you?'

'I'm enjoying every minute Bill, Sue's a lovely lady.'

'So, we'll soon be hearing the sound of tiny feet, will we Danny?'

Danny said nothing, but his silence spoke volumes.

Bill, as usual, was very sharp on the uptake, 'No, she's expecting already? That's wonderful news Danny!'

He beamed a big smile and raised his glass towards Danny.

Danny touched the glass with his own and both men took another sip of the whiskey.

Danny said, 'We've only just found out Bill, so it's early days. I'd appreciate it if you didn't say anything to anyone just yet.'

Bill smiled, 'Mum's the word Danny. Literally!'

He burst out laughing at his own joke.

When his laughter subsided, he became serious again and said, 'What about your other cases, Danny?'

'We're pretty clear at the moment. Now this has been resolved I want to devote a bit more time to finding our friend Jimmy Wade. I've had two detectives up there at Rampton working on the case, while the rest of the Unit has been tucked up with the Jenkins enquiry. I'm expecting an update from them in the morning. Hopefully, they'll have been able to make some progress. I've always had this nagging suspicion that Wade stayed local. I know it doesn't make any sense, but I've always had a feeling that he's still around here somewhere.'

'Well, keep me posted, Danny. I won't delay you getting home to your lovely wife any longer. Please pass on my congratulations to Sue. Goodnight, Danny.'

'I will do, goodnight, Bill.'

Five minutes later, Danny swallowed the last of the whiskey in his glass, slipped his jacket on, switched off the office light and went home.

CHAPTER 77

2nd July 1986
South Lodge, Retford

The first rays of the morning sun were beginning to stream into the master bedroom at South Lodge. A naked Melissa Braithwaite snuggled into the side of Jimmy Wade as they lay together in the huge double bed.

They had awoken thirty minutes before and had immediately made love, now spent, they cuddled together, enjoying the feel of skin to skin contact and a post coital cigarette.

Melissa had finished with her cigarette and had placed the butt in the ashtray on the drawers next to her side of the bed.

With her right hand she began to slowly caress Wade's stomach just below his navel. She made small circles on his skin, softly drawing them with her fingernails.

It was something she knew Wade enjoyed.

As she caressed him she said, 'I think we're making a mistake going after this detective, Jimmy. It's one thing getting even with the other three, nobody's even missed them yet, but if you abduct and kill a police officer everyone in the country will be searching for you. Let's just get away to Ireland and start a new life while we can.'

Wade remained silent, he lay on his back staring at the ceiling.

A week or so ago he wouldn't have tolerated Melissa having any sort of opinion let alone expressing one.

He had noticed a distinct change in her over the last few days.

Although lucid and able to articulate herself, she looked slightly unhinged and came across as being very intense.

She fidgeted constantly and appeared on edge.

Wade put the change in her down to the magnificent job he had done when breaking her spirit. He believed Braithwaite was now on the verge of either a full nervous breakdown or worse, insanity.

He reached over to the bedside drawer next to him and retrieved his half-smoked cigarette from the ashtray.

He took a long drag from the cigarette, blew the smoke towards the ceiling and said, 'Maybe you're right Mel, Rachel Moore is yesterday's news. I suppose I could get by if I never saw her again. I was thinking about it last night and I've already won. I'm already enjoying the freedom that her and the other cops tried to deny me.'

He felt Melissa's fingernails dig a little deeper in approval. The small circles she drew with her nails moved ever closer to his manhood.

He said, 'I'll get rid of Ainsworth's car later today, then we can start making plans and getting things in place ready to go to Ireland later this week.'

The fingernails had worked their magic and Wade felt a familiar stirring.

He stubbed out his cigarette in the ashtray and said, 'In the meantime, come here you.'

He turned over in bed to face Melissa, who immediately kissed him hard on the mouth.

She then whispered softly, 'I love you, Jimmy Wade.'

CHAPTER 78

2nd July 1986
Retford Police Station, Nottinghamshire

Throughout their time working together on the Wade enquiry, Tina Prowse and Rachel Moore had used the CID office at Retford Police Station as a base.

All their enquiries were in this part of the county, so it made sense to go on and off duty there rather than travelling to Mansfield every day to then drive to the Retford area.

Today was no different, the two detectives had arrived bright and early at the police station in the bustling market town.

They had arrived at just after seven thirty and the CID office was still empty. The first local detectives would normally arrive for duty around eight thirty in the morning.

Ever since they'd arrived at the station, the local officers had made Tina and Rachel feel very welcome and had told them to use the station and the facilities as they would their own.

In response to the offer, both detectives had made a cash donation to the CID office tea fund, so they could help themselves to a hot drink whenever they wanted one.

As Rachel poured the hot water from the kettle into the two mugs she said, 'How many sugars do you take in coffee, Tina?'

'It's one, and if you still need to ask me that after all the time we've worked together, you need to make the drinks more often.'

Tina smiled at Rachel, her brevity masking her nervousness.

She wasn't looking forward to making the phone call to Danny Flint this morning.

Although they had both been diligent in their enquiries into the escape of Jimmy Wade they hadn't made much progress.

Rachel handed the mug of steaming hot coffee to Tina and picking up on her colleague's mood she said, 'Listen Tina, Danny will be fine. He's not an ogre!'

'I know that, but we haven't made much progress have we?'

'Tina, stop worrying. Don't forget when Jimmy Wade first escaped the whole MCIU failed to make any significant progress. At least we've found a possible lead with this sighting of the mystery blonde at the pub when Barnes went missing. You never know, there's still time for Stewart Ainsworth to show up yet.'

'I doubt it.'

'You must tell Danny about this Melissa woman, that Ainsworth had the hot date with, don't forget to mention that.'

'I won't. It's nearly eight o'clock, I'll finish this coffee then phone him.'

'Don't worry Tina, it'll be fine.'

The clock on the wall finally showed eight o'clock.

Reluctantly Tina picked up the telephone and dialled the number for Danny Flint's office.

It was answered on the third ring, 'Good morning, DCI Flint.'

'Good morning sir, it's Sergeant Prowse.'

'Hello Tina, I've been expecting your call, good to see you're nice and prompt, I've got an appointment in the city first thing this morning. So, how's it going on the Wade enquiry?'

Tina took a deep breath and said, 'To be honest sir, it's pretty slow going. We've followed up all the enquiries on the disappearance of Jack Williams, but made no headway. A second male nurse, Fred Barnes, has also now been reported missing. Barnes also worked closely with Jimmy Wade when he was first transferred to Rampton. Our enquiries so far have revealed that Wade may have been assaulted by Barnes and Williams when he first arrived at the hospital. It would appear that a blind eye was turned towards these assaults by the powers that be inside the hospital.'

'Tell me about the second missing nurse, Fred Barnes. Have you carried out all the follow up enquiries on that?'

'Yes, we have.'

'Anything interesting come to light?'

'Barnes was last seen drinking in his local, the Crown and Anchor pub on Eastern Avenue in Retford. We've made enquiries there and spoken to the barman who was working that night. He recalls seeing a very attractive, young, blonde woman come into the pub. This woman had a look round and walked straight back out, this happened just before Barnes left. The barman had never seen the woman before.'

'Have you any idea who this woman is?'

Feeling slightly deflated Tina said, 'No sir, we haven't. We've drawn a complete blank, but we do believe that Barnes was abducted just outside the pub.'

'Why is that Tina?'

'We recovered his cigarette lighter from the gutter just outside the front door of the pub. Apparently, this lighter is one of his most prized possessions. It's something he treasures and would never let it out of his sight. The barman at the pub told us that the lighter was a gift to Barnes from his regiment when he left the army.'

'Is that as far as you've got Tina?'

'There's one other thing sir. We had made arrangements to see Stewart Ainsworth yesterday. He was Wade's social worker and responsible for his welfare inside Rampton. We questioned him briefly a couple of days ago, about the allegations of assault that were starting to come to light about Barnes and Williams. He denied there had been any such assaults.'

'Have you got a statement from Ainsworth?'

'No sir.'

'Why not Tina? I thought you said you'd spoken to him a couple of days ago?'

'We did speak to him, but we didn't get a statement from him that night as he had to be somewhere.'

'What was so important?'

'He didn't want to be delayed as he had a first date with a woman called Melissa Braithwaite, he didn't want to stand her up.'

'Bloody hell Tina! We don't do our enquiries around people's social lives!'

'Sorry sir.'

'You said you'd made arrangements to see him yesterday, how come you still haven't got the statement?'

'Because Ainsworth hasn't shown up for work since we saw him a couple of days ago, sir.'

'Hang on a minute, so now we've possibly got three members of staff who worked closely with Jimmy Wade, all unaccounted for?'

'Yes sir.'

Danny was quiet for a moment, deep in thought.

'Tina, tell me again the name of the woman Ainsworth was going to see.'

'Braithwaite. Melissa Braithwaite, why?'

'I'm sure I've seen that name in the Wade enquiry before. Give me ten minutes and I'll call you back.'

Danny put the phone down and walked into the main office.

Fran Jefferies was already at her desk, head down typing away on the computer's keyboard.

'Good morning Fran, are you logged on to the system already?'

'Yes, sir.'

'Do me a quick favour, go into the Wade enquiry database. See if there's any record of the name Melissa Braithwaite in the enquiry please?'

Fran's fingers flew over the computer keyboard and after a brief pause she said, 'Here we are sir. Melissa Braithwaite. She was seen by Dc Phil Baxter and Dc Martin Harper quite early on in the enquiry. Phil and Martin were tasked to trace, interview and eliminate Braithwaite from the enquiry. The pre-cursor to this enquiry was when visitor's records revealed that Braithwaite had visited Jimmy Wade on quite a few occasions.'

'What was the outcome?'

'They traced her to her home address, which is shown as South Lodge, Retford. They interviewed her and took a brief statement showing her whereabouts on the day of the escape. The reasons for her visits to Wade were for research into a master's degree course she was doing.'

'So, no concerns then?'

'Not according to this, sir.'

'Did they search the premises?'

'It says here, a discreet search was made that revealed no male presence at the property, apparently she lived alone at the address.'

'Thanks Fran, I thought the name rang a bell.'

Danny started to walk away, then suddenly stopped in his tracks.

He turned and said, 'Fran, did Phil and Martin complete a Personal Descriptive Form for Braithwaite?'

Again, her fingers were a blur on the keyboard, 'Yes, they did sir.'

'Briefly, what's the description of Braithwaite according to the PDF?'

'Very briefly, the woman was in her late twenties, petite, blonde hair, 5' 2", medium build.'

'Okay Fran, thanks.'

Danny returned to his office picked up the telephone and dialled the number for Retford CID.

Tina answered the phone, 'Hello Retford CID, Sgt Prowse speaking.'

'Tina, it's Danny. Melissa Braithwaite's known to Jimmy Wade, she was a regular visitor of his at Rampton. Her description's similar to the woman you described going into the pub where Barnes was abducted.'

'Oh my God sir, have we let Ainsworth walk into a trap?'

'I don't know Tina, but we need to start looking at this woman closely, she could be assisting Wade. I want you and Rachel to go and reconnoitre her home address at South Lodge, Retford. Do not under any circumstances go to the house itself. Just have a look, then get back to me. If Wade's hiding there I want to set up on the property properly, so there's no chance of him slipping away again. Do the recce this morning and then get straight back to Retford nick. In the meantime, I'll talk to the Special Operations Unit and see if they've got the capability to do an armed raid today. Good work Tina, I wouldn't have made the connection without the sighting of the blonde at the pub. It still might turn out to be just a coincidence, but it's got to be checked out properly.'

'We're on our way sir, we'll go out to the lodge in my own car, it won't stand out so much.'

'Okay Tina, like I said, I just want a recce. No heroics.'

'No heroics sir.'

CHAPTER 79

2nd July 1986
South Lodge, Retford

The two detectives had spent an age studying the ordnance survey map of the area around South Lodge at Retford.

The cottage was located in the centre of what was once the vast Retford Hall Estate. It backed onto the meandering River Poulter and was surrounded by vast areas of woodland.

The former estate was now owned almost entirely by the Forestry Commission and the woodland that surrounded the cottage was strictly managed and consisted mainly of row upon row of conifer trees, with smaller areas of native deciduous trees planted in pockets to preserve the natural wildlife.

The area was interlaced with a myriad of lanes and dirt tracks and this was the reason for the time spent poring over the map. The last thing the detectives wanted to do on a recce was blunder upon the cottage. They needed to know exactly how to get there and where to park their vehicle so they could complete the recce by approaching the cottage on foot.

Having satisfied themselves of the best route in, they had set off from Retford police station on the twenty-minute drive to the edge of the estate.

Tina was driving her own Vauxhall Astra very carefully along one of the potholed lanes.

The dark maroon coloured hatchback was her pride and joy. There were one or two spots of rust starting to show on the wheel arches at the front, but it was good runner and a solid car. She kept it immaculately clean and tidy inside and out.

Rachel sat in the passenger seat with the folded ordnance survey map in her lap.

Rachel held up her right hand, 'Take the next track on the right, according to the map South Lodge is on that track. Once you've made the turn find somewhere to pull off the track and park up, the cottage is about three hundred yards further along.'

'I'm so glad I put my flats on today, I wouldn't fancy walking through these woods in heels.'

'I keep telling you to wear practical shoes for work Tina, some of your heels are ridiculous.'

'It's part of me Rachel, not all of us can look as glamourous as you do in flats.'

Rachel shook her head and smiled.

Tina turned right and drove the car onto the final track, finding a place to pull over and stop after another fifty yards. The two women got out of the vehicle and were surprised at just how dark the area was.

Surrounded on all sides by tall conifers, hardly any daylight penetrated the thick canopy. It felt really cool, even though the sun was out and the weather was set fair for another hot day. The smell of the pine trees was heady and strong. The ground underfoot felt soft and spongy, from the fallen needles that formed a brown carpet.

Rachel said quietly, 'Jesus, if Wade's hiding out here it's no wonder we haven't found him. This place is definitely the back of beyond.'

'It's bloody creepy too, have you noticed there aren't any birds singing?'

'No, I hadn't until you mentioned it, but you're right it's definitely creepy in here. Why would anyone choose to live right out here on their own?'

'Come on Rachel, the cottage should be down here, watch your footing.'

The two detectives stealthily made their way along the side of the single dirt track. After almost two hundred yards the conifer forest abruptly stopped and was replaced by deciduous planting.

The trees here were smaller.

The planting was native species of Birch, Beech and Oak.

Immediately, the detectives felt warmer as they emerged into the dappled sunlight.

Suddenly Rachel stopped and squatted down, Tina immediately followed suit.

Rachel whispered, 'The lodge is over there, look.'

Tina looked passed Rachel and could see the small sandstone cottage some forty yards ahead. The tree line stopped ten yards in front of the detectives.

The cottage stood alone in a clearing framed on the other three sides by heavy conifer planting. The pines here were mature and offered a very dark backdrop to the small stone cottage.

'Let's get a little closer', whispered Tina.

The women edged themselves slowly forward until they were behind the last of the trees. From their new vantage point they had a clearer view of the property and were still in good cover. They could hear the sound of running water from their immediate left, they knew the sound would be the small stream that was shown on their map as the River Poulter.

The map showed the stream clearly adjacent to the rear of the property. Here the birds were singing loudly, a marked contrast to the dark, almost lifeless conifer forest.

'Look Tina, can you see the wisps of smoke from the chimney, somebody's at home.'

'I see it, let's not disturb them.'

'There are outhouses at the back of the cottage that aren't shown on the map, I'll make a note of them on here'

She took a biro from her jacket pocket and quickly drew two rectangles onto the folded map, marking the location of the outbuildings.

Tina pointed towards the front of the cottage, 'There's a couple of vehicles parked outside the front of the cottage. If we skirt around the tree line back that way, I think we should be able to get close enough to get a clear look at the registration numbers?'

'Take your time Tina, be careful.'

Never taking their eyes off the cottage, the two detectives began to circumnavigate the property, sticking to the tree line. Eventually, they reached a position almost opposite the front door where they could clearly see the registration numbers of the two vehicles.

One of the vehicles was a Fiat Uno, the other a Ford Transit van. Rachel scribbled the numbers down on the back of the map.

'I think we've seen enough Tina, let's not push our luck.'

'You're right. Come on, let's make our way back to the car and get out of here.'

Moving stealthily, they skirted back around to their original position and then backed into the woods away from the cottage. Staying on the side of the track they began to make their way back to Tina's Vauxhall Astra.

Suddenly, from behind them they heard a car door slam, then a second.

A car engine burst into life, followed by the lower rumble of a diesel engine.

Rachel grabbed Tina and pulled her off the track into the trees, 'Come on Tina, get in here.'

They scrambled deeper into the woods, got down and looked back towards the track. Both the Fiat Uno and the Transit van were being driven along the track. Although they both craned their necks to see, neither of the detectives were close enough or in a position to see who was driving the two vehicles.

As soon as the Uno and the Transit had passed them Rachel said, 'Come on Tina, move!'

Both detectives stood up and began to carefully make their way through the woodland back to where they had left their car.

Jimmy Wade driving Ainsworth's Fiat Uno saw the Vauxhall Astra parked at the side of the track and slowed his vehicle. It wasn't unusual to see vehicles parked in the woods. The place was often frequented by dog walkers, runners and bird watchers.

He stopped the Uno and jumped out to look at the car.

Braithwaite stopped the Transit behind him and wound the window down, 'What's up sweetheart?'

'I'm just checking this motor out, won't be a second.'

Wade cupped his hands and peered through the driver's window of the Astra. The inside of the car was completely sterile. There were no clues who may own the vehicle anywhere on view. There was a hatchback boot, but no sign of dog stuff anywhere.

He turned back to Melissa, 'Could be someone walking a dog I suppose, there's nothing in it.'

'Come on Jimmy, let's go and get rid of the Uno. We've still got a lot of planning to do.'

'I'm coming.'

Wade opened the car door, got back in the Uno, started the engine and drove off followed by Braithwaite.

From a distance of seventy-five yards the two detectives had seen the man snooping around the car. From that distance they were unable to make out any facial features and could only see the man's long dark hair. The driver of the van remained in the vehicle, totally out of sight.

Tina whispered to Rachel, 'Jesus, I'm glad I decided to drive my own car here and not the CID car. Do you think that was him?'

'Jimmy Wade with long dark hair? I don't think so Tina. I couldn't really see who it was. If you remember though, Ainsworth's got long dark hair, hasn't he? Let's get back to Retford nick and get these vehicle numbers checked, then we can phone the boss and tell him what we've seen, it'll be up to him then.'

As they drove through the woodland, Rachel was deep in thought.

Were they going off on completely the wrong tangent? Was it just an infatuation between Stewart Ainsworth and Melissa Braithwaite? Were they just a young couple spending a romantic time together at her secluded home?

Finally, they emerged from the forest, turned the car onto a tarmac road and began the short journey back to Retford police station.

CHAPTER 80

2nd July 1986
Retford Police Station, Nottinghamshire

It was approaching twelve o'clock by the time Rachel and Tina drove back into the car park at Retford police station.

Tina parked her Vauxhall Astra, got out and frowned at the mud spatters all along the side of car.

'Look at that Rach, it's bloody filthy!'

'Never mind the mud, it's a bloody good job you took it.'

'I know what you mean, can you believe that? Another couple of minutes and we would've been sat in the bloody car as they drove by.'

'Whoever they are?'

The two women walked into the police station and went straight to the control room.

Rachel handed the map she had written the car registration numbers on, to one of the control room operators and said, 'I need two PNC owners checks on these numbers please. As a matter of urgency, if you can?'

The civilian operator took the map, noted the two registration numbers on a pad and then handed the map back.

He tapped the relevant code into the computer and a few seconds later said, 'The first number relates to a Fiat Uno, no markers on the vehicle, registered keeper is a Stewart Ainsworth. The address shown is a local one, 23 Grosvenor Road, Retford.'

Rachel scribbled down the information.

'The second number comes back as a Ford Transit, again there are no markers on the vehicle. Another local keeper, Melissa Braithwaite. Her address is South Lodge, Retford. Can you give me the reason for the checks, detective?'

'Ongoing crime enquiries, thanks.'

Armed with the information from the vehicle checks, the two women made their way upstairs to the CID office to phone Danny Flint.

The first door they passed on the first floor led into the office used by the station Superintendent. As they walked by the door a gruff voice said, 'In here, ladies.'

Tina opened the door wider.

Sitting in the office with Superintendent Stringer were Danny Flint and Rob Buxton.

Tina said to Danny, 'Hello sir, we were just about to call you.'

Danny answered, 'As soon as I'd seen Tania Jenkins this morning, I thought I'd better come up to Retford to see how things were progressing for myself. I was just explaining to Superintendent Stringer that we may have a lead on the whereabouts of Jimmy Wade.'

Rachel said, 'It may be a bit too soon to say that sir. I've just done PNC checks on two vehicles we saw at South Lodge. A Fiat Uno which is registered to Stewart Ainsworth and a Ford Transit which is registered to the owner of South Lodge, Melissa Braithwaite. We actually managed to get a glimpse of the driver of the Fiat Uno and the driver fitted the description of Ainsworth. We could only see the driver from a distance, so we couldn't be sure whether it was Ainsworth or not.'

Stringer growled at Danny, 'Doesn't sound all that encouraging to me Chief Inspector. Please feel free to use the CID office to firm up your information.'

It was one of the most courteous dismissals Danny had ever heard. He was left in no doubt that the superintendent's office should be vacated immediately.

'No problem sir, I'll keep you informed of any developments.'

Superintendent Stringer didn't look up from the report he was now busy reading.

The four detectives left the office and made their way along the corridor to the CID office. The only person in the office was Angie Wilbraham, the local Detective Sergeant. She was also busily reading reports that had been left on her desk. She looked up when she saw the door to the office open.

Seeing Rachel, she said, 'Hello again Rachel, what's happening?'

'Hi Angie, this is my boss Detective Chief Inspector Flint and Detective Inspector Buxton. You already know Tina. We need to use the office for a while, sorry.'

Angie turned to Danny and said, 'No problem sir, if you need any local knowledge on whatever it is you're doing today just give me a shout. I'll be next door in the DI's office, he's not in today.'

Danny nodded and said, 'Thanks, sorry to interrupt your work.'

Angie grabbed her paperwork and walked out of the office.

Danny said, 'Okay ladies, give me a full debrief on your recce. I can have a section of the Special Operations Unit armed and travelling if we think there's any possibility that Jimmy Wade is at this South Lodge address.'

It was Rachel who spoke up, 'There's no way of knowing boss. The only man we saw at the location didn't look anything like Wade, but he did loosely fit the description of our missing social worker Stewart Ainsworth and he was driving Ainsworth's motor.'

'Who was driving the Transit?'

'We couldn't see, whoever it was never got out of the vehicle.'

'Okay, tell me about South Lodge Tina.'

Tina replied, 'It's so far off the beaten track that unless you actually knew it was there, you'd never find it in a month of Sundays. It's a small stone cottage surrounded by acres of conifer woodlands that are owned by the Forestry Commission'

'And the cottage itself?'

'Like I said, it's very small, almost two up two down. Typical of the stone lodges that you see on old country estates. The windows are tiny and the front door is made of a heavy hardwood.'

'What about the grounds?'

'It's in a small clearing that's surrounded on three sides by a mature conifer plantation and on one side by deciduous trees. It's accessed by a single track that leads to the cottage and comes to a dead end at the property. There's only one way in and one way out. At the rear of the cottage is a small stream just before the conifers start. There's a small stone bridge over the stream.'

'Is that it?'

'Yes sir.'

Rachel said, 'Don't forget the outhouses at the back of the property.'

Danny said, 'Go on.'

'Sorry boss, there are also two stone outbuildings directly behind the property, about fifteen yards from the back of the cottage.'

'Rachel, could the property be easily contained by the Special Operations Unit?'

'Very easily boss. The woodland surrounding it is very thick, I'm sure the Unit would be able to get in quite close without being seen by the occupants.'

Danny was deep in thought.

He said, 'Tina, Rachel, can you give me and Rob a minute or two please? There's something I want to discuss with him, before I run it by you two.'

Both women nodded, stood up and walked towards the door.

At the door Tina turned and said, 'We'll be downstairs in the control room, sir.'

'Thanks Tina, this won't take long.'

Danny waited for the door to close properly then turned to Rob and said, 'I've got an idea, but I don't know if it's fair to ask Rachel.'

'Let's hear it Danny.'

'I'm thinking if Wade's in that cottage, we are going to need something to make him show himself.'

'Or someone?'

'Yes, someone. The one police officer, Wade would risk showing out for is Rachel.'

'I don't like this idea at all, Danny. After what happened last time, I think it's totally unfair to even ask her to act as a decoy for that monster.'

'Hear me out, Rob. I propose to have the Special Operations Unit surround the cottage to act as armed back up to Rachel.'

'Why not just raid the cottage?'

'What if we're wrong and Wade isn't there? We haven't got enough evidence yet to justify an armed raid on a cottage that could just be occupied by two young lovers having fun. If Rachel goes in and discovers something else, then the armed team would be able to respond immediately.'

'Would immediately be fast enough though Danny?'

'I don't know, what do you think?'

'I know, I don't like it Danny. Couldn't we send a different officer to check out the property? Does it have to be Rachel?'

'We've already sent two other officers to the property. Dc Baxter and Dc Harper never saw hide nor hair of Wade. My biggest fear is that he would just disappear again. I want Rachel to make a telephone call to Melissa Braithwaite and tell her she needs to come and see her about Ainsworth. I want her to ask when it's convenient to come and see her at South Lodge. My guess is, if Wade's there he'll tell Braithwaite to play for a little time, so he can set a trap for Rachel. If it's Ainsworth who's there, my guess is she'll say come over straight away.'

'It could work Danny, but I think you need to ask Rachel what her thoughts on it are. I don't think you can order her to do something like that.'

'I would never dream of ordering her to do it Rob, if she's not happy about any part of it we'll find a different way. Call the control room and get them both back up here.'

A couple of minutes later, Rachel and Tina walked back into the CID office.

Danny outlined his plan to Rachel and asked what she thought.

Rachel though for a moment and said, 'And the Unit lads surrounding the cottage would be armed?'

'Yes, I could get authority for an armed containment.'

'What about comms?'

'We could utilise the covert radios used by the Special Ops lads, so everyone would be on the same channel. At any given moment if you were unhappy about the situation, we could have an armed response into the lodge within seconds.'

Rachel thought for a moment, then said quietly, 'I'll do it.'

CHAPTER 81

2nd July 1986
South Lodge, Retford

The four two-man sniper teams from the Special Operations Unit were the first officers to be deployed into the woodland that now made up the old Retford Hall Estate.

Their immediate role would be to set up an armed containment on the property. Each of the two-man teams would set up an observation post on each side of the property.

As soon as Danny Flint had made the telephone call that morning to check the availability of the Special Operations Unit, Inspector Scott Powell had been making contingency plans.

That first call had been received just after eight thirty that morning. By the time the second phone call was received just before midday, Powell had already briefed C Section and the three added sniper teams that would be required for the operation. Each SOU section had a two-man sniper team, so Powell had also had to call out the three other teams from A, B and D section.

The equipment required, for such a woodland operation, had been quickly loaded onto the two white Transit vans and as soon as the necessary authorisation for a containment operation had been given by the Deputy Chief Constable, weapons were drawn from the armoury.

By one o'clock, the sixteen men were travelling towards Retford, with an eta for Retford police station of one thirty.

The two vans actually pulled into the car park at Retford police station at twenty minutes past one.

A further meeting then took place between Danny Flint and Inspector Powell. Also present during this meeting was Sergeant Mitch Buchan, the Tactical Firearms Advisor.

During this initial meeting Danny outlined his proposed plan for the operation.

It was Mitch Buchan who had suggested that the four sniper teams be deployed immediately.

As well as providing the control room with much needed intelligence, it meant that the teams could set up suitable covert observation posts in plenty of time before the proposed visit to South Lodge by Rachel Moore.

Each of the sniper teams were tasked with observing a different side of the property.

The sniper team from C Section were tasked with observing the Black side of the property.

That meant they would be manning an observation post set up in the dense conifer woodland on the far side of the River Poulter, overlooking the rear of the property, including the two outhouses.

Pc Russel Day and Pc Kevin Thomas were the two snipers deployed from C Section.

The two men had earlier drawn their individual Ruger M77 sniper rifles. These specialist weapons had telescopic sights that had been zeroed personally by them on their last classification shoot. They had also drawn their personal Smith and Wesson.38 revolvers and ammunition for both weapons.

In addition they carried a set of binoculars each, water bottles and camouflaged carry cases for the long weapons. As it was an operation in woodland the two men had dressed in full DPM camouflage clothing and each man had taken his own "head and shoulders ghillie suit".

The "head and shoulders" was a hessian hood covered with ties so that vegetation local to the plot could be attached. This was a vital piece of equipment that helped the sniper to disrupt the normal shape of his head and body, allowing them to blend in seamlessly with the surrounding environment.

Each man took fastidious care of this piece of equipment, it was a vital component of the snipers art.

After their briefing from Mitch Buchan, the two C Section snipers had prepared their equipment. When they arrived on the edge of the forest and before they made their way into the dense woodland, they had further adorned their head and shoulders with foliage taken from the surrounding area. The very last thing they did before moving off into the woods was to ensure that every area of exposed skin was covered with black and green camouflage cream.

Having been conveyed by van to the nearest access point on the rear side of South Lodge, the two men still had over half a mile to cover on foot to get to their proposed site for an observation point.

Carrying all their equipment the two snipers had set off on foot.

Following a compass bearing they moved stealthily, but with purpose through the dense conifer woodland.

After half an hour Russel Day stopped and squatted down.

Instantly, Kev Thomas mirrored his partners position, before moving forward slowly until he was alongside his partner.

Day said softly, 'I can hear running water Kev, we must be near the river. According to the briefing, on the bearing we've taken through the woods, the target premises should be just beyond the river. Stay here, I'll move forward and check it out.'

Thomas nodded and squatted down further.

Leaving the heavy carry case containing his rifle with his partner, Day started to move forward slowly.

He lay flat on his stomach and began to inch forward towards the edge of the tree line. He could tell that he was crawling on a gentle downward slope. He guessed the slope would eventually take him right to the water's edge.

The line of conifer planting stopped ten yards short of the river, which at this point was only three yards wide.

Immediately in front of him, between the tree line and the river was an area of low shrubs and bushes that offered perfect concealment and would make the perfect covert observation post.

On the far side of the river, Day could see an area of knee length grass that led up to two stone outbuildings. There was a significant rise in the land between the small river and the outhouses. There was a small stone bridge to his immediate right that crossed the river.

Beyond the small stone buildings, was South Lodge, the target premises.

Day rolled slowly over onto his back and gestured for Thomas to join him.

From the position he'd selected, Day was in an area that offered excellent concealment. He had a clear view of the back door of the cottage, as well as views of the doors into both outbuildings.

Moving slowly, he took out his binoculars and began to scan the rear aspect of the property, paying particular attention to the doors and windows of the buildings.

There was single door at the rear of the cottage that was currently closed. Both doors to the outbuildings were also closed.

To the left side of the back door he could see one solitary window.

Through the binoculars, he could see the chrome heads of two taps beyond the panes of glass. It was possibly the kitchen. The door at the rear of the property would open directly into that room.

The cottage had a first floor with two windows facing the rear of the property.

Both windows were small and covered with a very fine net curtain.

As soon as his partner had crawled into position to the left of him, Day began to draw forward the carry case, that held his rifle.

Very carefully and very deliberately the sniper removed the M77 Ruger rifle and began to adorn it with small pieces of foliage, adding to the strips of black, brown and green hessian cloth that already hung from the weapon, disrupting its outline and cancelling out any tell-tale shine.

When the rifle was sufficiently camouflaged, Day placed the rifle on it's attached bipod and removed the two black screw caps from the telescopic lens. He then took a piece of dark beige coloured muslin from his DPM camouflage jacket and carefully placed it over the far lens.

Moving carefully, he then took up the weapon into his shoulder and peered through the scope.

He then very slowly traversed the weapon from one side of the plot to the other. From the position he'd chosen, he had clear lines of sight to every window and the door at the rear of the cottage. He also had clear lines of sight to the doors of both the outhouses.

Feeling satisfied with their position, he replaced the butt of the weapon on the ground.

Day then gently squeezed the button in the palm of his left hand that controlled his radio and spoke softly into the throat mike he was wearing, 'This is Sniper Team Charlie. We've established an O.P. facing the Black side of the target premises. We are in position. Report these signals. Over.'

In his covert ear piece, Day instantly heard the reassuring voice of Sergeant Rodgers, the SOU sergeant tasked with controlling the comms for the operation, 'Sniper Team Charlie roger that, your signal strength is ten and clear, over. I will require a sit-rep from you every ten minutes. Time check is now 1410. Over.'

'Roger that, 1410. Over.'

Having established communications, the two men of the sniper team settled down for what could be a long wait. Through their covert ear pieces, the men could hear the other sniper teams making comms checks as they too established OP's on the other three sides of the target premises.

Day was the designated sniper for this operation and Thomas his spotter, they would work as a team throughout.

It would be the responsibility of Thomas to ensure the ten-minute sit-reps were maintained.

Day then began plotting out the distances from their location to various points of the property.

Everything was within one hundred yards of their position, there was no wind of any significance as the cottage sat in a clearing surrounded on all sides by tall trees.

Day knew, that if he was forced by circumstances to pull the trigger and take a shot from his location, he would be able to achieve it easily.

CHAPTER 82

2nd July 1986
Retford Police Station, Nottinghamshire

Sergeant Rodgers nodded towards Danny and said, 'They're in position now sir.'

He had just received confirmation from the main SOU raid party being led by Inspector Powell that they were at the forward rendezvous point. They had taken up a position some fifty yards back from the target premises on the designated Red side of the property.

It would be the responsibility of these men to provide immediate back up for Rachel Moore if she required it.

The sniper teams covering all four sides of South Lodge also offered her protection from a distance.

Sniper team Bravo covering the front of the property had given an update approximately half an hour before, that the Ford Transit van seen earlier by the two detectives had returned to the property.

All the sniper teams had been given photographs of Melissa Braithwaite, Stewart Ainsworth and Jimmy Wade during the briefing.

Sniper Team Bravo had quickly identified that the driver of the Ford Transit was indeed Melissa Braithwaite. They had a partial view of the passenger in the vehicle and could not give a positive identification. They only saw him as he walked away from their position towards the front door of the cottage. The long dark hair they could see on the male, favoured the identity being the missing social worker, Stewart Ainsworth.

There had been no other sightings of either person since and no sign of the Fiat Uno that had been seen during the earlier recce by Rachel and Tina.

Danny looked across to Rachel and said, 'It's time Rachel, are you ready to make the call to Braithwaite?'

She nodded and picked up the telephone.

Danny raised his hands and said loudly, 'Everyone, not a sound! I don't want any background noise while this call's being made, understood?'

Everyone in the room nodded, radios were turned off and nobody moved a muscle.

Danny said, 'Go ahead, Rachel.'

Rachel dialled the number.

On the second ring the phone was answered.

A female voice said, 'Hello, South Lodge.'

Rachel took a deep breath and said, 'Hi, I'm trying to contact Melissa Braithwaite?'

'Speaking.'

'Hi Melissa, my name's Dc Rachel Moore. I'm sorry to disturb you but I'm trying to locate a man by the name of Stewart Ainsworth. He told me that he was meeting you a couple of days ago and nobody's heard from him since. Have you seen him?'

Jimmy Wade always insisted that all calls into the Lodge were on loudspeaker and he was listening intently to the call.

When he had heard the name Rachel Moore, he spun round and now stood right in front of Melissa.

He gestured for her to cover the ear piece of the telephone and whispered, 'Tell her he's gone out to the shops, but will be back later.'

Having been given the instruction Melissa said quietly, 'Stewart's been here with me, but he's had to go out this afternoon. You've only just missed him. Is there any message?'

'No thanks, there's no message, but I do need to see him today. Do you know what time he'll be back?'

Wade held up two fingers and silently mouthed the words two hours.

Melissa frowned and scowled at Wade, then she said, 'He's had to go over to Sheffield for something or other, but he shouldn't be any longer than two hours.'

Rachel looked at the clock on the office wall.

It was now almost three o'clock.

'If it's not an inconvenience Melissa, would it be okay for me and my partner to come over and have a quick chat with Stewart after five o'clock today? It shouldn't take long.'

Jimmy Wade nodded.

Melissa shook her head and mouthed the word, no.

Wade scowled, put his hand over the phone and whispered menacingly, 'Do it.'

Melissa knew she daren't argue and said meekly, 'Yeah, that should be fine, shall we say five thirty?'

'That's great Melissa, thanks.'

'And you're sure there's no message for him?'

'No, there's no message, we'll see you later.'

Rachel heard the click on the phone as Melissa ended the call, she placed her own handset back on the receiver and breathed out a huge sigh.

She turned to Danny and said, 'Braithwaite's lying boss. She told me that Stewart Ainsworth had been there, but that he'd gone out and that I'd only just missed him. Nobody's been seen leaving the property. There was something else too, it was almost as if she was receiving instruction on what to say. Too many long pauses, followed by a very effected response, too friendly, too nice.'

'What's your gut instinct, Rachel?'

'Jimmy Wade's in that cottage boss. I think Ainsworth might be in there too though.'

'Why do you think that?'

'The sighting earlier was nothing like Wade, and the man with the long hair hasn't gone anywhere. I think Ainsworth could still be in there.'

Danny frowned, 'Which means it's probably too risky, to send in an armed raid team to search the cottage.'

'I've made the appointment for five thirty, why don't we stick to the original plan?'

Tina spoke up, 'I'll tell you why Rachel, because it's way too risky, that's why.'

'Police work's always risky, Tina. It's got to be me. If Wade's in there, he'll only show out if he sees me. The armed teams are all in place, it will be fine.'

Danny said, 'You don't have to do this, Rachel.'

She replied, 'Yes I do, he'll be expecting me to arrive at five thirty. If I don't turn up now, Wade could wait until darkness and slip away again. Even with the armed containment on the cottage, it's so dark around that cottage there's a real possibility that he could slip through the net again. Don't worry boss, I'll make sure I'm careful and I won't put either myself or Tina at any unnecessary risk.'

Danny said, 'Okay Rachel. We've got just over two hours to plan this properly and plan for all contingencies, let's get cracking.'

CHAPTER 83

2nd July 1986
South Lodge, Retford

'Jimmy, I don't understand you, what is it about that bloody detective?'

'It doesn't concern you Melissa, it's my decision. I say what's going to happen around here, not you. I've given you way too much freedom lately, I can just as easily take that back, if that's what you want?'

'What I want is for us to leave together and go to Ireland like we planned.'

'I know you do and it's what I want too, trust me.'

'I sense a but coming.'

'There are no buts Mel! We'll be going to Ireland, just as soon as I've dealt with Rachel bloody Moore.'

'We've talked about this for hours already, you don't need to deal with her. We can walk away right now, you've already won, you can be free and we can start our life together away from here.'

'We can do all that anyway, afterwards.'

'After what?'

'After I've made her pay. I know you don't understand Mel, but I can't be satisfied until that scheming bitch is dead. Why don't you get it?'

'I'm just worried that it could be a trap. You said yourself she's a scheming bitch, don't you think it's a little strange that she's contacted me now?'

'No, I think it's perfectly natural, you heard that prick Ainsworth before he died, he said he should've been seeing Rachel and the other one. She's just following up on her enquiries like a good little detective. She won't have a clue that I'm actually living here with you. It will be a piece of piss to lure her in and finish her off once and for all.'

'And what about the other detective? She won't be coming here alone, will she?'

'Her too, I'll finish them both. We can't afford to leave any witnesses behind, there's plenty of room next to Barnes and the others. We'll need to leave for Ireland as soon as I've buried them. We need to be over the water before the pair of them are missed.'

'I don't like it Jimmy.'

'I don't care whether you like it or not, it's a simple choice Mel, you either help me or I'll leave you here, cold in the ground next to Barnes and the others.'

'You wouldn't do that to me, Jimmy.'

Wade reached out with one strong hand and gripped her throat, 'Why are you continually testing me, bitch?'

As his grip intensified, she could feel her windpipe constricting and her eyes starting to bulge.

She was powerless to do anything.

Desperately, she tried to drag in a breath and said hoarsely through her crushed voice box, 'I'm sorry Jimmy, I'll help you. Sorry.'

Instantly he released his grip, leaving her spluttering and gasping for breath.

She collapsed to the floor and Wade stood over her.

Jabbing an index finger in her direction he shouted angrily, 'Don't ever argue with me again! I don't mind taking you with me if you do as you're told. If you want to argue, I'll make sure you stay here for good! Do we understand each other?'

Tears streamed down her face and she gasped, 'Okay, okay.'

In that single moment, she realised that despite all the horrendous acts she had forced herself to do, the killings she had taken part in purely to ingratiate herself with him, Jimmy Wade would still snuff her out in a heartbeat.

Wade stormed into the kitchen leaving her on the floor of the living room. Turning on the cold tap at the sink, he filled a tumbler glass full of cold water and took a long drink, trying to calm himself down.

As he swallowed the cold water he came to a decision.

That was it, he'd had enough of her whining.

He would definitely leave for Ireland that night just as soon as he'd despatched Rachel Moore, her partner and the annoying Melissa Braithwaite.

Deep down he'd always known that eventually Melissa would become a liability. He knew if he took her with him to Ireland, she would soon be an encumbrance. It was the right thing to do. He could travel much quicker and easier on his own.

CHAPTER 84

2nd July 1986
South Lodge, Retford

It was now approaching five thirty in the afternoon.

The sun was still far from sinking below the trees.

Outside the car, the temperature was close to twenty-seven degrees and it felt even warmer inside. Rachel was understandably tense, she felt a single bead of sweat trickle down the back of her neck.

Tina was driving the CID car very carefully down the dirt track that led to South Lodge.

The track was potholed and dusty.

The small Ford Fiesta wasn't designed to tackle rough terrain like this, any one of the deep pot holes could spell disaster.

Just before the car reached the clearing that housed the small stone cottage, Tina stopped the car.

She turned to Rachel and said, 'It's not too late to turn back, Rachel. You don't have to go through with this.'

'Don't you get it yet Tina? This is exactly what I've got to do. This is my job and yes, it's dangerous, but I know I can catch this bastard, if he's still in there. This is our one and only hope of finding Ainsworth and the other two, if they're still alive.'

'And what if they're already dead? You're risking your life here Rachel.'

'I know that, but until we've seen the bodies, I've got to believe they're all still alive.'

'It doesn't have to be you though Rachel, you've been through enough already.'

'I'm not discussing it anymore Tina. I want you to pull up outside the cottage and wait in the car.'

'What! Have you lost your mind? I'm not letting you walk in there on your own.'

'Trust me Tina. If Jimmy Wade's in there, he won't immediately attack me. He's going to want to talk to me. He won't be able to resist gloating, telling me how much smarter than me he is, it's his nature. I'll have plenty of time for back up to get in there and get him.'

'That won't change just because I'm in there with you.'

'Yes, Tina it will. He'd have absolutely no qualms about killing you before he started to talk to me. Don't you understand yet. It's personal between me and Wade, in a way that it's not with you.'

'I don't like it, Rachel.'

'Look, nobody's going to feel bad towards you because you didn't go in with me. I've already discussed this with Danny before we left. He totally agrees with me, he understands the psyche of Wade. His instruction was that you're to wait in the car until I call for back up. Danny also said to tell you that whatever happens, you're not to get in the way of the armed teams going in. Do you understand?'

'I understand Rachel, I think you're bloody crazy though.'

'At least that's one thing we agree on. Come on, we've wasted enough time here, let's get this done.'

Tina slipped the car into first gear and trundled slowly along the track until they came to a stop directly outside the cottage.

As the car stopped, Rachel pressed the switch in the palm of her right hand. The small black button operated the throat mike she was wearing beneath her high-necked blouse.

In an even voice she said, 'This is Dc Moore to control, report signals, over.'

She immediately heard a calm voice in her covert earpiece respond to her request, 'Your signals are clear, over. Every member of the operation can hear everything you say Rachel. Good luck, we're watching your every step.'

She pressed the switch twice in an acknowledgement, turned to Tina and said, 'Don't worry, I'll see you soon.'

With that she opened the passenger door of the car and got out. She straightened and took a deep breath before shutting the door and stepping towards the garden gate.

Inside the car Tina whispered, 'I'll see you soon, crazy woman.'

CHAPTER 85

2nd July 1986
South Lodge, Retford

Inside the cottage Jimmy Wade watched as the Ford Fiesta was driven up the track towards the property.

He stared hard through the fine mesh of the net curtains, trying to make out who was in the car. Momentarily, the car stopped on the track about thirty yards from where the trees opened up into the clearing.

What was the delay, he wondered?

Just as he began to get concerned, he saw the car move forwards again.

A broad grin spread across his features as the car once again came to a stop, this time directly outside the front of the cottage.

Melissa sat in silence, brooding on the settee behind him.

He watched intently as the passenger door finally opened and almost let out an audible gasp when he saw Rachel Moore get out of the car.

She paused and stretched.

She was wearing a cream cotton blouse that was buttoned up to the top. Navy suit trousers and black flat shoes. She wasn't carrying anything, no bag and no radio to be seen.

He admired the curves of her body as she stretched and said, 'It's definitely her Melissa, remember what I told you, I don't want you to say a word until you see her. Quickly, get out the back, you need to be in the outhouse so she comes looking for you.'

Melissa did as she was instructed.

The soreness around her windpipe a constant reminder of what would happen if she didn't obey instantly.

She quickly got to her feet and walked from the small lounge into the kitchen.

Wade continued to watch the car, but it quickly became apparent that her partner was staying put.

He waited until Rachel reached the front gate before quickly checking that the front door of the cottage had been left ajar.

He then followed Melissa out of the lounge, through the small kitchen and out the back door.

Wade opened the nearest outhouse door and bundled Melissa inside, 'You know what you've got to do. Don't make a sound. If she calls out to you, just ignore her. Let her come looking for you. Do you understand me?'

She nodded sullenly and backed away from the open door deeper into the gloom.

Wade wedged the door of the outhouse open and then made his way into a thick clump of rhododendron bushes situated to the left of the back door.

He had one last quick glance around, then squatted down in the bushes. From his hiding position, he knew he couldn't be seen by anyone emerging through the open back door.

As he squatted down, he felt the ballpein hammer in his waist band dig into the small of his back.

He grinned and growled menacingly, 'Come on Rachel sweetheart, don't keep me waiting all evening.'

CHAPTER 86

2nd July 1986
South Lodge, Retford

From their location at the rear of the cottage Pc Russell Day and Pc Kev Thomas had watched the events unfolding.

Russell Day had observed through the scope of his Ruger M77 sniper rifle whilst his spotter Kev Thomas had watched through his powerful olive-green binoculars.

They had heard the transmission from Rachel as she checked her signals and had almost immediately witnessed the small blonde-haired woman and the taller dark-haired man bolt through the door at the rear of the cottage.

Russel Day watched intently as the man bundled the woman into one of the outhouses before wedging the door open. The man then quickly moved back towards the cottage and squatted down, concealing himself in a thick clump of rhododendron bushes.

Kev Thomas spoke on his covert handset, 'Sniper Team Charlie to control permission?'

'Sniper Team Charlie go ahead, over.'

'From Sniper Team Charlie we have movement on Black side of the target premises. We've had a male and a female emerge from the door on Black. I've identified the female as the target Melissa Braithwaite. She left the property through the rear door and is now in the first outhouse at the rear of the property, so far?'

'All received, go ahead with the rest of your message, over.'

'An unidentified white male has also emerged from the rear of the property and has now hidden himself in bushes close to the rear of the property, over.'

'Received, over.'

Kev turned to Russell and said in hushed tones, 'I couldn't make that guy out Russ, what do you reckon, was that Ainsworth?'

'Couldn't tell, I never got a clear look at his face. The bloke's hair is right, could be him, but it's not enough for a positive ID.'

'I don't get it though, why would Ainsworth try and hide from the detective.'

I don't know, but I need Rachel to keep some distance between herself and those bushes where the bloke's hiding. That way, I'll have a chance to react and deal with any threat he may pose.

Russel pressed the switch in the palm of his hand and said, 'Sniper Team Charlie to control. Permission, over.'

'Sniper Team Charlie go ahead, over.'

'Advise Dc Moore that as and when she emerges from the rear of the cottage she needs to keep some distance between herself and the rhododendron bushes on her left, over.'

'Control to Dc Moore. Be advised if you go out of the rear of target premises keep a distance between yourself and the rhododendron bushes on your immediate left, over.'

The sniper team heard two clicks on the radio which meant that the young detective had received the message.

By relaying the message through control, the sniper had in effect sent the message over the air twice. Which ensured Dc Moore would definitely get the message.

Russell Day lay in a comfortable prone position with the rifle butt fitting snug in his shoulder. He still had a clear line of sight through the scope to the area of the bushes where the unidentified male had hidden himself.

He said quietly to his spotter, 'I'm going to make ready Kev. This whole picture doesn't look right to me. I see that guy in the bushes as a threat.'

'I think you're right Russ. Have you got the distance to those bushes mapped?'

'Yeah, I make it ninety yards, nil wind.'

'That's what I've got too.'

Very deliberately, Russell Day slowly slid back the bolt action of the rifle.

This action prompted a round to emerge from the top of the five-round magazine and align itself in the breach.

As the sniper smoothly pushed the bolt forward the round was fed fully into the breach. The final part of the movement saw him press the bolt down the side of the weapon.

The rifle was now made ready.

There was no safety catch on the sniper rifle

Day kept his index finger outside of the trigger guard so there was no chance of a negligent discharge.

The sniper was now totally in the zone and would rely on his spotter for updates on events unfolding in the area of the plot he couldn't see through the telescopic sight. His concentration was fixed solely on the unidentified male. If at any time he became a threat towards the detective, it would be down to him to deal with that threat and keep her safe.

Kev Thomas whispered, 'I've got your back Russ. I'll give you the pictures on the plot mate, you stick with the target.'

Day did not reply.

He was now concentrating on regulating his breathing, getting relaxed, letting the rifle become one with him.

CHAPTER 87

2nd July 1986
South Lodge, Retford

Rachel Moore had almost reached the front door of the cottage, when she heard the sniper teams update about the male and the female exiting the rear of the property.

She had listened carefully to the description of the male; long dark hair didn't sound like Jimmy Wade.

She'd also heard and acknowledged the transmission that the male was now hiding in bushes at the rear of the cottage.

Rachel forced herself to concentrate.

The male hiding in the bushes could easily be Ainsworth. The social worker could have taken the opportunity to escape from Wade and was now hiding from the psychopath outside the cottage.

As she reached the front door, she realised that it was ever so slightly ajar.

Pressing the switch in her right palm she said in a voice that was barely a whisper, 'The front door's open, I'm going in.'

The only sounds she heard in her covert earpiece were the two clicks in acknowledgement of her message.

Using the back of her left hand, she pushed the heavy wooden door until it was fully open.

She already knew that Melisa Braithwaite was outside the back of the cottage, but she still shouted out, 'Hello! Ms Braithwaite, are you home?'

There was no reply.

She could barely will her legs to move. The tension she felt was almost palpable.

Slowly, she stepped over the threshold and into the cottage.

Once inside the cottage it felt instantly cooler and she shuddered involuntarily.

Save for the sound of dripping water coming from upstairs, the property was totally silent. The air felt heavy and there was a strange, pervasive musky smell that reminded her of sitting in an old church.

Her training kicked in and she realised that she had to check the upstairs of the cottage before moving through into the kitchen.

The small staircase led directly up from the front door. There was no handrail on the side of the stairs that opened into the lounge. Moving slowly and keeping her back to the wall she climbed the flight of stairs. Her flat shoes felt slippery on the polished wooden stairs and she concentrated hard on moving carefully, so she didn't fall.

At the top of the stairs, Rachel saw three doors that were all slightly open.

She pushed open the door facing her and as it opened she saw that it was the bathroom. She stepped inside and saw a cream coloured bath fitted with an overhead shower, a toilet that smelled strongly of bleach and a sink that had been set into a pale, wooden vanity unit. She saw that on the vanity unit, either side of the sink, were two toothbrushes and a variety of both male and female toiletries.

Looking down at the cream coloured sink she could now see that it was the cold-water tap causing the dripping sound.

She stepped forward and twisted the chrome tap until it was closed off properly. The dripping water instantly stopped.

She then checked the next room.

This was a tiny box room barely big enough to accommodate the single bed and wardrobe it contained. There were all kinds of disused articles and other rubbish strewn on the bed, it was obvious the room was never used.

Undeterred, Rachel still checked under the bed and inside the wardrobe.

Nothing.

With a growing feeling of trepidation, she made her way across the landing to the last room.

She felt for the radio button in the palm of her right hand and moved her middle finger next to it, ready to press it and scream for help.

Every nerve ending in her body was on fire, her mouth was dry and her senses were on maximum, it felt as though she could almost smell and taste the presence of Jimmy Wade.

She pushed the door open.

The small window on the far wall only let in partial sunlight, she furrowed her brow and squinted, willing her eyes to adjust quickly to the gloom. From her position in the doorway, she could see a huge double bed that was unmade, the sheets crumpled and unwashed.

The room smelled of sweat and dirty clothes.

On the floor at each side of the bed were piles of dirty, discarded clothes waiting to be washed. There was a huge double wardrobe that dominated the entire wall opposite the window. The bed itself was a drawer divan so there was no space for anyone to be hiding beneath the bed.

Moving further into the room, Rachel turned around and saw on one side of the door was a dressing table, on the other side stood a chest of drawers.

Stepping over to the double wardrobe she opened the first door.

A coat hanger containing a heavy jacket fell out of the wardrobe as she opened the door.

She half jumped and half fell backwards onto the bed and almost hit the radio button in panic, before she realised it was just a jacket.

Jumping to her feet, she quickly cleared the rest of the bedroom and made her way downstairs.

As soon as her breathing and heart rate had calmed down a little, she pressed the radio button and whispered, 'I've checked the upstairs of the cottage, it's clear, I'm checking downstairs now.'

Again, the only reply was the two clicks on the radio.

She stepped into the living room from the bottom of the stairs and checked behind the settee and the chairs. Finally, she opened the door that led into the kitchen.

The kitchen was one of the largest rooms in the property.

At one end she could see a round wooden dining table and four wooden chairs all made from pine and varnished to a shine.

As soon as she walked into the kitchen, Rachel saw that the back door was wide open. The bright sunlight outside flooded in through the open door. Looking out of the door she could see the field that led down to the river and the tall conifers beyond.

She knew that somewhere in those conifers, there was a sniper team watching her every move, probably with their weapons trained on her.

It gave her no comfort.

Again, she pressed the button in her palm, 'The cottage is clear, I'm moving outside.'

This time there was a reply to her signal, she recognised Danny's voice, 'Rachel, it's Danny. I've been speaking with the Tactical Firearms Advisor. Whatever happens you are not to go into that outhouse where we know Braithwaite is. Do you understand?'

'Understood. I'm making my way outside now.'

CHAPTER 88

2nd July 1986
South Lodge, Retford

Jimmy Wade shifted uncomfortably.

He was still squatting on his haunches and remained hidden in the middle of the rhododendron bushes.

What was keeping Rachel?

He'd carefully staged everything inside the cottage so she would quickly realise the property was empty and would make her way outside into the garden, where he could spring his trap.

He hadn't expected her to take so long to get through the cottage. The muscles in his thighs were beginning to ache and burn.

Just as he was about to change position he saw movement in the doorway.

Finally, he got a clear unobstructed view of Rachel; this time there were no net curtains or other obstructions in the way.

In the bright sunlight he thought she looked wonderful.

From where he was hiding, he could clearly see the fear etched onto her face. Fine lines had formed at the corners of her eyes as she squinted against the bright sunlight.

Even though she was undeniably stressed, she still maintained an unbowed demeanour. Her spirit was there for all to see, even in the face of a real and present danger.

In any other scenario he would have tried to make her his own, but he knew it was that very spirit and courage, being demonstrated now, that meant he would never be able to own her in the way he wanted to.

He would always be doomed to fail and Jimmy Wade loathed failure.

He understood that the only way he could ever truly possess her, was by killing her.

The whole situation felt intolerable to him, because he genuinely believed she was a magnificent woman.

As she stepped a few yards further outside, away from the kitchen door and out into the bright sunlight, he involuntarily hunched down lower.

She paused again, looking around her at the sights and sounds outside the cottage.

The air outside was completely still.

The only sounds to be heard were the gentle waters of the River Poulter as it flowed over the stones in the shallows and the songbirds singing in the treeline.

There wasn't a breath of wind, so even the normally ever-present whisper of the breeze, as it passed through the pine forest, was silent.

CHAPTER 89

2nd July 1986
South Lodge, Retford

Rachel moved further away from the cottage door and suddenly felt even more exposed. She had the feeling that a thousand eyes were upon her, watching her, scrutinising her.

Suddenly there was an overwhelming urge to rush back inside the cottage.

The old stone building that only minutes before, had felt like a place of menace and threat, had suddenly transformed into a sanctuary that offered safety and salvation.

Fighting her instincts, she moved further away from the cottage and walked towards the nearest outhouse.

Remembering the words of the sniper team, she gave a wide berth to the large dark green leaved rhododendron bushes on her immediate left.

The plants still held the remnants of the large purple headed flowers that had bloomed earlier in the year. The flowers were almost all dead and the once vibrant purple was now tinged with brown.

She could see no movement or any other perceived threat in the bushes, but in deference to the received warning she maintained a good distance from them as she walked down the narrow path towards the outhouse.

Rachel paused on the path and shouted, 'Melissa, where are you?'

There was no reply.

She tried again, still no reply.

Moving forward, she could now see that the heavy wooden door on the first of the outhouses was wedged open. She could see the new stainless steel hasp on the door, where a padlock would fit.

She speculated over the reason Danny had instructed her not to enter the outhouse under any circumstances.

If she somehow ended up locked inside with Wade, the armed teams wouldn't be able to rescue her quickly and it would also make the sniper team redundant.

She manoeuvred around until she could see inside the outbuilding, but still remained five yards from the doorway.

From her position in bright sunlight it was difficult to see inside the dark outbuilding. As she peered into the gloom, she could finally make out a figure sitting on the floor over by the far wall.

Rachel could make out the blonde hair on the figure and she shouted, 'Is that you, Melissa?'

A very timid frightened voice said, 'Yes.'

'Why are you in there, Melissa? What's happening?'

'You've got to help me, I'm chained up in here. It's Jimmy Wade, he's holding me prisoner. Help me, get these chains off me, please.'

Rachel started to move towards the outhouse door so she could go inside and release Melissa, when she heard a calm voice through her covert earpiece.

'Sniper Team Charlie to Dc Moore, be advised you have the unidentified dark-haired male approaching you from behind. Over.'

Rachel spun around and saw the man walking towards her from the direction of the bushes.

He was no more than twenty yards away.

Instantly, she recognised the features of Jimmy Wade.

The psychopath had significantly changed his appearance, but it was definitely Wade.

Pressing the button in the palm of her right hand Rachel said loudly, 'Stay where you are, Wade. The cottage is surrounded by armed police.'

Jimmy Wade stopped, spread his arms wide, palms open and smiled benignly.

Suddenly, Rachel had a memory of sitting in Wade's house sipping coffee as she asked him questions about the death of the miner Albie Jones in 1984. He had smiled at her in exactly the same way then. It was the smile of the python just before it ate the rabbit.

He was now fifteen yards from Rachel, still moving slowly towards her.

'Oh, please Rachel, you can do better than that surely?'

'I mean it Wade, they're already moving forward through the woods as we speak.'

He stopped momentarily and said in a mocking voice, 'You see Rachel, the problem I'm having with this conversation is that I don't believe you. I watched you both arrive, just you and your skinny female partner. Not a handgun or a rifle between you. While we're on the subject of your skinny partner, where is she? Still sitting in the car? Didn't she fancy having a chat with the lovely Melissa in our little outbuilding? Left it all for you to sort out, did she?'

Inexorably, he started edging towards her again.

Wanting to appear confident and trying to disguise the tremor in her voice she said, 'I mean it Wade, stay where you are. Stand still.'

Her middle finger remained pressed down on the transmitter button whenever she spoke.

She released the pressure momentarily and heard a soft, reassuring voice through her earpiece, 'If he comes directly at you Rachel, do not run. Stand still. You'll want to run, but I need you to just stand still, okay.'

She said nothing, but in her mind, she heard herself replying to the soothing voice, 'Okay.'

CHAPTER 90

2nd July 1986
South Lodge, Retford

Pc Russel Day had watched the detective as she moved out of the cottage and made her way towards the outhouse.

Eventually, she'd moved out of his vision, out of the view offered by the telescopic sight fitted to the Ruger sniper rifle.

His spotter, Pc Kev Thomas, had maintained a softly spoken commentary on the detective's subsequent movements, so the sniper was fully appraised on what was happening to her while he maintained sight picture on the area of bushes where the man had disappeared.

As Russell maintained his watch on the bushes he became aware of movement.

Suddenly, the man hiding there had stood up.

As the sniper watched him, the man crouched over and began to move towards the detective. Looking through the telescopic sight on the rifle he followed the man's movements. Through his earpiece, he heard his spotter say over the radio, 'Sniper Team Charlie to Dc Moore, be advised you have the unidentified dark-haired male approaching you from behind. Over.'

By the time the detective turned to face the male, he was no further than twenty yards away from her.

The sniper could now clearly see both the detective and the unidentified male within the confines of his telescopic sight.

He then heard the voice of the detective through his ear piece, 'Stay where you are, Wade. The cottage is surrounded by armed police.'

She had definitely said the name Wade, there was no mistaking it.

The sniper heard his spotter whisper, 'She said Wade, that's Jimmy Wade down there, you'd better be ready Russ.'

Russel Day said nothing, he was now totally concentrated on the male figure. He blinked often and focussed on the figure through the telescopic sight, carefully placing the point of the stick sight onto the left ear of Jimmy Wade.

He could see that Wade continued to inch closer towards the detective as he spoke to her and that he was feeling for something behind his back.

To the sniper it was obvious that Wade was about to launch an attack.

He opened the transmitter of his own covert radio by pressing his left palm against the stock of the rifle which caused pressure on the switch in the palm of his hand.

He said in a whisper, 'If he comes directly at you Rachel, do not run. Stand still. You'll want to run, but I need you to just stand still, okay.'

As he calmly spoke to the detective, he maintained the sight picture on the suspects head, slipped his index finger within the trigger guard and took up first pressure.

CHAPTER 91

2nd July 1986
South Lodge, Retford

Rachel was now once again staring into those all too familiar, cold, emotionless blue eyes that she'd seen in so many of her nightmares.

Wade grinned cruelly and said, 'It really is just you and me now Rachel, it's time we became re-acquainted.'

Her mind was racing, think Rachel think.

She blurted out, 'Where's Stewart Ainsworth, Jimmy?'

'Don't worry about our friendly social worker Mr Ainsworth. He's still here. He's in the field lying next to his two best mates, Barnes and Williams.'

He gestured over towards the field that ran down towards the river, 'They all had to answer for the way they disrespected me.'

Rachel knew she had to try and keep him talking, she knew the firearms team would be getting closer.

'What did you do to them?'

'Me? I didn't do anything to them, Rachel. Fred killed Jack and Melissa killed Fred and Stewart. As always, I'm an innocent man. Anyway, as much as I'd love to tell you exactly what happened to those three no marks, I think we've talked long enough. Come on Rachel, we both know how all this has to end. You cheated me once, Rachel, you won't do it again.'

Rachel saw him reach behind his back and remove a heavy ballpein hammer from the waistband of his jeans.

Wade grinned and tossed the hammer from hand to hand, feeling the weight.

Suddenly, without warning Wade launched himself towards her holding the hammer aloft, ready to crash it down on to the top of her skull.

Fighting every fibre of her own survival instincts, that were screaming at her to flee, Rachel remained rooted to the spot.

She stared directly into the maniacal eyes of the onrushing psychopath.

Just as the heavy ballpein hammer started on its downward arc towards her head, Wade's face suddenly disintegrated before her eyes.

A fraction of a second after Wade's head literally exploded, she heard the crack of the rifle round as it was discharged. The sound of the shot arrived fractionally after the bullet smashed through Wade's head, killing him instantly.

Wade's forward momentum caused his already dead body to crash into Rachel knocking her backwards onto the grass.

In her ear piece she heard the same calm voice saying, 'All units Wade's down, but so is Dc Moore, get in there fast.'

Rachel was lying flat on her back winded; all the air had been knocked from her body.

She felt moisture on her face and wiped her hand across her left cheek. Looking at her hand, she recoiled in horror when she realised her face was covered in bone fragments, blood and brain matter from Jimmy Wade's destroyed head.

Crawling backwards away from the dead psychopath, she managed to press the radio transmitter in her palm and splutter, 'I'm okay, I'm okay. Wade's dead.'

As she tried to stand, she saw the first of the black clad Special Operations Unit officers emerging from the woodland, racing towards her with their H&K Mp5 weapon's in the shoulder, pointing towards the body of Wade.

Suddenly, Rachel saw Tina emerging from the back door of the cottage.

'I'm okay Tina, I'm okay.'

'Thank God for that. That was too bloody close, Rachel. You could have been seriously injured or killed.'

'But I wasn't, so it's all good. Braithwaite's in the outhouse chained up, go and help her Tina. I'm okay, honestly.'

Seconds later Tina emerged from the outhouse with Melissa Braithwaite, who was sobbing quietly repeating the words, 'Is he dead?'

Tina said quietly, 'Did you say she was chained up?'

'That's what she said, why?'

'Because she wasn't, she was just sitting there in the dirt, crying.'

'I don't know. I probably misheard her, it's been a pretty stressful last five minutes.'

As Rachel finished her sentence, her voice broke with emotion.

Suddenly everything that had happened overwhelmed her and she felt her legs buckle.'

Tina quickly grabbed her colleague and said, 'Come over here out of the way. Sit down, take some deep breaths.'

Through her ear piece Rachel could hear Danny Flint barking out instructions to preserve the scene of the shooting.

For a split second she imagined him giving out the same orders to preserve the scene of her murder at the hands of Jimmy Wade.

Suddenly, Rachel felt very cold and very alone.

CHAPTER 92

5th August 1986
Eakring Road, Mansfield, Nottinghamshire

'Oh, it's you. You'd better come in.'

The voice belonged to Rachel Moore's brother Joe.

The powerful, squat Royal Marine commando reluctantly stepped aside and allowed Danny Flint to step into the hallway of the three-bedroom semi-detached house owned by his sister.

'Wait here Mr Flint, I'll see if she wants to see you.'

Danny waited patiently in the hallway.

He knew Rachel had been deeply affected by the shooting of Jimmy Wade. At first, she'd seemed fine and had continued on the case working alongside Tina Prowse, making enquiries into the deaths of Stewart Ainsworth, Fred Barnes and Jack Williams.

Then the night before last, Rachel had been found in the middle of the night, sitting alone in her car quietly sobbing in the car park at Mansfield Police Station.

She had refused to speak to any of the officers who found her, but was eventually coaxed out of the car and taken to hospital by very worried uniform colleagues. The officers had immediately contacted Rachel's brother Joe, who lived in Poole, Dorset and informed him of his sister's condition.

Joe had obtained an emergency forty-eight hour leave pass from his commanding officer and travelled directly to Kings Mill Hospital.

The doctor who attended to Rachel at the hospital diagnosed the problem as a classic case of post-traumatic stress and prescribed some tranquilisers and immediate rest in the short term and advised that she would require professional help and counselling in the long term to try and rectify the issues that had caused the stress.

Everyone on the force knew exactly what the cause of the stress was.

Danny was notified of Rachel's illness the next morning, but he was on a Senior Investigators course in Newcastle, Tyne and Wear and was due to give a lecture that morning on the extradition procedures that followed the arrest of Jimmy Wade when he was first identified in New South Wales, Australia.

He set off back to Nottinghamshire the moment he'd finished the lecture and had driven directly to Rachel's house.

He hadn't been surprised to see Joe standing in the doorway, he recalled how close he was to his older sister.

Joe came back into the hallway and said, 'It's against my better advice, but she wants to see you, Mr Flint.'

Danny went to walk into the living room of the house, but was prevented from walking past the tough marine. Joe gripped Danny's forearm, stopped him in his tracks and whispered menacingly, 'I used to respect you, Danny. Why the fuck would you allow my sister to face that psycho on her own and put her in harm's way like that?'

Danny was tired from the drive and feeling irritable already, this he didn't need.

He pulled his arm away from Joe's vice like grip and growled back, 'She wasn't on her own Joe, that's why she's still here and alive to tell the tale. With rank, there sometimes comes an onerous responsibility. I had an opportunity to capture one of the most dangerous killers we've had in this country for a long long time. I knew that Rachel was the only person who could delay Wade long enough for back up to get in to help her and we just might have had the opportunity to rescue four possible hostages. Don't you see Joe? For some reason your sister's very existence had struck a personal note with Wade. He was unable to resist her, when given the opportunity to get close to your sister, he lost all of his usual animal cunning.'

'When you use that phrase, "get close". What you're actually saying is giving Wade the opportunity to kill my sister.'

'Yes Joe, I suppose that's exactly what it boils down to and it's testament to your sister's courage that she still accepted the task of going into South Lodge even when she was offered the chance to back out.'

'But what choice did she really have Danny?'

'She had every choice Joe. I would never order any of my staff to go into such a dangerous situation. This isn't the military; my staff don't follow orders that put themselves in harm's way. Police officers choose to do it, they do it because they care and because they know it will make a difference. Now if you don't mind Joe, I've just driven three and a half hours to see your sister.'

'Okay Danny, I'm sorry for what I said and just for the record, I know that you really do care for her.'

'No apology needed. I understand you're upset. Of course, I care about her, I care about all my staff in the same way and I promise you I'll ensure that Rachel takes as long as she wants and gets all the help she needs to get back to being her old self.'

'Thanks Danny, I know you will.'

'Don't worry Joe, your sister means an awful lot to me. Her recovery will be entirely at her own pace, she will only come back to work if and when she's ready to, okay.'

'Danny, I get it. Now stop talking to me and get in there and visit my sister, it will do her good to see you.'

CHAPTER 93

5th August 1986
Mansfield, Nottinghamshire

Danny heard the car door slam outside his house.

He glanced at the clock on the mantlepiece above the open fire. It was only just coming up for eight o'clock, he knew that Sue wasn't due to finish work for at least another couple of hours.

He took another drink from the cut glass tumbler full of Bushmills whiskey, stood up and walked to the window.

It was still light outside and Danny could see the unmistakeable bulky figure of Detective Chief Superintendent Wainwright standing by the side of his BMW car on the driveway.

For a split second, an icy chill swept over him and he strained his eyes to see if there was a woman police constable also in the car.

Inwardly, he breathed a sigh of relief when he realised that Bill Wainwright wasn't visiting him at home as the bearer of the worst possible news.

Danny walked to the front door and opened it just as Bill Wainwright was about to ring the doorbell.

Danny said, 'Hello Bill, come in, come in. What brings you here at this time of night?'

Wainwright stepped inside the hallway, far enough past Danny to allow him room to close the front door. As soon as

Danny had shut the door Wainwright said, 'I was visiting my sister at her house in Warsop and I thought I'd drop in and pay you a visit on my way home, you don't mind do you?'

'Of course not, come through to the front room. Can I fix you a drink?'

Wainwright gestured at the whiskey glass in Danny's hand and said, 'A small one of those would do the trick. I can't have too much though, I've still got to drive home.'

He smiled then continued, 'Your lovely good lady not at home Danny?'

'She's on a late shift this evening, I'll be lucky to see her before eleven o'clock.'

Danny walked over to the drinks cabinet and poured Bill a small measure of the Irish whiskey and dropped in a couple of ice cubes.

He held up the cut glass tumbler and said, 'Would you like a splash of water in it Bill?'

'No thanks Danny, the ice will be fine.'

Handing his boss the glass Danny said, 'Grab yourself a seat, Bill.'

As soon as the big Scot sat down, Danny also sat and said, 'Is it just a social call?'

'It is and it isn't. I do have some news for you, but like I say I was passing anyway.'

'What's the news?'

'Before I left work this evening I had sight of the Independent Police Complaints Commission report into the fatal shooting of Jimmy Wade.'

'I see. Anything controversial in it?'

'Not really Danny, well nothing for us to worry about anyway. The sniper team have been totally exonerated.'

'I should think so too, they did a fantastic job and without doubt saved Rachel's life.'

Bill took a sip of the fiery whiskey, allowing the heat of the liquor to slowly dissipate over his tongue before saying, 'They do have a few words of criticism though, Danny.'

'Really?'

'The IPCC are of the opinion that the firearms operation should have been handled differently.'

'In what way for Christ's sake?'

'Don't worry Danny, it's only in the form of a recommendation and not a discipline issue.'

'Go on Bill, what do they say?'

'They believe the operation may have resulted in no fatalities had the cottage been raided by a firearms team in a conventional manner rather than sending in a lone Dc.'

'And what about the possibility of rescuing any hostages?'

'They acknowledge that was part of the thought process Danny and that's the reason their report is only advisory.'

'Well hallelujah! Hindsight's always twenty-twenty vision isn't it?'

'We both know that Danny, as far as I'm concerned, and this also goes for the rest of the command corridor, what you did was spot on. There will be absolutely no criticism of the way the operation was handled from the command of Nottinghamshire Police. In fact, now that the IPCC report is about to come out exonerating the force, the Chief Constable was busy drafting out commendations for the sniper team, Rachel Moore and yourself as I left the office.'

'Well I appreciate that Bill, but it's still galling when they pass these comments from their ivory towers months after the event.'

'How is Detective Moore? I heard she'd been troubled and unwell lately.'

'I went to see her earlier today when I got back from Newcastle. She's got her brother Joe staying with her, looking after her. The doctor who saw her at the hospital has diagnosed PTSD, no doubt as a result of the incident with Jimmy fucking Wade!'

'Prognosis?'

'It's good Bill. The doctor has told her that with the correct counselling and support there's no reason why she shouldn't make a full recovery.'

'Well that's good news. I'll make sure that young woman gets whatever she needs Danny. Are you aware that the Chief has nominated her to receive the Queens Police Medal for Gallantry?'

'That's the first I've heard of it. I hope he has, because if anyone deserves that recognition it's Rachel. She knew exactly what Wade was capable of and still volunteered to go in and get him.'

'The final decision will be made by the Home Secretary, but I think she stands a good chance of being awarded the honour.'

'That would be great Bill. Can I top up your glass?'

'Go on then, if you're twisting my arm, I will. Better make it half a small one this time though. Thanks.'

As Danny topped up the glasses Bill said, 'Is everything tied up with the Tall Trees case now?'

'Very much so. All the suspects involved in the death of Evan Jenkins have been arrested and charged. All of them are now on remand pending a trial date, which should be sometime early next year.'

'Can you believe that woman running the home Danny, what was her name, Christine something?'

'You mean Caroline Short.'

'That's her, what an evil bitch.'

'I won't argue with those sentiments Bill, but the real organiser of the group and the driving force behind the child abuse offences was Grenville Slater, the solicitor.'

'He's another evil bastard, that's for sure, but you say you've got them all now?'

'Every single one of them. The last one to be arrested and charged was the anaesthetist William Baxter. He's made full admissions now like most of them, it's only Slater who hasn't admitted his part.'

'Who's doing the file for the job?'

'It's a massive job Bill, but Brian Hopkirk's bringing it all together.'

'A good man, Brian. Very capable. What about the Wade case?'

'Rob Buxton's bringing that one together for the coroner.'

'I understand there was some confusion about this Braithwaite woman, what's the news with that Danny?'

'When she was eventually interviewed after the shooting, she stated that she had been held prisoner by Wade ever since his escape from Rampton Hospital. She denied helping in the escape and we couldn't prove otherwise. She stated that Wade had found his own way to her remote cottage and had remained there for the duration of the time he was on the run. The story she provided to the interviewers was horrendous. Apparently, she was repeatedly raped by Wade and beaten into submission to the point where she obeyed him without question.'

'What about the sighting of the blonde woman at the pub where the first nurse was abducted? Was that her?'

'She admits being there when both nurses were abducted, but she was too terrified to do anything else. All her actions were as a direct result of the extreme duress she felt in Wade's presence.'

'And we're satisfied that's the case, are we?'

'We have no evidence to dispute her story, Bill. It would appear that she was as much a victim as the two nurses and the social worker. I'm sure that Wade would have killed her too, just as soon as she stopped being useful to him.'

'Didn't I read somewhere that Wade told Dc Moore that it was Braithwaite who had killed one of the nurses and the social worker?'

'That's what Wade said, but that would be just the sort of manipulative games that psycho would play. Braithwaite stated during her interview that she was forced by Wade to watch him murder the three men, after he'd held them captive for a few days torturing them.'

'After the bodies of Barnes, Williams and Ainsworth were recovered at South Lodge, did the post mortem findings bear out her version of events?'

'Totally, in as much as it showed that the three men had all been tortured, prior to being killed.'

'So, what's happened to Braithwaite now then?'

'She's been treated as a witness and provided a detailed statement for the coroner. Last I heard, she's sold her story to a newspaper and made a lot of money. You know the type of thing, my sheer hell living with the monster Wade. Blah! Blah! Blah!'

'Well, for some reason that kind of stuff does sell newspapers. Is she still in the area?'

'I'm not sure Bill. She's definitely not at South Lodge anymore. The cottage is up for sale.'

'I do have one last piece of very good news for you Danny.'

'That sounds interesting, I could always do with some good news.'

'I was chatting with the Chief the other day and I've informed him that within the next eighteen months, my intention is to retire.'

'Congratulations Bill, you've earned a long and happy retirement.'

'That's not the news Danny. When I told him of my intention, the Chief told me he that intends to create a new post of Assistant Head of CID with the rank of Superintendent. He wants you to accept this new role with a view to becoming my successor when I retire.'

'Bloody hell Bill! I didn't see that coming!'

'It's perfect for you Danny. You've got a new baby on the way, you'll have more money and another promotion within eighteen months. You and Sue would be set fair financially and you'd get to spend more time at home with Sue and your baby.'

'I don't know what to say.'

'There's only one thing to say Danny. Yes.'

'What about the MCIU?'

'Your position would be advertised, but both Rob and Brian would make excellent Chief Inspectors running the Unit.'

'How long have I got to make a decision?'

'I was rather hoping you'd say yes straight away Danny. What are you worried about?'

'It really is a fantastic opportunity Bill, but my concern is I wouldn't be a detective anymore, that's all.'

'Danny, think about it logically. You would have the best of both worlds. You would be working sociable hours for ninety percent of the time and having weekends off with your family. You would still be able to dip in and out of the MCIU, as you would remain the Units immediate line supervisor. Trust me on this Danny, you could never stop being a detective.'

'In that case Bill, I'll give you my answer now. It's a definite yes. When's it all likely to happen?'

'I'll talk to the Chief tomorrow and tell him you want the job. All things being equal you should be promoted into your new post within a month. Congratulations, I look forward to working alongside you, Superintendent Flint.'

EPILOGUE

16th November 1986
Moraira, Costa Blanca, Spain

The woman was gazing out to sea, watching the two sailing boats near the horizon.

With large dark glasses protecting her eyes against the glare of the sun on the ocean, she was the only customer at the tables.

The small intimate coffee shop was situated right on the water's edge overlooking the marina at Moraira.

Since arriving in the small town and renting a spacious apartment that overlooked the medieval tower and the town's beach, the woman had made the short walk to the coffee shop most mornings

Moraira was a sleepy place, especially in the winter months. A lot of the tourist shops and bars had already closed for the winter.

It suited the woman in the dark glasses perfectly.

As was her habit, she had ordered the Churros con Chocolat and now waited patiently for the waiter to bring the cup of piping hot chocolate and the sugary lengths of dough to her table.

Melissa Braithwaite had completely changed her appearance before leaving England five weeks ago, to start her new life on the Costa Blanca.

The distinctive blonde bob hairstyle had gone and been replaced by very short, dyed black hair. She had continued to lose weight due to the stress of her situation and some of her curves had disappeared. The lines etched into her face caused by her months living with Wade made her look older than her years.

She had holidayed in both Moraira and neighbouring Javea as a small child with her parents. In those days the town of Moraira was little more than a coastal village relying on the small fishing boats to bring cash into the economy.

With the expansion of tourism starting to spread down the coast from the larger towns of Benidorm and Calpe, the area had in recent years grown rapidly.

The Costa Blanca was now serviced by two large airports at Alicante and Valencia.

Because the area held such pleasant memories for Melissa, it had seemed the perfect location to escape all the media attention following the death of Jimmy Wade.

In the immediate aftermath of the psychopath's death, she had worried that the police would in some way find out that she had been responsible for the deaths of at least two of the men and had played a major role in the abduction of all three.

Melissa Braithwaite had feared she would be spending many years in prison.

As the police interviewed her, it soon became apparent to the intelligent Braithwaite that the police had absolutely no evidence linking her to the killings.

Everyone involved in that horrific chain of events was now dead.

Very quickly she had taken on the role of being the fourth victim of Jimmy Wade.

She had invented a story that somehow Wade had tracked her down to her secluded woodland home.

Again, there was no one to dispute her version of events and very soon the police took a witness statement from her and offered her counselling for the trauma suffered at the hands of the escaped psychopath Wade.

Braithwaite had immediately placed South Lodge on the market, unable to face returning to the secluded property.

She already had two cash buyers interested in the property and had left instructions with her solicitor to sell the property to the highest bidder in the shortest time possible. He was then to transfer the money from the sale to her new Spanish bank account.

She had used the money she made from selling her story to one of the red top tabloid newspapers to fund her move to the Costa Blanca.

As well as the newspaper money, a publisher had also approached her and paid her a substantial advance to write a book about her time spent as a prisoner of the notorious serial killer, Jimmy Wade.

Financially, she was in a very good place.

Finally, the Spanish waitress brought out her Churros con Chocolat.

Melissa made no attempt to speak to the young girl in either English or Spanish. She never even looked at the waitress and continued to stare out at the ocean.

The waitress placed the food and drink on the table and left.

As Melissa dipped the churros into the hot chocolate drink, she wondered if she would ever be able to totally shake off the murderous thoughts she continued to have.

The reoccurring thoughts were the legacy of what she had been forced to experience and endure whilst living at the cottage with Wade.

However hard she tried to force the memories of those experiences to the back of her mind, she could still vividly remember the tingle of pleasure she had felt as she snuffed out the lives of Barnes and Ainsworth.

It didn't matter how many times she told herself that the feelings were wrong and immoral, that the only reason she had killed the two men was to survive herself, deep down inside her she knew the truth was very different.

She was a changed and damaged woman.

The constant worry for Melissa, was that one day in the very near future, she would not be able to resist the urge to kill again.

About the author

Trevor Negus is a retired Police Officer who spent 30 years working with Nottinghamshire Police.

He worked both inner city and rural beats in uniform and spent the entire duration of the Miners' Strike of 1984 on a Police Support Unit.

He then spent six years as an authorised firearms officer and was a sniper on the Force's Special Operations Unit. The last eleven years of his Police career were spent as a detective on the CID, where he was involved in numerous murder enquiries. During his time on the CID he was trained as a specialist interviewer, involved in the planning and interviews of murder suspects.